Jim & Gerry:

"LORD, Your Words were found and I ate them, and Your Word became for me a joy and the delight of my heart..."

Jer. 15:16

Ron & Marsha Harvell

Dr. Ron & Marsha Harvell

The WATCHMAN *on the* WALL

Volume 2

Daily Devotions for Praying God's Word Over Those You Love

The WATCHMAN on the WALL—VOLUME 2

Daily Devotions for Praying God's Word Over Those You Love

DISCLAIMER: These devotions are reflections of personal faith as they relate to contemporary events and do not represent the views of the Department of Defense or the United States Air Force.

Printed in the USA

Cover Design & Layout by Wendy K. Walters | www.wendykwalters.com

ISBN (Hardcase): 978-0-9916104-8-8

ISBN (Paperback): 978-0-9916104-9-5

ISBN (EPub): 978-0-9982711-1-8

ISBN (ePDF): 978-0-9982711-0-1

Library of Congress Control Number: 2016956724

Published By

Xaris Publications
Amarillo, Texas

To Contact the Authors:

www.GodsGreaterGrace.com

DEDICATION

To our dads, James Mills and Kenneth Harvell,
who have faithfully watched over and cared
for their families for 60 years.

Thank you for being Titus 1 men who unceasingly
love their wife, children, grandchildren,
and great-grandchildren.
We thank God for you;
you are an example to us all.

*Devote yourselves to prayer, keeping alert in
it with an attitude of thanksgiving.
Let the Word of Christ richly dwell within you, and
hear the LORD say, "Because you prayed …"*

—Colossians 4:2; 3:16; Isaiah 37:21

CONTENTS

$\mathcal{I}$NTRODUCTION

Welcome fellow Watchman to the Wall. There are over 6,000 prayer warriors lifting up requests to the LORD using His Word and *The Watchman on the Wall, Volume 1* (WOW-1). Through God's leadership, we are excited to open another arsenal of 366 more Swords of the Holy Spirit for your use with *The Watchman on the Wall, Volume 2* (WOW-2).

If the LORD permits, there will be a total of four WOW books to cover the entire Bible with prayers from each of the 1,189 chapters. This means there will be times when we write new prayer devotionals for books of the Bible previously covered. It is amazing how many prayers can be found in every chapter of God's Word! In addition, the LORD has led us to bring in New Testament books to follow Old Testament books to give more complete understanding of His Word.

For example, you prayed *Hebrews* in WOW-1 as part of the 21 New Testament letters section. This time you will pray through *Exodus* and *Leviticus* and then go right into *Hebrews*. *Hebrews* will add "wow!" to your prayer time as you appreciate Jesus for fulfilling every aspect of the sacrificial system.

WOW-2 also has a special season of praise and worship, your "Summer of Psalms," 100 days of praying Psalms 1 through 100. Finally, you will study and pray through *1 and 2 Samuel* as you approach Christmas. You will see Jesus through God's relationship with and promises to David. December ends with *1, 2, and 3 John* preparing for *Revelation* in WOW-3.

Whether you are already familiar with praying as a Watchman on the Wall, or if you are just starting to take your place on the Wall, we hope the following words of encouragement and tips will help you pray. These ideas will make you a powerful prayer warrior as you stand firm in the LORD and His Word.

Pray the Word of God

Learn how to pray God's Word for others. The Bible is the greatest prayer book ever written. It contains everything you would ever want or need to pray over someone.

For the next 366 days, you will mine the Word of God for treasure verses that you can pray for yourself and others. You will be able to say the words confidently because they will be the very words of God—containing His will over every situation. By the end of the year, you will be in the holy habit of finding Bible verses to pray, so for the rest of your life, you can constantly pray God's Words back to Him.

Pray With God

Prayer is a gift and a privilege from the LORD. Have faith as you pray that God is greater than any issue of this world, that He cares about you, and He will answer your prayers. Praying is faith. "And without faith it is impossible to please **Him,** for he who comes to God must believe that **He** is and that **He is a rewarder** of those who seek **Him**" (Hebrews 11:6).

As you pray, seek the LORD. He loves it! As you go closer to Him, your faith will supernaturally grow as a result. It is amazing the God of all creation would not only give you permission to talk to Him, but would desire to converse with you as well, to be in intimate nonstop communication with you. Proverbs 3:32 says, "The Lord is intimate with the upright." *Intimate*

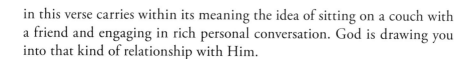

in this verse carries within its meaning the idea of sitting on a couch with a friend and engaging in rich personal conversation. God is drawing you into that kind of relationship with Him.

Pray with Context

For the devotions and prayers to be most fully understood, take the time to read the chapters in which they are written to get the best context for the prayers. If you do so faithfully, you will read nearly 1/3 of the Bible by the end of the year. The devotions flow directly through entire books of the Bible.

Pray at a Dedicated Time

If *The Watchman on the Wall* is your primary devotional for this year, then using it in the mornings can help tune you with the LORD before you walk through the rest of the day. Having your "connect with God time" only at night is like a violinist tuning their violin after the concert is over. Certainly, anytime with God is good and having dedicated prayers during many parts of the day is encouraged.

Pray Alone or With Others

If possible and fitting for your situation, consider praying with others, perhaps a friend or family member. We heard testimonies of couples married for over 50 years who began praying and reading their Bibles together for the first time with WOW-1! What a powerful team you will be! The prayers are easily modified to 'we' and 'us' in place of ' _____ and me.'

Pray with Persistence

God has called you to be a prayer warrior for the sake of others. Isaiah 62:6-7 says God has appointed watchmen who all day and all night never keep silent. These watchmen on the walls of Jerusalem are constantly reminding the LORD to establish Jerusalem. The watchmen refuse to take any rest for themselves, and they refuse to give God any rest until He establishes and makes Jerusalem a praise in the earth. Who does God want you to constantly remind Him to establish and make their life a praise to Him?

Pray Standing Firm and Faithful

Just like the watchmen in Isaiah keep talking and talking to God about Jerusalem, you keep talking and talking to God about the people He wants you to watch over in prayer. Remind the LORD of His promises, of His good Word, of His good Name. Refuse to back down or take a break. As a watchman, appointed by God, continually intercede until God establishes your loved ones and makes them a praise in the earth. See from your place on the Wall the glory of the LORD as He answers your prayers and changes the landscape of eternity before your eyes in the lives of those you love.

We pray this prayer from Colossians 1:9-12 for you:

> *For this reason also, since the day we heard of it,*
> *we have not ceased to pray for you and to ask that*
> *you may be filled with the knowledge of His will in*
> *all spiritual wisdom and understanding,*
> *so that you will walk in a manner worthy of the LORD,*
> *to please Him in all respects, bearing fruit in every good*
> *work and increasing in the knowledge of God;*
> *strengthened with all power, according to His glorious might,*
> *for the attaining of all steadfastness and patience;*
> *joyously giving thanks to the Father,*
> *who has qualified us to share in the inheritance of the saints in Light.*

We thank the LORD for you,

Ron AND *Marsha* HARVELL

JANUARY

On your walls, O Jerusalem,
I have appointed watchmen;
All day and all night they
will never keep silent.
You who remind the LORD,
take no rest for yourselves;
And give Him no rest until He establishes
And makes Jerusalem a
praise in the earth.
ISAIAH 62:6-7, NASB

JANUARY 1

Please read Exodus 1.

Meditate on verse 17.

> *But the midwives feared God, and did not do as the king*
> *of Egypt had commanded them, but let the boys live.*

Genesis ends with the death of Joseph (Genesis 50:26). Exodus begins by remembering Joseph's death and fast-forwarding 400 years to the continuation of Israel's story, one of enslavement to the Egyptians. Despite affliction and abuse, the Israelites multiplied, and the Egyptians dreaded them. In order to stop their population increase, the king of Egypt ordered Hebrew baby boys be put to death as they were being born. These horrific orders were given to two midwives, Shiphrah and Puah, who feared God more than they feared Pharaoh—they refused to kill the babies.

With whom do you identify from this chapter? Are you like the Egyptians in opposition to God's work, or are you a Godly and courageous Shiphrah and Puah, willing to defy orders that are contrary to God's Word?

As you desire to see God establish your family this year in His righteousness and holiness, be willing to obey His Word and walk in His ways.

Pray Exodus 1:17 and 20-21 over yourself and those for whom you stand guard as a faithful, prayerful watchman (Isaiah 62:6-7).

> *"LORD, help _____ and me to fear only You*
> *and not the commands of men who oppose You.*
> *Help us do things that help others live!*
> *Be good to us, God; multiply us and make us mighty.*
> *Establish our family because we fear You.*
> *In Your name, Jesus~"*

JANUARY 2

Please read Exodus 2.

Meditate on verse 23b.

> *And the sons of Israel sighed because of the*
> *bondage, and they cried out;*
> *and their cry for help because of their bondage rose up to God.*

Exodus 2 is an action-packed chapter about the first 40 years of Moses' life (Acts 7:17-29). He was one of the Hebrew babies saved at birth because of brave midwives like Shiphrah and Puah, who refused to kill baby boys (Exodus 1:15-17). After his birth, Moses' family hid him from Pharaoh. Miraculously, he was found and adopted by Pharaoh's daughter. The remainder of the chapter tells of Moses killing an Egyptian, Pharaoh trying to kill Moses, and Moses running for his life.

As Moses was saved and raised by God for even more adventure, the children of Israel remained in bondage to the Egyptians where they cried to the LORD for help. God heard their cry and noticed them.

Are you and/or someone you love in bondage? Are you a slave to sin? Are you controlled by something instead of Christ? God sees you and those you love. He is waiting for you to cry to Him for help.

Pray Exodus 2:23-25 over yourself and those for whom you stand guard as a faithful, prayerful watchman (Isaiah 62:6-7).

> *"LORD, I am sighing and crying out*
> *because _____ and I are in bondage.*
> *Let our cry for help rise up to You, God.*
> *God hear our groaning,*
> *and God remember Your covenant with us.*
> *God see us and take notice of us.*
> *For the sake of Your name, Jesus~"*

Please read Exodus 3.

Meditate on verse 4.

> *When the LORD saw that he turned aside to look,*
> *God called to him from the midst of the*
> *bush and said, "Moses, Moses!"*
> *And he said, "Here I am."*

Forty years passed after Moses fled for his life to the wilderness (Acts 7:29-30). As he pastured his father-in-law's flock in the area of Mt. Sinai, he came upon an incredible sight: a bush burning with blazing fire, but not being consumed. Moses turned and took notice. When he did, the LORD responded to him, calling Moses by name.

Notice how timing is key in verse four: "<u>When</u> the LORD saw that he turned aside to look," God began speaking to Moses, telling him the plan that would take Moses through the next 40 years of his life. I wonder what the LORD would have done if Moses had not turned to look, but just gone about his sheep herding ways and not noticed God.

What is God doing right now in your life that He wants you to notice? The LORD desires to talk to you and reveal His will to you. Turn aside from the distractions and pay attention to Him.

Pray Exodus 3:3-4 over yourself and those for whom you stand guard as a faithful, prayerful watchman (Isaiah 62:6-7).

> *"LORD, _____ and I must turn aside now*
> *and see the marvelous sight of what You are doing in our lives.*
> *LORD, see that we are turning aside to look at You.*
> *Call us by name! Here we are, LORD!*
> *In Your name, Jesus–"*

JANUARY 4

Please read Exodus 4.

Meditate on verse 11.

> *The LORD said to him, "Who has made man's mouth?*
> *Or who makes him mute or deaf, or seeing or blind?*
> *Is it not I, the LORD?"*

Exodus 4 is about obedience. The LORD was angry with Moses twice in this chapter. The first time was when Moses reasoned with God that His choice to make Moses His spokesman was a poor one. The second was prior to the emergency circumcision of Moses' son. Moses obviously did not obey God's command to circumcise him when the boy was eight days old (Genesis 17:10-14). A disobedient Moses resulted in an angry God.

Sin makes God mad. It is not to be toyed with and taken lightly. Is there sin in your past that you need to confess to the LORD, seeking His forgiveness? What is God asking you to do that you are ignoring and avoiding? Do you have a list of excuses for your disobedience?

God created you. He knows you better than you know yourself. He knows what is best for you and what you need to do to live a full and amazing life with Him. Since God made your mouth, use it to ask Him what to say and do to please Him today.

Pray Exodus 4:12 over yourself and those for whom you stand guard as a faithful, prayerful watchman (Isaiah 62:6-7).

> *"LORD, may _____ and I*
> *be obedient when You tell us to go.*
> *Be with our mouths and teach us what we are to say.*
> *For the sake of Your name, Jesus~"*

Please read Exodus 5.

Meditate on these questions from verses 2 and 22.

> *Who is the LORD that I should obey His voice ... ?*
> *O LORD, why have You brought harm to this people?*
> *Why did You ever send me?*

Exodus 5 contains some interesting questions; some that you may have asked as well.

Pharaoh asked the first question, "Who is the LORD that I should obey His voice to let Israel go?" (v. 2a). Rather than letting the LORD reply, Pharaoh was quick to give his own answer, "I do not know the LORD, and besides, I will not let Israel go" (v. 2b).

Pharaoh will soon learn who is LORD, and he will be forced to obey Him. Pray for those you love to know and obey the LORD with a willing heart.

Moses asked the last two questions. He knew the LORD, and he had an honest conversation with Him, asking Him difficult questions. "O LORD, why have You brought harm to this people? Why did You ever send me?" (v. 22).

As you walk in intimacy with the LORD today, talk to Him about everything and don't be afraid to ask Him tough questions. As you continue to read His Word, you will learn the answers to the three questions from Exodus 5, and the LORD will give you answers to your questions as well.

Use the words from Exodus 5:2 to pray for yourself and those for whom you stand guard as a faithful, prayerful watchman (Isaiah 62:6-7).

> *"LORD, let _____ and me know You*
> *that we will obey Your voice.*
> *In Your name, Jesus~"*

JANUARY 6

Please read Exodus 6.

Meditate on this phrase from verses 2, 6, 7, 8, and 29.

I am the LORD.

God said, "I am the LORD" five times in Exodus 6. He said it as a statement of fact, as a name by which He would make Himself known, as an assurance that He would deliver and redeem His people from bondage, as a guarantee that He would keep His Word, and as the reason Moses was to obey and speak all that the LORD spoke to him.

Notice the responses of the people to the LORD. Because of their bondage and state of despondency, the Israelites refused to listen to what the LORD said through Moses (v. 9). And Moses continued to make excuses for not wanting to obey the LORD (v. 12, 30).

"I am the LORD." This is God, the self-existent, eternal Master who has supreme power and authority over you. His Word to Moses is His Word to you: "I am the LORD. I will keep My Word. I want to deliver and redeem you from your bondage. Obey Me as Master, Ruler, King, and LORD of your life."

Pray Exodus 6:6-7 and 29 over yourself and those for whom you stand guard as a faithful, prayerful watchman (Isaiah 62:6-7).

"You are LORD.
Bring _____ and me out from under our burdens
and deliver us from our bondage.
Redeem us with an outstretched arm and with great judgments.
Take us as Your people and be our God.
Let us know that You are the LORD our God
who brought us out from under our burdens.
Help us to obey all that You speak to us.
Because You are LORD Jesus~"

January 7

Please read Exodus 7.

Meditate on verse 3.

But I will harden Pharaoh's heart
that I may multiply My signs and My wonders in the land of Egypt.

As you read and observe the next seven chapters of Exodus, notice there were times when the LORD hardened Pharaoh's heart, and there were times Pharaoh hardened his own heart. You may find this hardening of a heart difficult to understand, but take God at His Word. He does not need you to make excuses for Him, justify His actions, or change the text of Scripture to fit your idea of what He does or does not do. He is LORD.

Let these verses prompt you to examine your own heart. Would the LORD describe your heart as hard and stubborn, not attending to His Word? Or do you have a tender heart that desires to hear, heed, and obey the Word of the LORD?

Use the words from Exodus 7:3 and 13-14 to pray for yourself and those for whom you stand guard as a faithful, prayerful watchman (Isaiah 62:6-7).

"LORD, please do not harden _____ and my hearts.
Do not let us harden our own hearts.
Help us listen to You.
Let us not have stubborn hearts that refuse to let go.
In Your name, Jesus~"

JANUARY 8

Please read Exodus 8.

Meditate on these phrases from verses 29 and 32.

Do not let Pharaoh deal deceitfully again ...
But Pharaoh hardened his heart this time also ...

Frogs, gnats, and insects! Ugh! Have you ever been plagued by something or someone? Have you begged and begged the LORD to deliver you, making promises to Him if He would take you out of your distressful circumstances? After He gave you relief, did you find yourself behaving not much differently than Pharaoh did 3,500 years ago?

Oh the hardhearted state of mankind!

For I know that nothing good dwells in me, that is, in my flesh;
for the willing is present in me, but the doing of the good is not.
Wretched man that I am! Who will set me
free from the body of this death?
Thanks be to God through Jesus Christ our LORD!
—Romans 7:18, 24-25a

Thankfully the LORD Jesus Christ saves your hard heart, changing it into a heart that can know, love, and serve Him. Reread Exodus 8. Can you relate to Pharaoh? Ask God to reveal areas in your life where you are dealing deceitfully with Him and others.

Pray Exodus 8:10, 15, and 29 over yourself and those for whom you stand guard as a faithful, prayerful watchman (Isaiah 62:6-7).

"There is no one like You, LORD our God.
May _____ and I know that truth.
When You give us relief, do not let us harden our hearts
and stop listening to You.
Do not let us deal deceitfully again.
For Your name's sake, Jesus~"

Please read Exodus 9.

Meditate on verses 20-21.

> *The one among the servants of Pharaoh*
> *who feared the word of the LORD*
> *made his servants and his livestock flee into the houses,*
> *but he who paid no regard to the word of the LORD*
> *left his servants and his livestock in the field.*

The LORD warned the people of Egypt He was sending a hailstorm that would kill every person and animal left outside. He gave them 24 hours notice, so they and their livestock could flee to safety. Amazingly, there were those who paid no attention to the word of the LORD, leaving their servants and animals to die in the fields.

The LORD still warns people, today. His Word says:

> *The LORD Jesus will be revealed from heaven*
> *with His mighty angels in flaming fire,*
> *dealing out retribution to those who do not know God*
> *and to those who do not obey the Gospel of our LORD Jesus.*
> —2 Thessalonians 1:7b-8

You have His Word. Will you pay attention to it and tell others what God says? The lives of those you love are dependent on obedience to God's Word.

Pray Exodus 9:14 and 20-21 over yourself and those for whom you stand guard as a faithful, prayerful watchman (Isaiah 62:6-7).

> *"LORD, there is no one like You in all the earth.*
> *May _____ and I fear Your Word*
> *and obey when You command us to flee.*
> *Let us regard and obey Your Word.*
> *In Your name, Jesus~"*

JANUARY 10

Please read Exodus 10.

Meditate on this question from verse 3.

> *Thus says the LORD, "How long will you*
> *refuse to humble yourself before Me?"*

By chapter 10 of Exodus, Pharaoh's refusal to humble himself before God resulted in:

- ❧ dead fish
- ❧ foul drinking water
- ❧ frogs in beds and bowls and heaps of dead frogs
- ❧ dust that became gnats throughout all the land
- ❧ houses swarming with insects
- ❧ horses, donkeys, camels, herds, and flocks dead from severe pestilence
- ❧ boils on animals and people
- ❧ hail that killed every man, beast, and plant left in the fields
- ❧ tree eating locusts and houses filled with locusts
- ❧ three days of darkness so dark it could be felt

Pharaoh did not submit to God, resulting in misery, darkness, and death to countless plants, animals, and people. Now examine yourself and the situations going on around you. How would others describe you? Are you a prideful person who brings darkness and misery to others? Or, are you a humble follower of Jesus who brings light and life to others?

Using the words from Exodus 10:1-3, pray for yourself and those for whom you stand guard as a faithful, prayerful watchman (Isaiah 62:6-7).

> *"LORD, do not let _____ and my hearts be hardened.*
> *Help us tell our children and grandchildren*
> *about the signs You perform among us*
> *that we may know You are the LORD.*
> *May we humble ourselves before You.*
> *Because You are LORD Jesus~"*

JANUARY 11

Please read Exodus 11.

Meditate on verses 6-7.

> *Moreover, there shall be a great cry in all the land of Egypt,*
> *such as there has not been before and such as shall never be again.*
> *But against any of the sons of Israel a dog will not even bark,*
> *whether against man or beast, that you may understand*
> *how the LORD makes a distinction between Egypt and Israel.*

The LORD makes distinctions. The Hebrew word, *palah*, translated as "distinction" in Exodus 11:7 is also used in Psalm 4:3:

> *But know that the LORD has set apart the Godly man for Himself;*
> *the LORD hears when I call to Him.*

God sets apart and distinguishes those who belong to Him. The distinction God made between Egypt and Israel was made apparent by death for the Egyptians and life for the Israelites. Tomorrow's devotional will teach what the LORD required of the Israelites to be given that life distinction as children of God.

It is eternally important for you to be distinguished as belonging to the LORD. Has the LORD set you apart for Himself? Are you a person of distinction because you belong to Christ?

Pray Exodus 11:3 and 7 over yourself and those for whom you stand guard as a faithful, prayerful watchman (Isaiah 62:6-7).

> *"LORD, give _____ and me favor in Your sight*
> *and in the sight of others.*
> *Let us be greatly esteemed where You put us.*
> *Make a distinction between the world and us.*
> *Because of Your name, Jesus~"*

JANUARY 12

Please read Exodus 12.

Meditate on verses 13 and 1 Corinthians 5:7b.

> *The blood shall be a sign for you on the houses where you live;*
> *and when I see the blood, I will pass over you,*
> *and no plague will befall you to destroy you*
> *when I strike the land of Egypt.*

> *For Christ our Passover also has been sacrificed.*

Exodus 12 is the picture of salvation from sin through the sacrifice of Jesus. People are enslaved to sin like the Israelites were enslaved to the Egyptians. Jesus, the Passover Lamb, came into Jerusalem on the day the Jewish people were choosing their lambs (John 12:12-15). Five days later when the lambs were slain, "the Lamb of God who takes away the sin of the world" (John 1:29), cried with His last breath, "It is finished!" (John 19:30).

> *Now in Christ Jesus, you who formerly were far off*
> *have been brought near by the blood of Christ,*
> *sprinkled with His blood, redeemed with precious blood,*
> *as of a lamb unblemished and spotless, the blood of Christ.*
> —Ephesians 2:13; 1 Peter 1:2b, 18b, 19

Just as He did over the Jews, the LORD will also pass over you when He returns in judgment, if He sees the blood of the Lamb covering you.

Pray Exodus 12:23 over yourself and those for whom you stand guard as a faithful, prayerful watchman (Isaiah 62:6-7).

> *"LORD, when You pass through to smite those who do not know You,*
> *thank You that You will see Your blood on*
> *the lives of _____ and me.*
> *LORD, pass over us and do not allow the destroyer*
> *to come into our homes to smite us.*
> *Because of Your blood, Jesus-"*

JANUARY 13

Please read Exodus 13.

Meditate on verse 8.

> *You shall tell your son on that day, saying,*
> *"It is because of what the LORD did for*
> *me when I came out of Egypt."*

The story of your salvation continues in Exodus 13. The day after eating the Passover lamb, the Israelites removed anything with leaven (yeast) from their midst. Paul explained the symbolism behind this Feast of Unleavened Bread in 1 Corinthians 5:6-8:

> *Do you not know that a little leaven leavens the whole*
> *lump of dough? Clean out the old leaven so that you may*
> *be a new lump, just as you are in fact unleavened.*
> *For Christ our Passover also has been sacrificed.*
> *Therefore let us celebrate the feast, not with old leaven,*
> *nor with the leaven of malice and wickedness,*
> *but with the unleavened bread of sincerity and truth.*

Before becoming a Christian, you were enslaved to sin. When you chose the Lamb of God, Jesus Christ, He took away your sins, freeing you from enslavement to them. God's glorious freedom in Christ lets you remove leaven (sin) from your life as you wholeheartedly live for Him.

Pray Exodus 13:7-8 over yourself and those for whom you stand guard as a faithful, prayerful watchman (Isaiah 62:6-7).

> *"LORD, do not let any leaven (sin) be seen*
> *among _____ and me.*
> *Let us tell others we are getting rid of sin*
> *because of what You did for us*
> *when You brought us out of slavery to sin.*
> *Because of You, our Passover Lamb, Jesus~"*

JANUARY 14

Please read Exodus 14.

Meditate on verses 13a and 14.

> *... do not fear! Stand by and see the salvation of the LORD*
> *which He will accomplish for you today ...*
> *The LORD will fight for you while you keep silent.*

The Israelites boldly left Egypt, but their confidence quickly turned to fear as the Egyptians had a change of heart and chased after them.

Can you relate to the Israelites? Have you ever been delivered by the LORD from a difficult situation? You feel confident, "going out boldly" (v. 8); when suddenly, another attack comes from the enemy, and your confidence quickly dissolves into gut-wrenching fear.

"The LORD will fight for you while you keep silent" (v. 14). God wants you to let Him fight for you, so He will get the credit and glory for the victory in your life. Notice the response of the professional Egyptian warriors when the Israelites let the LORD do their fighting:

> *He caused their chariot wheels to swerve,*
> *and He made them drive with difficulty;*
> *so the Egyptians said, "Let us flee from Israel,*
> *for the LORD is fighting for them against the Egyptians."*
> —Exodus 14:25

Pray Exodus 14:13-14 over yourself and others in fearful situations as a faithful, prayerful watchman (Isaiah 62:6-7).

> *"LORD, help _____ and me not to fear!*
> *Let us stand by and see the salvation You will accomplish for us today.*
> *LORD, fight for us!*
> *Help us to keep silent as we watch You do it.*
> *In Your name, Jesus~"*

JANUARY 15

Please read Exodus 15.

Meditate on verses 2-3.

> *The LORD is my strength and song, and He has become my salvation;*
> *this is my God, and I will praise Him;*
> *My father's God, and I will extol Him.*
> *The LORD is a warrior; the LORD is His name.*

Carefully observe God in Exodus 15. He is:

- highly exalted (v. 1)
- your strength, your song, and your salvation (v. 2)
- a warrior (v. 3)
- majestic in power, shattering the enemy with His right hand (v. 6)
- overthrowing those who rise up against Him in the greatness of His excellence (v. 7)
- majestic in holiness; awesome in praise; working wonders (v. 11)
- leading His redeemed people in lovingkindness and guiding them in His strength to His holy habitation (v. 13)
- causing the people He purchased to pass over and be planted in the mountain of His inheritance (vs. 16-17)
- reigning forever and ever (v. 18)
- the LORD, your healer (v. 26)

Remember these truths when you are tempted to grumble against the LORD like the Israelites did at Marah. Memorize at least one of the actions and attributes of your LORD and meditate on Him all day.

Pray Exodus 15:26 over yourself and those for whom you stand guard as a faithful, prayerful watchman (Isaiah 62:6-7).

> *"LORD our God, help _____ and me*
> *give earnest heed to Your voice.*
> *Let us do what is right in Your sight and*
> *give ear to Your commandments,*
> *and keep all Your statutes.*
> *LORD, You are our healer; keep us from sin sickness.*
> *In Your name, Jesus~"*

JANUARY 16

Please read Exodus 16.

Meditate on this statement from verse 8.

> *This will happen when the LORD gives you meat to eat in the evening*
> *and bread to the full in the morning,*
> *for the LORD hears your grumblings*
> *which you grumble against Him.*

There are two repeated words in Exodus 16: *grumbling* and *gathering.* Exactly one month passed since the Israelites saw the LORD destroy Pharaoh's army on their behalf. They sang a song of praise, but their gratitude quickly turned to grumbling when they romanticized their past because their present had hit a rough spot. Again, God miraculously met their needs, commanding them to gather His daily blessings of manna and quail. Gathering is a good remedy for grumbling.

Examine your life. Are you a grumbler or a gatherer? The LORD promises to "supply all your needs according to His riches in glory in Christ Jesus" (Philippians 4:19). Instead of grumbling, gather God's daily provisions. Start by daily gathering from His Word and talking to Him continuously throughout the day. As you gather God's blessings, let your grumbling become words of gratitude to your generous LORD.

Pray Exodus 16:12 over yourself and those for whom you stand guard as a faithful, prayerful watchman (Isaiah 62:6-7).

> *"LORD, I know You hear the grumblings of* _____ *and me.*
> *LORD, forgive us. At twilight let us eat what You provide,*
> *and in the morning, let us be filled with Your bread.*
> *May we know that You are the LORD our God.*
> *In Your name, Jesus, the Bread of Life~" (John 6:35)*

Please read Exodus 17.

Meditate on verses 2a and 4a.

Therefore the people quarreled with Moses…
So Moses cried out to the LORD, saying,
"What shall I do to this people?"

As you continue reading Exodus, observe Moses and his leadership style. There is much to be learned from the life of Moses as he led grumbling people from the land of slavery to the land of promise.

God freed the Israelites from the Egyptians with miraculous signs and wonders. He killed a mighty Egyptian army, burying them in the mud of the Red Sea. The LORD provided fresh water, manna, and quail. He consistently made His presence known with a pillar of cloud and a pillar of fire. Yet, when the people arrived at Rephidim with no sign of drinking water, they grumbled against Moses to the point he thought they would stone him. Notice Moses' response. He took his grumbling people and trying situation to his miraculous LORD. The LORD told Moses what to do and promised to stand before him in the presence of the people.

What impossible situation are you facing? Cry out to your LORD. He is waiting for you to come to Him for His solution.

Pray Exodus 17:4, 6, 13, and 15-16 over difficult situations in your life and the lives of those for whom you stand guard as a faithful, prayerful watchman (Isaiah 62:6-7).

"LORD, what shall _____ and I do?
Stand before us, LORD! Overwhelm our situations!
LORD, You are our Banner; You have sworn, and You will do it.
Because of Your name, Jesus~"

Please read Exodus 18.

Meditate on verse 9.

> *Jethro rejoiced over all the goodness which*
> *the LORD had done to Israel,*
> *in delivering them from the hand of the Egyptians.*

Deliver is used five times in Exodus 18 and means "to snatch away, rescue, and save."[1] Moses told his father-in-law, Jethro, about the difficulties he and the Israelites faced and how the LORD delivered them. Jethro rejoiced in the LORD's deliverance and acknowledged, "Now I know that the LORD is greater than all the gods" (v. 11a).

What difficult situation are you or someone you love facing? The LORD wants you to ask Him for help. He is your deliverer.

> *I love You, O LORD, my strength.*
> *The LORD is my rock and my fortress and my deliverer …*
> —Psalm 18:1-2a

As you trust in God and wait for Him to deliver, others will see the LORD working, and they will give Him praise, recognizing He is greater than all.

Call on God, your help, and pray Exodus 18:8-11 over yourself and those for whom you stand guard as a faithful, prayerful watchman (Isaiah 62:6-7).

> *"God, my help, please deliver _____ and*
> *me from all the hardship*
> *that has befallen us. We rejoice over all the*
> *goodness You have done to us.*
> *We will rejoice again as you deliver us from*
> *the hand of _____.*
> *Blessed be You, LORD, who delivers us. I*
> *know You are greater than all.*
> *Because You are Jesus-"*

---

1.   Retrieved from www.blueletterbible.org/lang/lexicon/lexicon.cfm?Strongs=H5337&t=NASB

JANUARY 19

Please read Exodus 19.

Meditate on verses 5-6a.

> *Now then, if you will indeed obey My voice and keep My covenant,*
> *then you shall be My own possession among all the peoples,*
> *for all the earth is Mine; and you shall be to Me*
> *a kingdom of priests and a holy nation.*

In order to belong to God, the Israelites had to obey Him and keep His covenant. In order for you to belong to God, you must obey His command to come to Him through a covenant relationship with Jesus Christ (John 14:6). You have access to something even more wonderful than the Israelites—that covenant relationship lets you abide in God, not just gaze up at Him from the foot of a mountain. Jesus Himself said, "In that day, you will know that I am in My Father, and you in Me, and I in you" (John 14:20).

When you belong to God, He says words to you that are similar to what He said to the children of Israel:

> *But you are a chosen race, a royal priesthood, a holy nation,*
> *a people for God's own possession, so that*
> *you may proclaim the excellencies*
> *of Him who has called you out of darkness into His marvelous light;*
> *for you once were not a people, but now you are the people of God ...*
> —1 Peter 2:9-10a

As a faithful, prayerful watchman, pray Exodus 19:5-6 over someone who needs to be in a covenant relationship with the LORD.

> *"LORD, let _____ obey Your voice and keep Your covenant.*
> *May they become Your own possession*
> *and a part of Your kingdom of priests and holy nation.*
> *Through You, Jesus Christ, our Savior~"*

Please read Exodus 20.

Meditate on verse 2.

> *I am the LORD your God,*
> *who brought you out of the land of Egypt,*
> *out of the house of slavery.*

Exodus 20 contains the Ten Commandments, laws God gave His people so they would know how to live with Him and others. These commands came after the LORD rescued the Israelites from 400 years of slavery in Egypt.

The LORD saved His people first, then gave them His commandments. God followed the same pattern when He saved you. First He rescued you from your slavery to sin, then He wrote His laws on your heart (Hebrews 10:16-17). Keeping God's law will not save you; only Jesus saves. Once you are in a saving relationship with Jesus, you will want to spend the rest of your life pleasing and obeying Him.

Pray Exodus 20:2-3, 6, and 20 over yourself and those for whom you stand guard as a faithful, prayerful watchman (Isaiah 62:6-7).

> *"LORD, thank You for bringing _____.*
> *and me out of slavery to sin.*
> *Let us have no other gods before You.*
> *As we love You and keep Your commands,*
> *show lovingkindness to us and our families.*
> *May we always fear You, so that we may not sin.*
> *In Your name, Jesus~"*

Please read Exodus 21.

Meditate on verses 15 and 17.

He who strikes his father or his mother shall surely be put to death.
He who curses his father or his mother shall surely be put to death.

Besides the Ten Commandments, God gave the people an additional 603 rules to help them live with Him and others. Over the next few days, you will read many of these 613 laws. Do not be tempted to skip reading these chapters, for the Law reveals what pleases the LORD and what He hates.

The meditation verses sound severe, but it is important to remember that these are the very words of God as recorded by Moses. Jesus even reminded the Pharisees and scribes of these rules:

For God said, "Honor your father and mother," and
"He who speaks evil of father or mother is to be put to death."
—Matthew 15:4

Would children treat their parents differently if they knew God views disrespect of parents as an offense worthy of the death penalty? When our children were young, we taught them what the Bible says about obeying and honoring parents. God's Word shaped their attitudes and behaviors in ways pleasing to Him.

Pray Exodus 21:15 and 17 over yourself and those for whom you stand guard as a faithful, prayerful watchman (Isaiah 62:6-7).

"LORD, let _____ and me never
strike or curse our father or mother.
Help us put to death thoughts, attitudes,
and actions that displease You.
Because of Your name, Jesus~"

JANUARY 22

Please read Exodus 22.

Meditate on verse 31a.

You shall be holy men to Me ...

God gave Moses laws for His people. These rules governed the behavior of people who belonged to the LORD.

In Exodus 22, you observe that God expects you to take responsibility for things entrusted to your care. If you borrow something and it breaks, do not return it broken; fix it or replace it (v. 14).

The LORD wants you to have nothing to do with witchcraft or sorcery (v. 18). Many popular books, shows, and movies revolve around this theme. Do you let yourself and your family to be entertained by it? What do you allow into your heart and mind?

When you became a Christian, God made you holy and set apart for Jesus; this distinction should be obvious by your behavior. The LORD wrote His laws on your heart (Hebrews 10:16); be sensitive to obey them as you observe them in His Word.

Pray Exodus 22:27b and 31a over yourself and those for whom you stand guard as a faithful, prayerful watchman (Isaiah 62:6-7).

"LORD, thank You that when _____ and I cry out to You,
You hear us because You are gracious.
We cry out to You for _____.
Make us holy people to You.
In Your name, Jesus~"

JANUARY 23

Please read Exodus 23.

Meditate on verse 13a.

*Now concerning everything which I have
said to you, be on your guard ...*

As you continue to read the laws in Exodus, observe that the LORD is the one speaking. You are reading the words of Almighty God, not the opinions of Moses or any other human. As you ponder the Words of the LORD, ask God to give you His heart to know Him more intimately and to understand the importance of His 613 laws.

Notice God promises to guard you when you obey Him (vs. 20-21). People want God's blessings. Blessings come from walking in obedience to the LORD, serving the LORD, and not rebelling against Him.

As you continue to learn God's Word, be on your guard to keep God's Word. When we obey God, it goes well with us (Jeremiah 7:23).

Pray Exodus 23:2a, 13, and 25 over yourself and those for whom you stand guard as a faithful, prayerful watchman (Isaiah 62:6-7).

*"LORD, do not let _____ and me
follow the masses in doing evil.
Let us be on our guard concerning everything You have said to us.
Do not let us mention the name of other gods,
nor let them be heard from our mouth.
Let us only serve You, LORD our God.
Please bless our bread and water,
and remove sickness from our midst.
In Your name, Jesus~"*

Please read Exodus 24.

Meditate on verse 12a.

> *Now the LORD said to Moses,*
> *"Come up to Me on the mountain and remain there …"*

How close do you want to be to God? In Exodus 24, the LORD was on Mount Sinai, and the people were at the foot of the mountain looking up at His glory. Aaron, Nadab, Abihu, and seventy elders went up the mountain with Moses and ate and drank in God's presence. Then God invited Moses to come further up and remain with Him. Notice that Joshua joined Moses to be with the LORD. I love that Joshua went with Moses even though his name was not personally on the invitation. Joshua wanted to be with God.

Where are you in relationship to the LORD? Do you watch from a distance the relationship others have with Christ, perhaps envying the intimacy they enjoy with Him? Do you occasionally eat and drink with Jesus when you partake of the LORD's Supper, but that closeness to God is reserved for days when you go to church? Or do you have an abiding relationship, spending your days walking and talking with God?

God extends the invitation to you to come to Him and remain there. What is your response?

Pray Exodus 24:7, 11, and 12 over yourself and those for whom you stand guard as a faithful, prayerful watchman (Isaiah 62:6-7).

> *"LORD, help _____ and me to be obedient*
> *and do all that You have spoken.*
> *Let us see You and eat and drink with You.*
> *We want to come to You and remain there.*
> *Because of our relationship with You, Jesus~"*

Please read Exodus 25.

Meditate on verse 8.

Let them construct a sanctuary for Me,
that I may dwell among them.

Exodus 25:8 is the first time *sanctuary* is mentioned in the Bible. It means a "holy place." Since the beginning of creation, God desired to live with people. When sin entered the world, God who is perfect could no longer live among sinful humans. Yet His desire did not change, and the construction of the sanctuary/tabernacle provided a way for God to dwell among His people. As you continue to read Exodus, you will learn what is required for humans to have their Creator live with them.

Each piece of furniture in the tabernacle was a picture and foreshadowing of Jesus Christ. For example, the tabernacle contained a table with the bread of the Presence on it (v. 30). Jesus is "the living bread that came down out of heaven; if anyone eats of this bread, he will live forever" (John 6:51).

As you continue to read about the tabernacle, ask Jesus to reveal Himself to you, and thank Him for dwelling with you.

Pray Exodus 25:8, 22, and 30-31 over yourself and those for whom you stand guard as a faithful, prayerful watchman (Isaiah 62:6-7).

"LORD, make _____ and me a
sanctuary for You; dwell among us.
Meet with us and speak to us about all Your commandments.
Jesus, be the bread of the Presence and the lampstand of our lives.
In Your name, Jesus~"

Please read Exodus 26.

Meditate on verses 33b-34.

> *The veil shall serve for you as a partition between*
> *the holy place and the holy of holies.*
> *You shall put the mercy seat on the ark of*
> *the testimony in the holy of holies.*

Holy God made special provision to keep Himself separated from sin. As you read the words "curtain," "board," "bar," "veil," and "screen" 60 times in Exodus 26, you probably felt the distance put between God and man. But notice in the midst of separation, God placed the mercy seat over the ark. God provided a place of mercy where people can be freed from sins and reunited with Him.

Knowing Exodus 26 helps you understand what happened 1,500 years later when Christ was crucified.

> *And Jesus uttered a loud cry and breathed His last.*
> *And the veil of the temple was torn in two from top to bottom.*
> —Mark 15:37-38

Jesus cut through all the curtains, boards, bars, veils, and screens, so you can "draw near with confidence to the throne of grace to receive mercy" (Hebrews 4:16). Jesus entered inside the veil "to save forever those who draw near to God through Him" (Hebrews 6:19; 7:25).

Use the words from Exodus 26:33-34 and praise Jesus for being the Way to get to the mercy seat and into the presence of God.

> *"Jesus, thank You for removing the partition*
> *between the holy place and the holy of holies.*
> *LORD, You are my Mercy Seat.*
> *Please let _____ accept You as their Mercy Seat.*
> *In Your name, Jesus~"*

Please read Exodus 27.

Meditate on verse 21.

> *In the tent of meeting, outside the veil which is before the testimony,*
> *Aaron and his sons shall keep it in order from evening until*
> *morning before the LORD; it shall be a perpetual statute*
> *throughout their generations for the sons of Israel.*

As you continue reading about the tabernacle, ask the LORD to show you how these words written 3,500 years ago apply to your life. Compare today's meditation verse to 1 Corinthians 6:19-20:

> *Or do you not know that your body is a temple*
> *of the Holy Spirit who is in you,*
> *whom you have from God, and that you are not your own?*
> *For you have been bought with a price;*
> *therefore, glorify God in your body.*

The detailed instructions for the tabernacle are a picture of the details accomplished by Christ on the cross in order for you to become the temple/tabernacle where the Spirit of God dwells. What are you doing to keep the temple in order? Do you meditate on God's Word day and night (Joshua 1:8)? Do you "devote yourself to prayer, keeping alert in it" (Colossians 4:2)?

Ask the LORD to reveal areas where you need to let Him put His tent of meeting in order. Pray Exodus 27:20-21 over yourself and those for whom you stand guard as a faithful, prayerful watchman (Isaiah 62:6-7).

> *"LORD, let Your light burn continually in _____ and me.*
> *Help us keep our bodies, the tent of meeting,*
> *in order from evening to morning before You, LORD.*
> *Make this a perpetual statute of our lives throughout our generations.*
> *Because You live in us, Jesus~"*

Please read Exodus 28.

Meditate on verses 2 and 3b.

> *You shall make holy garments for Aaron your*
> *brother, for glory and for beauty.*
> *Make Aaron's garments to consecrate him,*
> *that he may minister as priest to Me.*

Now meditate on these verses from the New Testament:

> *Put on the LORD Jesus Christ.*
> *You also, as living stones, are being built up as a*
> *spiritual house for a holy priesthood, to offer up spiritual*
> *sacrifices acceptable to God through Jesus Christ.*
> —Romans 13:14a; 1 Peter 2:5

Being a Christian means you put on Jesus, just like Aaron put on holy garments, setting him apart as God's priest. God says that when you put on Jesus, you became part of His priesthood to minister for Him. These truths are important to know as you live in Christ.

Aaron also wore a turban on his head containing the words: "Holy to the LORD." In Christ, you are also "Holy to the LORD." Let that phrase be on your mind, governing what you think, say, and do.

Pray Exodus 28:3, 12, 29-30, 36, and 38 over yourself and those for whom you stand guard as a faithful, prayerful watchman (Isaiah 62:6-7).

> *"LORD, thank You for making me a priest to minister before You.*
> *I bear the names of _____ before*
> *You, LORD; remember them.*
> *I carry the names of _____ over*
> *my heart before You continually, LORD;*
> *may they choose to follow You and not incur Your judgment.*
> *Let it always be on our mind that we are holy to You.*
> *Because You are holy, Jesus~"*

Please read Exodus 29.

Meditate on verse 44.

> *I will consecrate the tent of meeting and the altar;*
> *I will also consecrate Aaron and his sons to minister as priests to Me.*

Consecrate is used ten times in Exodus 29. It means to set apart as holy and dedicated to the LORD.[1] It is used in the context of great sacrifice: bulls, rams, and lambs killed and much blood applied in order to be consecrated as God's priest. About 28 sacrificial steps are listed in this chapter.

Yesterday, you learned that in Christ, you are God's priest. It is in the context of great sacrifice that you have this privilege.

> *By this will, we have been sanctified through the offering*
> *of the body of Jesus Christ once for all. For by one offering*
> *He perfected for all time those who are sanctified.*
> —Hebrews 10:10, 14

Jesus' death met all of the sacrificial requirements of the Old Testament Law. Your acceptance of this perfect sacrifice sets you apart as God's dwelling place and His priest (1 Corinthians 3:16; 1 Peter 2:5, 9). Live your life dedicated to the One who accomplished everything for you!

Pray Exodus 29:43-46 over yourself and those for whom you stand guard as a faithful, prayerful watchman (Isaiah 62:6-7).

> *"LORD, meet with _____ and*
> *me. Consecrate us by Your glory.*
> *Consecrate us to minister as priests to You.*
> *Dwell among us and be our God. We know*
> *that You are the LORD our God*
> *who brought us out of the land of our sin,*
> *that You might dwell among us.*
> *Because You are the LORD our God, Jesus~"*

---

1.   Retrieved from www.blueletterbible.org/lang/lexicon/lexicon.cfm?Strongs=H6942&t=NASB

JANUARY 30

Please read Exodus 30.

Meditate on verse 8b.

*There shall be perpetual incense before the LORD
throughout your generations.*

Inside the tabernacle, the altar of incense was placed in front of the veil separating the Holy Place from the Holy of Holies. The fragrance of incense went over the veil into the room containing the Ark of the Covenant, the place where God's presence dwelled. For the priests to be in God's presence, they had to smell good.

For you to be in God's presence, you have to smell good. Sin makes you stink, and God cannot be in the same room with stinky sin. If you are a Christian, then you have put on Jesus Christ; you not only look like Him; you also smell like Him. Amazing!

*For we are a fragrance of Christ to God among those who
are being saved and among those who are perishing.*
—2 Corinthians 2:15

You probably try to talk and act like Jesus throughout the day. Add the sense of smell to your journey into Christlikeness. Do you smell like Jesus? Ask the LORD to show you areas of your life that need to be permeated with the sweet aroma of Him.

Pray Exodus 30:6b, 8, and 10b over yourself and those for whom you stand guard as a faithful, prayerful watchman (Isaiah 62:6-7).

*"LORD, _____ and I want to meet with You.
May we be perpetual incense before You.
Make the generations that come after us
be perpetual incense, too.
Make us most holy to You, LORD.
Because we smell like You, Jesus~"*

Please read Exodus 31.

Meditate on verse 18.

> *When He had finished speaking with him upon Mount Sinai,*
> *He gave Moses the two tablets of the testimony,*
> *tablets of stone, written by the finger of God.*

It is fascinating to observe the finger of God throughout Scripture. Exodus 31:18 and Deuteronomy 9:10 both record God writing His Words with His finger on tablets of stone. Daniel 5 tells about a prideful king whose imminent death and the death of his kingdom were foretold by fingers writing on a wall. Jesus declared that He "cast out demons by the finger of God" (Luke 11:20). And when Jesus wrote on the ground with His finger, accusers eager to stone a woman caught in adultery, quickly dropped their rocks and left the scene realizing they, too, had committed sins worthy of death (John 8:3-11). The same finger of God that wrote "You shall not commit adultery" on tablets of stone, touched men with hearts of stone and the heart of a sinful woman with mercy, grace, and the command to "sin no more" (Exodus 20:14; John 8:11).

Has the finger of God touched your life? Ask the LORD to search your heart and use His finger to cut out anything that displeases Him.

Pray Exodus 31:2-3 and 6 over yourself and those for whom you stand guard as a faithful, prayerful watchman (Isaiah 62:6-7).

> *"LORD, call _____ and me by name.*
> *Fill us with Your Spirit, God,*
> *in wisdom, in understanding, in knowledge,*
> *and in all kinds of craftsmanship.*
> *Appoint us, LORD, and put in our hearts*
> *the skill to do all that You have commanded us.*
> *Because Your finger has touched our lives, Jesus~"*

FEBRUARY

On your walls, O Jerusalem,
I have appointed watchmen;
All day and all night they
will never keep silent.
You who remind the LORD,
take no rest for yourselves;
And give Him no rest until He establishes
And makes Jerusalem a
praise in the earth.
ISAIAH 62:6-7, NASB

February 1

Please read Exodus 32.

Meditate on verses 7-8a.

> *Then the LORD spoke to Moses, "Go down at once, for your people,*
> *whom you brought up from the land of Egypt,*
> *have corrupted themselves.*
> *They have quickly turned aside from the*
> *way which I commanded them.*

Exodus 32 is the continuation of the story that began in Exodus 24. The last thing the people said to Moses before he went up the mountain to receive God's law was, "All that the LORD has spoken we will do, and we will be obedient!" (Exodus 24:7). Well, the people quickly got out of control, corrupting themselves in idol worship.

God was furious, and if His compassion for these obstinate people had not overcome His wrath for their sin, He would have totally destroyed them.

Do you ever feel like an Israelite, saying you will obey the LORD but quickly turning aside from the way He tells you to go? Exodus 32:25, 29, and 32 tells you how to stop sinful behavior:

1. Recognize when you are out of control.
2. Dedicate yourself, today and everyday, to the LORD.
3. Ask the LORD to forgive you.

Pray Exodus 32:7-8, 25-26, 29, and 32 as a prayer of confession for yourself and a prayer of intercession for those whom you stand guard as a faithful, prayerful watchman (Isaiah 62:6-7).

> *"LORD, _____ and I have corrupted ourselves.*
> *We have quickly turned aside from the way*
> *which You have commanded us.*
> *Help us recognize when we are out of control and come to You.*
> *We dedicate ourselves today to You, LORD.*
> *Please forgive our sins.*
> *Because of Your mercy, Jesus~"*

Please read Exodus 33.

Meditate on verse 18.

Then Moses said, "I pray You, show me Your glory!"

The people committed heinous idolatry in Exodus 32, and the LORD told Moses to take them to the Promised Land without Him. He would provide an angel to guide them on their way, but He would not be in their midst because He might destroy them for being obstinate. The people grieved at the thought of God not with them, and Moses refused to go without Him.

Observe carefully the intimate, honest, face-to-face conversation between Moses and God in Exodus 33:11-23. Moses knew God and His ways. He knew the words God had spoken, and he boldly reminded God of His promises. The LORD granted Moses' requests, promising to go with him and give him rest.

As a follower of the LORD Jesus Christ, you also have access to an intimate relationship with God. You have His spoken Word written in the Bible. You have the Holy Spirit inside you to teach and remind you of the Words of Christ (John 14:26). Get to know God and His Word better this year. Use His Words as you engage in intimate conversation with Him throughout the day.

Pray Exodus 33:13-14 and 18 over yourself and those for whom you stand guard as a faithful, prayerful watchman (Isaiah 62:6-7).

> *"LORD, let _____ and me know*
> *Your ways that we may know You,*
> *so that we may find favor in Your sight.*
> *Let Your presence go with us and give us Your rest.*
> *Show us Your glory!*
> *In Your name, Jesus~"*

Please read Exodus 34.

Meditate on verse 8.

Moses made haste to bow low toward the earth and worship.

Carefully observe the LORD in Exodus 34.

1. He stood with Moses as he called on the name of the LORD (v. 5).
2. He is compassionate, gracious, slow to anger, abounding in lovingkindness and truth (v. 6).
3. He keeps lovingkindness for thousands and forgives iniquity, transgression, and sin (v. 7).
4. He does not leave the guilty unpunished, and He visits the iniquity of fathers on children and grandchildren to the third and fourth generations (v. 7).
5. He performs miracles that have never been done before (v. 10).
6. His name is Jealous; He is a jealous God (v. 14).

Apply that knowledge to your life:

1. Call on the LORD by name; He will stand with you.
2. Know the LORD's actions and attributes, and bow and worship Him.
3. Live pleasing to the LORD for the sake of future generations.
4. Ask the LORD to let you see His miraculous works.
5. Worship no other gods because the LORD is jealous for you.

Pray Exodus 34:6 and 9 over yourself and those for whom you stand guard as a faithful, prayerful watchman (Isaiah 62:6-7).

"LORD God, You are compassionate, gracious, slow to anger,
abounding in lovingkindness and truth.
O LORD, may _____ and I find
favor in Your sight; go along in our midst.
Help us stop being obstinate, and pardon our iniquity and our sin.
Take us as Your own possession.
For the sake of Your name, Jesus~"

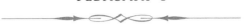

Please read Exodus 35.

Meditate on verse 5.

> *Take from among you a contribution to the LORD;*
> *whoever is of a willing heart, let him bring*
> *it as the LORD's contribution:*
> *gold, silver, bronze, ...*

The word *heart* is used six times in Exodus 35. It is used in the context of God looking for people with willing hearts to contribute the materials and talents needed to build His tabernacle. The LORD's contribution came from people with hearts moved and stirred by Him to give freely.

The Hebrew word translated as *willing* in Exodus 35:5 also means "generous, magnanimous, and noble."[1] Examine your heart. How would the LORD describe it? Is it generous and willing, or selfish and begrudging?

Ask the LORD to make your heart more and more like His. Pray Exodus 35:29-30 and 34-35 over yourself and those for whom you stand guard as a faithful, prayerful watchman (Isaiah 62:6-7).

> *"LORD, move _____ and*
> *my hearts to do all You command*
> *and to bring You a freewill offering.*
> *Call us by name, LORD, and fill us with Your Spirit*
> *in wisdom, in understanding and in*
> *knowledge, and in all craftsmanship.*
> *Also put in our hearts to teach.*
> *Fill us with skill to perform every work as You desire.*
> *In Your name, Jesus–"*

---

1.   Retrieved from www.blueletterbible.org/lang/lexicon/lexicon.cfm?Strongs=H5081&t=NASB.

FEBRUARY 5

Please read Exodus 36.

Meditate on verse 7.

*For the material they had was sufficient
and more than enough for all the work to perform it.*

"The work" is repeated twelve times in Exodus 36. It is the Hebrew word *melakah* meaning "work, service, and ministry."[1] It was first used in Genesis 2:2-3 when God completed His work and rested from all the work He had created and made.

The work in Exodus 36 was building God's tabernacle. Just reading the description of the work can be overwhelming. But notice God did not expect the people to make 915 feet of curtains, 1,050 loops and clasps, 1,920 board feet of wood overlaid with gold, 96 silver sockets, etc. in their own strength. The LORD put the skill and understanding into the people constructing the tabernacle, He strengthened them, and they had more than enough material to accomplish His work.

What ministry has the LORD asked you to perform? Do you feel overwhelmed? Ask God to give you the skill, understanding, and materials you need.

Pray Exodus 36:1-3 and 7 over yourself and those for whom you stand guard as a faithful, prayerful watchman (Isaiah 62:6-7).

*"LORD, put the skill and understanding
into _____ and me that we may
know how to perform all the work You have commanded.
Stir our hearts and give us the ability to come
to Your work to perform it well.
Bring all the resources needed to perform the work;
let them be sufficient and more than enough
for all Your work to complete it.
For the glory of Your name, Jesus~"*

1.   Retreived from www.blueletterbible.org/lang/lexicon/lexicon.cfm?Strongs=H4399&t=NASB.

THE WATCHMAN on the WALL | 41

Please read Exodus 37.

Meditate on verse 2.

And he overlaid it with pure gold inside and out
and made a gold molding for it all around.

The LORD must really like gold. Eighty-eight verses in Exodus contain the word "gold." When the children of Israel left Egypt, God caused the Egyptians to give the them their gold (Exodus 12:35-36). This plundered gold was purified and used to overlay the LORD's tabernacle and its furnishings because this was the place where God dwelled among His people. He surrounded Himself with pure gold.

Interestingly, there are two things more precious to God than pure gold: the proof of your faith and the blood of His Son.

The proof of your faith, being more precious than gold ...
may be found to result in praise and glory
and honor at the revelation of Jesus Christ.
You were not redeemed with perishable things like silver or gold
from your futile way of life ... but with precious blood,
as of a lamb unblemished and spotless, the blood of Christ.
—1 Peter 1:7, 18-19

As a Christian, you are now the temple of the Holy Spirit, the place where God dwells. You were bought with a price worth more than all the pure gold in the world, the blood of Christ (1 Corinthians 6:19-20).

Use the words from Exodus 37:29 to dedicate yourself and those for whom you stand guard as a faithful, prayerful watchman to the LORD (Isaiah 62:6-7).

"LORD, do the work of a perfumer in _____ and me.
Pour Your holy anointing oil on us.
May our lives be a pure, fragrant incense of Your work in us.
Because of You, Jesus-"

Please read Exodus 38.

Meditate on this phrase from verse 21.

… the tabernacle of the testimony …

The LORD expected His tabernacle, His residence or dwelling place, to be made exactly the way He desired. God gave detailed instructions for how the construction was to be done, and it was costly in materials and time. Amazingly, these 3,500-year-old plans were preserved for you to read. Ponder how important they must be that the LORD saved these blueprints for us—they are much more than a history lesson.

The tabernacle described in Exodus no longer exists; however, God is not homeless.

Do you not know that your body is a temple
of the Holy Spirit who is in you,
whom you have from God, and that you are not your own?
For you have been bought with a price;
therefore, glorify God in your body.
—1 Corinthians 6:19-20

You are now the tabernacle of the testimony; you are the temple of God. Your life gives testimony to the fact that God exists; He is "Christ in you, the hope of glory" (Colossians 1:27). And, in the same way God was intricately involved in the planning and building of the tabernacle 3,500 years ago, He is intricately and intimately involved in every detail of your life. Live to glorify the One who lives in you.

Pray Exodus 38:22 over yourself and those for whom you stand guard as a faithful, prayerful watchman (Isaiah 62:6-7).

"LORD, may _____ and I be like Bezalel,
doing everything You command us to do.
As a testimony of You, Jesus~"

Please read Exodus 39.

As you read, keep in mind that you are not only the temple of God (1 Corinthians 3:16; 6:19; 2 Corinthians 6:16); you are also a priest to God (1 Peter 2:5, 9; Revelation 1:6; 5:10; 20:6).

Meditate on verse 30.

> *They made the plate of the holy crown of pure gold,*
> *and inscribed it like the engravings of a signet, "Holy to the LORD."*

In order for Aaron and his sons to minister as priests of God, they had to wear special clothing. Exodus 39 describes these holy garments beautifully designed by the LORD. The ephod, breastpiece, robe, and turban set the priests apart as belonging to the LORD for the purpose of ministering in His tabernacle on behalf of His people.

When you became a Christian, Jesus took your sins, described as a filthy garment (Isaiah 64:6), and clothed you with garments of salvation (Isaiah 61:10). Jesus, your high priest (Hebrews 9:11), wraps you in His robe of righteousness (Isaiah 61:10), making you "holy to the LORD" (v. 30).

Meditate on these truths and let them affect the way you live for Christ.

The phrases "just as the LORD had commanded" and "all that the LORD had commanded" are repeated ten times in Exodus 39. As a priest holy to the LORD, use those phrases to pray for yourself and those for whom you stand guard as a faithful, prayerful watchman (Isaiah 62:6-7).

> *"LORD, help _____ and me to do*
> *all that You have commanded*
> *just as You have commanded.*
> *Because we are holy to You, Jesus-"*

Please read Exodus 40.

Meditate on verse 9.

> *Then you shall take the anointing oil and anoint*
> *the tabernacle and all that is in it,*
> *and shall consecrate it and all its furnishings; and it shall be holy.*

The tabernacle was a long rectangle. A single door led inside the courtyard to the altar of burnt offering, the place of sacrifice. Next there was a laver (large bowl) for washing. The priests offered sacrifices for their sins and washed before entering the tent of meeting. Inside the tent of meeting was a table with bread, a lampstand, an altar of incense, and then a veil. Behind the veil was the ark of the testimony; on its lid was the mercy seat. The LORD's glory came and rested on the ark and filled the tabernacle.

Through Jesus Christ, you get to tabernacle with God. Consider how Jesus fulfills every aspect of the tabernacle.

- The **door:** Jesus is the door (John 10:7).
- The **altar of burnt offering**: Jesus is the sacrifice for sin (John 1:29).
- The **laver**: Jesus washes you clean (John 13:8).
- The **table of bread**: Jesus is the Bread of Life (John 6:35).
- The **lampstand**: Jesus is the Light of the world (John 8:12).
- The **altar of incense**: Jesus is the fragrant aroma (Ephesians 5:2).
- The **veil**: Jesus entered through the veil, that is, His flesh (Hebrews 10:19-20).
- The **ark of the testimony**: Jesus is the glory of God (John 1:14).
- The **mercy seat**: Jesus saves according to His mercy (Titus 3:5).

Through Jesus you become the temple where His Spirit dwells (1 Corinthians 3:16).

Pray Exodus 40:35b over yourself and those for whom you stand guard as a faithful, prayerful watchman (Isaiah 62:6-7).

> *"LORD, as Your tabernacle, let Your glory fill _____ and me.*
> *Because of You, Jesus~"*

You are beginning the Christian season called Lent, the 40 days (not counting Sundays) prior to Easter. It is a time for meditation, fasting, and prayer to remember the suffering, crucifixion, and resurrection of Jesus.

In order to better understand what Christ did for you on the cross, you will spend the next 27 days reading *Leviticus*. It contains the LORD's requirements for sinful people to approach Him, the Holy God. You will read a lot about sin, blood, and sacrifices. The book screams, "We need a Savior!" As you read and pray this amazing book, allow your heart to overflow with gratitude for your LORD and Savior Jesus Christ who fulfilled every word of *Leviticus*, so you can be holy as He is holy (Leviticus 19:2).

FEBRUARY 10

Please read Leviticus 1.

Meditate on verses 3b-5.

> *He shall offer a male without defect; he shall offer it at the doorway*
> *of the tent of meeting, that he may be accepted before the LORD.*
> *He shall lay his hand on the head of the burnt offering, that it*
> *may be accepted for him to make atonement on his behalf. He*
> *shall slay the young bull before the LORD; and Aaron's sons the*
> *priests shall offer up the blood and sprinkle the blood around*
> *on the altar that is at the doorway of the tent of meeting.*

In the Old Testament, if a person wanted to be accepted by God, he offered a sacrifice, a perfect male animal. He brought it to the door of the tabernacle, then placed his hands on the animal's head, showing the transferance of his sins to the animal. Then he killed it; the animal died for the sins of the person, and its blood was sprinkled on the altar by the tabernacle door. The animal served as a sacrifice for sin. Once the sacrifice was made and received—cleansing the sin—only then did the LORD accept the person.

This is the picture of the sacrifice of Jesus Christ for your sins. Jesus, a male without defect, became the sins of all mankind (2 Corinthians 5:21). He was killed for your sins, and His blood was sprinkled on you (1 Peter 1:2). God accepts you because of the sacrifice of His perfect Son (Hebrews 9:26). No one gets through the door to God except through Jesus (John 14:6). Jesus is the door! (John 10:9).

Have you asked Jesus to forgive your sins; have you walked through the door so you can live the rest of eternity with Him?

Use the words from Leviticus 1:3-4 to pray over someone who needs Jesus.

> *"LORD, let _____ ask You*
> *to make atonement (reconciliation)*
> *on their behalf, so they can be accepted before You.*
> *Through Your blood, Jesus~"*

Please read Leviticus 2.

Meditate on these repeated phrases from verses 1-5, 7, and 9-10.

Fine flour
A soothing aroma to the LORD
A thing most holy

Offerings are important to God, and He gives His requirements for holy offerings in *Leviticus*. Chapter 2 describes the LORD's offerings as made of fine flour, without leaven, and seasoned with salt. In Scripture, leaven is often a picture of sin (1 Corinthians 5:8). Salt is used to purify and make things enduring. The LORD requires offerings to be pure and sinless in order to bring a soothing aroma to Him.

If you have come to God through the sacrifice of Christ, then the rest of your life is a holy offering lived wholly for the LORD.

Therefore I urge you, brethren, by the mercies of God,
to present your bodies a living and holy sacrifice, acceptable to God,
which is your spiritual service of worship.
—Romans 12:1

Would the LORD describe what you offer Him as fine, holy, and soothing? Ask Him to reveal and remove leaven/sin in your life. Let Him make you the salt of the earth (Matthew 5:13). Live to be a pleasing aroma to God.

Pray Leviticus 2:2-3 over yourself and those for whom you stand guard as a faithful, prayerful watchman (Isaiah 62:6-7).

"LORD, make _____ and me like fine flour.
May the offering of ourselves be a soothing aroma to You.
Make our lives a thing most holy to You.
Because of You, Jesus~"

Please read Leviticus 3.

Meditate on two repeated sentences from verses 1-2, 7-8, and 12-13.

He shall offer it before the LORD.
He shall lay his hand on the head of his offering
and slay it before the tent of meeting.

For a person to be at peace with God, sacrifice was made. An animal without defect was brought to the door of the tabernacle, and the person laid his hand on its head then killed it. The symbolism is powerful. As the hand was placed on the perfect animal, it received the person's sins and took their punishment—death (Romans 6:23)—for them. Peace with God came with the sacrifice of the animal. One did not enter God's presence without first making peace with Him, and peace came through the death of sin.

Jesus Christ is the fulfillment of *Leviticus* and the sacrificial system. Jesus received all of your sins and died for them. His sacrifice allows you to enter the presence of God. You can live at peace with the LORD because your sin died in Christ on the cross. Meditate on these truths during this season called Lent (the forty days before the celebration of Christ's death and resurrection).

Pray Leviticus 3:1-2 as an offering of thanksgiving for what Jesus did for you and those for whom you stand guard as a faithful, prayerful watchman (Isaiah 62:6-7).

"Jesus, You are _____ and my sacrifice of peace.
You were offered without defect before the LORD.
All our sins were laid on Your head, and You were slain.
We are able to enter the tent of meeting with God
because of Your blood sprinkled on us.
Thank You, Sacrifice of Peace, Jesus~"

Please read Leviticus 4.

Notice the repeated words: *sin, sin offering,* and *blood.*

Meditate on verse 29.

> *He shall lay his hand on the head of the sin offering*
> *and slay the sin offering at the place of the burnt offering.*

"Without the shedding of blood there is no forgiveness" (Hebrews 9:22b). Every sinner: priests, leaders, common people, the whole congregation brought a sin offering to the tent of meeting, symbolically transferred their sins to the sacrificial animal, and then killed it. The animal's blood was sprinkled before the LORD in front of the veil, on the altar of incense, and on and around the altar of burnt offering—**so** many sin offerings and **so** much blood because of **so** much sin.

Picture these repetitive, sacrificial requirements; then ponder Jesus, the Lamb of God, who takes away the sin of the world (John 1:29).

> *Every priest stands daily ministering and offering time after time*
> *the same sacrifices, which can never take away sins,*
> *but He (Jesus) having offered one sacrifice for sins for all time…*
> *… perfected for all time those who are sanctified.*
> —Hebrews 10:11-12a; 14b

Without Christ, you would need a perfect bull for a sin offering right now. Spend the time you don't have to search for a bull thanking your Savior for His perfect and complete sacrifice that covers all of your sins.

Use the words from Leviticus 4:29-31 in thanksgiving to Jesus, your sin offering.

> *"Jesus, You are _____ and my sin offering.*
> *Thank You for pouring out Your blood for us.*
> *Thank You for making atonement and forgiving us.*
> *Because of Your sacrifice, Jesus~"*

FEBRUARY 14

Please read Leviticus 5.

Meditate on verse 19.

It is a guilt offering; he was certainly guilty before the LORD.

In order to be right with God, one had to bring Him not only burnt, grain, peace, and sin offerings, but also guilt offerings. Sins requiring a guilt offering are listed in Leviticus 5. Are you guilty of any of the following?

- ❧ Refusing to tell the truth (v. 1)
- ❧ Touching a dead animal (v. 2)
- ❧ Touching human uncleanness (v. 3)
- ❧ Thoughtless speech (v. 4)
- ❧ Unfaithful actions (v. 15)
- ❧ Doing anything God said not to do (v. 17)

Guilty! Guilty! Guilty! Can you even imagine how many rams were required to cover all of the guilt? Thankfully the blood of Jesus not only covers your sins; it also covers your guilt, so you can live for Christ without a guilty conscience.

How much more will the blood of Christ,
who through the eternal Spirit offered
Himself without blemish to God,
cleanse your conscience from dead works to serve the living God?
—Hebrews 9:14

Pray Leviticus 5:5 and 18 over yourself and those for whom you stand guard as a faithful, prayerful watchman (Isaiah 62:6-7).

"LORD, I confess that I am guilty in all of these sins.
Jesus, You are my guilt offering. Thank You
for making atonement (a covering)
for me concerning the errors in which I sin.
Thank You for forgiving me.
LORD, may _____ make You the guilt offering for their sin.
In Your name, Jesus~"

Please read Leviticus 6.

Meditate on verses 2a, 6a, and 7.

> *When a person sins and acts unfaithfully against the LORD ...*
> *Then he shall bring to the priest his guilt offering to the LORD ...*
> *And the priest shall make atonement for him before the LORD,*
> *and he will be forgiven for any one of the things*
> *which he may have done to incur guilt.*

The LORD made sure every sin was accounted for in *Leviticus*. Your holy God cannot be in the presence of any sin, even unintentional sin; it must be covered and forgiven.

Leviticus shows you how desperately you need a Savior. Continue to read saying, "Thank You, Jesus" after every sacrificial requirement.

> *Sacrifices and offerings and whole burnt offerings and sacrifices for sin*
> *You have not desired, nor have You taken pleasure in them*
> *(which are offered according to the Law),*
> *then He said, "Behold, I have come to do Your will ..."*
> *By this will, we have been sanctified*
> *through the offering of the body of Jesus Christ once for all.*
> —Hebrews 10:8-10

Pray Leviticus 6:2a, 6a, and 7 over yourself and those for whom you stand guard as a faithful, prayerful watchman (Isaiah 62:6-7).

> *"LORD, _____ and I have sinned*
> *and acted unfaithfully against You.*
> *Jesus, You are our guilt offering.*
> *Thank You for making atonement for us*
> *and forgiving us for all of the things we have done to incur guilt.*
> *In Your name, Jesus~"*

Please read Leviticus 7.

Meditate on verses 26-27.

> *You are not to eat any blood, either of bird or*
> *animal, in any of your dwellings.*
> *Any person who eats any blood, even that*
> *person shall be cut off from his people.*

After the flood, God allowed people to eat meat with the stipulation that it be fully cooked with no blood in it (Genesis 9:3-4). This command was given because there would be a time in the life of every individual to decide whether or not to drink blood. That time is when a person chooses to become a Christian. Blood is life, and Jesus said, "Unless you eat the flesh of the Son of Man and drink His blood, you have no life in yourselves" (John 6:53). You are a Christian if you have consumed Jesus, symbolically eating and drinking Him, so that Christ is your life (Colossians 3:4).

In *Leviticus*, the priests were allowed to eat from the sacrifices offered at the tabernacle, but they could not eat the entire sacrifice, and it was never to be a piece of rare meat. As a New Testament priest (Revelation 1:6), you have the privilege of devouring all of your saving sacrifice, the LORD Jesus Christ.

Does Jesus live in you? If not, make Him your life, today.

Pray Leviticus 7:15 in thanksgiving to Jesus.

> *"Jesus, You are the flesh of the sacrifice.*
> *This is my thanksgiving peace offering to You.*
> *On this day of my offering, I choose to eat all of You;*
> *I will not leave any of You until morning.*
> *Because You are my life, Jesus~"*

FEBRUARY 17

Please read Leviticus 8.

Meditate on verse 7.

> *He put the tunic on him and girded him with the sash,*
> *and clothed him with the robe and put the ephod on him;*
> *and he girded him with the artistic band of the ephod,*
> *with which he tied it to him.*

The fact that Aaron and his sons were priests to God was obvious by what they wore. Their tunic, sash, robe, breastpiece, and turban with the holy crown identified them as priests.

Keep in mind that you, too, are set apart to be a priest to God.

> *And they sang a new song, saying, "Worthy are You to take the*
> *book and to break its seals; for You were slain, and purchased*
> *for God with Your blood men from every tribe and tongue and*
> *people and nation. You have made them to be a kingdom and*
> *priests to our God; and they will reign upon the earth."*
> —Revelation 5:9-10

Like Aaron and his sons, the fact that you are a priest is obvious by what you wear. Your priestly garment is the LORD Jesus Christ (Romans 13:14). When people see you, do they see Jesus?

Pray Leviticus 8:12-13 and 36 over yourself and those for whom you stand guard as a faithful, prayerful watchman (Isaiah 62:6-7).

> *"LORD, pour Your anointing oil on _____ and me.*
> *Anoint us to consecrate[1] us.*
> *Clothe us and gird[2] us with Yourself.*
> *Bind us to You!*
> *And may we do all the things which You command.*
> *Because of You, Jesus~"*

---

1.   *Consecrate* means dedicated to a sacred purpose.

2.   *Gird* means to surround.

Please read Leviticus 9.

Meditate on verse 6.

> *Moses said, "This is the thing which the*
> *LORD has commanded you to do,*
> *that the glory of the LORD may appear to you."*

In order for God's glory to appear, a bull calf sin offering, a ram burnt offering, a male goat sin offering, a one-year-old calf and lamb burnt offering, an ox and a ram peace offering, and a grain offering mixed with oil were necessary. The offerings had to be perfect and offered precisely as the LORD commanded, with blood from the offerings dipped and poured to the LORD's specifications. After the animals were slaughtered and presented before God, "fire came out from before the LORD and consumed the burnt offering" (v. 24). Only then was the LORD pleased and His glory revealed.

Because of the complete sacrifice of Jesus Christ, you are no longer required to come with an unblemished lamb, ram, or goat before you can approach God. Faith in the fact that Jesus came to earth, died for your sins, and rose from the dead is the way you gain the glory of the LORD (2 Thessalonians 2:14).

Has God's glory appeared to you? If not, believe in Jesus today. If His glory has appeared to you, thank Him. Reading *Leviticus* helps you appreciate even more what your Savior did on the cross.

Pray Leviticus 9:22-24 over yourself and those for whom you stand guard as a faithful, prayerful watchman (Isaiah 62:6-7).

> *"LORD, You are _____ and my sin*
> *offering, burnt offering, and peace offering.*
> *Bless us and let Your glory appear to us.*
> *Let Your fire come and consume us.*
> *May we shout and fall on our faces before You.*
> *Because of Your unblemished sacrifice, Jesus~"*

Please read Leviticus 10.

Meditate on verse 10b.

> *Make a distinction between the holy and the profane,*
> *and between the unclean and the clean.*

For the past nine days, you have read what God requires to enter His presence. The LORD expected strict obedience to these rules. Well, Aaron, the priest, had two sons who did not take God at His word and decided to enter God's presence their own way. Scripture says they "offered strange fire before the LORD, which He had not commanded them" (v. 1). Nadab and Abihu's blatant disregard for God's Word so angered the LORD that fire came from His presence and consumed them.

As a Christian, it is important to understand Leviticus 10. God has a specific way to come into His presence, and that is through Jesus Christ (John 14:6). If you believe other paths lead to God, you believe in "strange fire." If you attend a church that compromises God's Word for the sake of political correctness, you are in the midst of "strange fire." And the LORD does not tolerate "strange fire."

Continue to read and study the Bible. Learn what pleases God; treat Him as holy, and honor Him before all people (v. 3).

Pray Leviticus 10:1, 3, and 10 over yourself and those for whom you stand guard as a faithful, prayerful watchman (Isaiah 62:6-7).

> *"LORD, do not let _____ and*
> *me offer You strange fire.*
> *As we come near You, help us treat You as holy*
> *and honor You before all the people.*
> *Teach us to make a distinction between the holy and the profane,*
> *and between the unclean and the clean.*
> *For Your name's sake, Jesus-"*

Please read Leviticus 11.

Meditate on verse 44.

For I am the LORD your God.
Consecrate yourselves therefore, and be holy, for I am holy.
And you shall not make yourselves unclean
with any of the swarming things that swarm on the earth.

God gave the children of Israel laws regarding edible animals and those not to be eaten by humans. God created inedible animals to clean the environment; some of the things they consume are not healthy for humans. In Christ, there is freedom to eat anything God created "if it is received with gratitude" (1 Timothy 4:4). However, if you are having health issues, obeying Old Testament dietary laws can be beneficial.

The LORD used the word "unclean" 32 times in Leviticus 11. And while it is okay to eat a bacon sandwich, there are unclean things swarming the world that are detestable to God and should be detestable to you, too. Ask the LORD to help you and your family discern unclean, detestable things and not be absorbed in the abhorrent.

Pray Leviticus 11:43-45 over yourself and those for whom you stand guard as a faithful, prayerful watchman (Isaiah 62:6-7).

"LORD, may _____ and I
not render ourselves detestable
through any of the swarming things that swarm around us.
Do not let us make ourselves unclean with
them so that we become unclean.
You are the LORD our God. Consecrate us
and make us holy, for You are holy.
Do not let us make ourselves unclean
with any of the swarming things that swarm the earth.
Because You are holy, Jesus~"

FEBRUARY 21

Please read Leviticus 12.

Meditate on verse 8b.

The priest shall make atonement for her, and she will be clean.

As you continue reading God's laws for cleanliness, ask Him to show you His purpose behind the rules. For example, a woman remained "in the blood of her purification" (v. 5) twice as long if she gave birth to a daughter than when a son was born. This law was for the mother's welfare; God gave her more days to recuperate before her husband would want to try for a coveted male child.

Mary and Joseph followed the laws of Leviticus 12 after Jesus was born.

And when eight days had passed, before His circumcision,
His name was then called Jesus …
And when the days for their purification
according to law of Moses were completed,
they brought Him up to Jerusalem to present Him to the LORD …
and to offer a sacrifice according to what was
said in the Law of the LORD,
"A pair of turtledoves or two young pigeons."
—Luke 2:21-24

The unblemished, spotless Lamb of God's earthly parents "performed everything according to the Law of the LORD" (1 Peter 1:19; Luke 2:39). That Lamb's precious blood redeemed you, thus completing your days of purification.

Use Leviticus 12:7 in thanksgiving for what Jesus, the Lamb, did for you and those for whom you stand guard as a faithful, prayerful watchman (Isaiah 62:6-7).

"Jesus, thank You for offering Yourself before the LORD
to make atonement for _____ and me.
You cleansed us from the flow of sin and completed our purification.
Only because of You, Jesus~"

Please read Leviticus 13.

Notice the repeated phrase: *The priest shall look.*

Meditate on verse 34b.

> *The priest shall pronounce him clean;*
> *and he shall wash his clothes and be clean.*

Leviticus 13 contains the criteria for diagnosing the infectious disease called leprosy. It is a condition that starts unnoticeably small and grows to affect and rot other parts of the body. It is a real condition, and it is a poignant picture of sin. Sin infects your life, starting small, but when left undiagnosed and unchecked, grows into a putrid decay that affects you and those around you.

Thankfully you have a High Priest, Jesus the Son of God, who sympathizes with your sinful weaknesses and delights to heal leprosy (Hebrews 4:14-15; Luke 5:12-14; 17:11-19). Humbly come to your Great High Priest and ask Him to look you over and reveal the infectious sin in your life. Ask Him to cut out the sin sickness and make you clean. Hear these words of your Priest:

> *I am the Alpha and the Omega, the first and the last,*
> *the beginning and the end. Blessed are those who wash*
> *their robes, so that they may have the right to the tree*
> *of life, and may enter by the gates into the city.*
> —Revelation 22:13-14

Pray Leviticus 13:34 over yourself and those for whom you stand guard as a faithful, prayerful watchman (Isaiah 62:6-7).

> *"LORD Jesus, You are my Priest.*
> *Look at _____ and me. Stop the spread of sin in us.*
> *Do not let it go any deeper. Pronounce us clean.*
> *We want You to wash our clothes and make us clean.*
> *Only because of You, Jesus~"*

Please read Leviticus 14.

Notice the repeated phrase: *the one to be cleansed.*

Meditate on verses 1-3a.

> *Then the LORD spoke to Moses, saying,*
> *"This shall be the law of the leper in the day of his cleansing.*
> *Now he shall be brought to the priest,*
> *and the priest shall go out to the outside of the camp."*

The LORD cares about lepers. He dedicated 116 verses to lepers and their dreaded disease. While leprosy is a condition caused by bacteria and is not sin, its parallels to sin's consequences and what God requires in order to be cleansed are not coincidental.

A leper was cleansed outside the camp through great sacrifice involving birds, blood, living water, oil, lambs without defect, clothes washed … And just like God cares about the individual cleansing of one leper, He cares about the individual cleansing of you from sin, going to great sacrifice to ensure you are "the one to be cleansed" (vs. 4, 7-8, 11, 14, 17-19, 25, 28-29, 31).

> *But God demonstrates His own love toward us,*
> *in that while we were yet sinners, Christ died for us.*
> *Therefore Jesus also, that He might sanctify the people*
> *through His own blood, suffered outside the gate.*
> *So, let us go out to Him outside the camp.*
> —Romans 5:8; Hebrews 13:12-13a

Use Leviticus 14:24-25 as a prayer of thanksgiving to your LORD and as a prayer of intercession over those for whom you stand guard as a faithful, prayerful watchman (Isaiah 62:6-7).

> *"Jesus, You are the Lamb of my guilt offering.*
> *You were slaughtered, and Your blood put on*
> *me, so I can be cleansed. Thank You!*
> *Let _____ accept You as their*
> *guilt offering to be cleansed of their sins.*
> *In Your name, Jesus~"*

Please read Leviticus 15.

Meditate on verse 25.

> *Now if a woman has a discharge (an issue) of*
> *her blood many days ... she is unclean.*

A discharge or an issue coming from a person's body made him/her unclean. Their issue made everything they touched unclean.

Knowing Leviticus 15 makes this story from Mark 5:25-34 even more marvelous.

A woman who had a hemorrhage (an issue of blood) for twelve years came up in the crowd behind Him (Jesus), touched His cloak, and the flow of her blood dried up. Immediately Jesus turned around in the crowd and said, "Who touched My garments?" The woman fearing and trembling, aware of what had happened to her, came and fell down before Him and told Him the whole truth. He responded, "Daughter, your faith has made you well; go in peace and be healed of your affliction."

This unclean woman touched Jesus in the middle of a large crowd. No wonder she feared and trembled! It was against the law for her even to be there. She was unclean—she risked contaminating hundreds of people hoping to touch Jesus and be healed. The moment she touched her gracious Savior, He healed her issue and gave her peace.

What issues are discharging in your life? Issues like anger, pornography, jealousy, lying ... can pour forth in your life, bringing uncleanness to you and those around you. Touch Jesus. Tell Him the whole truth; He wants to heal your afflictions and give you peace.

Pray Leviticus 15:2 (using the King James translation) as a prayer of confession.

> *"LORD, I am unclean in this issue of _____.*
> *My flesh runs with this issue.*
> *LORD, stop this issue in my flesh!*
> *Because You can make me clean, Jesus~"*

Please read Leviticus 16.

Notice the repeated phrase: *make atonement.*

Meditate on verse 30.

> *For it is on this day that atonement shall*
> *be made for you to cleanse you;*
> *you will be clean from all your sins before the LORD.*

The Day of Atonement was the day, every year, when blood sacrifices were made to cleanse the people from all their sins. Atonement simply means "at-one-ment."[1] The LORD wanted to be one with His people, but He could not be in the presence of sin. Leviticus 16 gives God's requirements to be "at one" with Him. The blood from the sin offerings covered sinful impurities, and a scapegoat was sent into the wilderness, symbolically bearing the sins of the people.

God's requirements to be at one with Him have not changed. Blood still must cover your sins, and you need a scapegoat. Jesus Christ is your sin offering and your scapegoat. The day Jesus became your Savior is your Day of Atonement. He is the only blood sacrifice that makes atonement for your sins, allowing you to be at one with God (Romans 3:23-25). He is the scapegoat bearing all your sins, taking them away, so you can live at one with Him in righteousness (1 Peter 2:24).

Pray Leviticus 16:30-31 in thanksgiving for your Day of Atonement and for those who need a Day of Atonement.

> *"LORD, thank You for the day You made atonement to cleanse me.*
> *Thank You that I am clean from all my sins before You.*
> *Thank You for the solemn rest that comes from You.*
> *Keep my soul humble before You.*
> *LORD, please let _____ desire*
> *their Day of Atonement with You.*
> *Because of Your blood, Jesus~"*

---

1. *Easton's Bible Dictionary.*

FEBRUARY 26

Please read Leviticus 17.

Meditate on verse 11, pronouncing atonement as three separate words: at-one-ment.

For the life of the flesh is in the blood,
and I have given it to you on the altar to
make atonement for your souls;
for it is the blood by reason of the life that makes atonement.

An animal's blood represented its life. That lifeblood was poured on the altar of sacrifice as a covering for sins to make atonement for the people, so they could experience at-one-ment with God.

Understanding Leviticus 17:11 brings richer understanding to Jesus' words.

He who eats My flesh and drinks My blood has eternal life.
He who eats My flesh and drinks My blood
abides in Me and I in him.
The glory which You have given Me I have
given to them, that they may be one,
just as We are one; I in them and You in Me,
that they may be perfected in unity …
—John 6:54a, 56; 17:22-23a

When you are in Christ, His blood covers you. You spiritually drink His lifeblood, making Jesus' life your life. You become one with Him.

Pray Leviticus 17:11-12 and 14 in thanksgiving for the flesh and blood of Jesus Christ given for you.

"LORD, the life of the flesh is in the blood.
Thank You for giving Yourself on the altar
to make atonement for my soul;
for it is Your blood by reason of Your life that makes atonement.
LORD, You prohibited eating the blood of any flesh, for the
life of all flesh is its blood. Thank You that this prohibition was
to protect the one time I would eat the blood of Your flesh on
the Day of Atonement when I became one with You, Jesus."

FEBRUARY 27

Please read Leviticus 18.

Meditate on verses 2b and 4.

> *I am the LORD your God.*
> *You are to perform My judgments*
> *and keep My statutes to live in accord with them;*
> *I am the LORD your God.*

The Israelites spent over 400 years living among the Egyptians who engaged in activities abominable to the LORD. Now they were entering another land full of perverse people with laws condoning lewd and impure behaviors. God commanded His people not to walk in the statutes of the Egyptians and the Canaanites; God's people were to obey His rules (vs. 3-4). He even gave laws for maintaining sexual purity.

Here is the LORD's list of those you are never to have intercourse with:

- Any blood relative (v. 6)
- Father or mother (v. 7)
- Stepmother (v. 8)
- Sister, stepsister, half-sister (vs. 9, 11)
- Aunt (vs. 12-14)
- Uncle (v. 14)
- Daughter-in-law (v. 15)
- Sister-in-law (vs. 16, 18)
- Grandchildren (vs. 10, 17)
- Neighbor's wife (v. 20)
- Anyone the same sex as you (v. 22)
- Any animal (v. 23)

Hear and heed the Word of the LORD. Nations' laws do not change God's Laws. Stand firm on His Truth.

Pray Leviticus 18:30 over yourself and those for whom you stand guard as a faithful, prayerful watchman (Isaiah 62:6-7).

> *"LORD, help _____ and me to keep Your charge,*
> *that we do not practice any of the abominable customs*
> *which are practiced before us, so as to defile ourselves with them.*
> *Because You are the LORD our God, Jesus~"*

Please read Leviticus 19.

Notice the repeated phrase: *I am the LORD your God.*

Meditate on verse 2b.

> *You shall be holy,*
> *for I the LORD your God am holy.*

If God is your LORD, you will be holy (sacred and set apart) because He is holy. Leviticus 19 contains behaviors exemplifying those who are set apart to God.

Examine your life. Do your attitudes, words, and actions give evidence that you belong to God, that He is the LORD over your life? As you read the commands in Leviticus 19, do any of them bring conviction to your heart?

- ⮞ Reverence your mother and father (v. 3).
- ⮞ Do not deal falsely (v. 11).
- ⮞ Do not show partiality (v. 15).
- ⮞ Do not hate your fellow countryman (v. 17).

Submit to Him any area where you falter. Rejoice! You can be holy because the LORD Jesus who lives inside of you is holy. Ask Him to give you His attitudes, words, and actions.

Pray Leviticus 19:2, 32b, and 37 over yourself and those for whom you stand guard as a faithful, prayerful watchman (Isaiah 62:6-7).

> *"LORD, make _____ and me holy,*
> *for You, LORD our God, are holy.*
> *Help us revere You; You are the LORD.*
> *Help us observe all Your statutes*
> *and all Your ordinances and do them.*
> *Because You are the LORD, Jesus~"*

FEBRUARY 29

Please read Leviticus 20.

Meditate on verse 26.

Thus you are to be holy to Me, for I the LORD am holy;
and I have set you apart from the peoples to be Mine.

Leviticus gives a vivid picture of God's heart and mind. He abhors child sacrifice, sexual immorality, disrespect of parents … God hates sin … but He loves people. He loves people so much that He created a sacrificial system to remove sin, making it possible for people to belong to Him.

Christ's death on the cross was the culmination of sacrifices for sin. His death forever satisfied the need for sacrifice. Jesus, as payment for your sins, was so costly and so complete that your faith in Him sets you apart to belong to God forever. As you grow in that eternal relationship, you will want to do things that please the LORD. Pleasing Him is so wonderful you will find you no longer desire things which He abhors.

Now those who belong to Christ Jesus
have crucified the flesh with its passions and desires.
—Galatians 5:24

Heed God's words and warnings from Leviticus 20 and pray verses 7-8, 23, and 25-26 over yourself and those for whom you stand guard as a faithful, prayerful watchman (Isaiah 62:6-7).

"LORD, consecrate _____ and me.
Make us holy, for You are the LORD our God.
Help us keep Your statutes and practice them.
Sanctify us, LORD!
May we not follow the customs of our nation, which You abhor.
Let us make a distinction between the clean and the unclean.
LORD, make us holy because You are holy,
and You have set us apart to be Yours.
Because of You, Jesus~"

MARCH

On your walls, O Jerusalem,
I have appointed watchmen;
All day and all night they
will never keep silent.
You who remind the LORD,
take no rest for yourselves;
And give Him no rest until He establishes
And makes Jerusalem a
praise in the earth.
ISAIAH 62:6-7, NASB

MARCH 1

Please read Leviticus 21.

Meditate on verse 12.

> *Nor shall he go out of the sanctuary nor profane the*
> *sanctuary of his God, for the consecration of the anointing*
> *oil of his God is on him; I am the LORD.*

The priests were anointed and consecrated (set apart) by God to work in His sanctuary, presenting offerings on behalf of the people. Such a high calling required stringent rules for maintaining purity and holiness among those who served in God's presence.

As a Christian, the LORD consecrated you to be a priest, but you are also a sanctuary.

> *He (Jesus) has made us to be a kingdom,*
> *priests to His God and Father...*
> —Revelation 1:6a

> *Or do you not know that your body is a temple of the*
> *Holy Spirit who is in you, whom you have from God,*
> *and that you are not your own? For you have been bought*
> *with a price; therefore, glorify God in your body.*
> —1 Corinthians 6:19-20

The life of Jesus paid for you to be both God's priest and His sanctuary, housing His glory. How precious you are to be bought with the blood of the One of eternal value! Let Christ's holiness and purity be evident by the way you glorify God in your body.

Pray Leviticus 21:12 over yourself and those for whom you stand guard as a faithful, prayerful watchman (Isaiah 62:6-7).

> *"LORD, do not let _____ and me go out from Your*
> *sanctuary (Your presence) nor profane Your sanctuary (our bodies),*
> *for the consecration of Your anointing oil is on us. You are the*
> *LORD, and You bought us with Your life, LORD Jesus~"*

MARCH 2

Please read Leviticus 22.

Meditate on verses 2 and 4.

> *Tell Aaron and his sons to be careful with the holy gifts of the*
> *sons of Israel, which they dedicate to Me, so as not to profane*
> *My holy name; I am the LORD. No man of the descendants*
> *of Aaron ... may eat of the holy gifts until he is clean ...*

Only priests were allowed to eat from the sacrifices, "the holy gifts" (v. 4), and they had to be clean before being allowed to eat. An unclean priest first "bathed his body in water," then ate of the holy (vs. 6-7).

Let these Old Testament insights be illuminated by the Light of New Testament understanding:

- ❧ Jesus is the Holy Gift, the Holy One of God (John 4:10; 6:69).
- ❧ Jesus washes you clean (John 13:8).
- ❧ In Christ, you are a priest offering spiritual sacrifices to God (1 Peter 2:5).
- ❧ As God's priest, you eat the Holy (John 6:53-56).

> *While they were eating, Jesus took some bread,*
> *and after a blessing, He broke it and gave it to the*
> *disciples, and said, "Take, eat; this is My body."*
> —Matthew 26:26

Pray Leviticus 22:31-33 over yourself and those for whom you stand guard as a faithful, prayerful watchman (Isaiah 62:6-7).

> *"LORD, help_____ and me keep Your commandments*
> *and do them. You are the LORD. Do not let us profane Your holy*
> *name. Let us sanctify (reverence and honor) You among the people.*
> *You are the LORD who sanctifies (purifies and cleanses) us. Thank*
> *You for bringing us out of the land of slavery to be our God.*
> *Because You are LORD, Jesus~"*

MARCH 3

Please read Leviticus 23.

Meditate on verse 2b.

The LORD's appointed times which you shall proclaim as
holy convocations—My appointed times are these:

The LORD gave details for eight holy convocations (sacred assemblies).
Just like Christ fulfilled every aspect of the tabernacle and the sacrificial
system, He has and will fulfill these holy convocations.

- ✖ The Sabbath rest – Jesus is your Sabbath rest (Hebrews 4:7-11).
- ✖ The LORD's Passover – Jesus died on Passover, and He is your
  Passover (1 Corinthians 5:7).
- ✖ Feast of Unleavened Bread – This feast began the day after Christ's
  crucifixion. His sacrifice removes the leaven (sin) in your life (1
  Corinthians 5:8).
- ✖ Feast of First Fruits – Christ rose from the dead on this feast day. He
  is the First Fruit raised from the dead (1 Corinthians 15:20).
- ✖ Feast of Weeks (Pentecost) – Fifty days after His resurrection, Jesus
  gave His Spirit to believers on this day, and 3,000 people were added
  to His church. The church is the new grain offering (Acts 2:1-47).
- ✖ Feast of Trumpets – Jesus will fulfill this feast when He returns with
  the sounding of God's trumpet (1 Thessalonians 4:16).
- ✖ Day of Atonement – Your Day of Atonement is when you make Jesus
  the sacrifice for your sins. It will come for Israel when they accept
  Jesus as their atoning sacrifice (Romans 11:25-29).
- ✖ Feast of Booths (Tabernacles) – The kingdom of the world will
  become the Kingdom of Christ, and He will tabernacle with you
  forever (Revelation 7:15; 11:15; 21:1-4). Glory!

Pray Leviticus 23:4 over yourself and those for whom you stand guard as a
faithful, prayerful watchman (Isaiah 62:6-7).

"LORD, You have appointed times for holy convocations. LORD,
let_____ and me not miss any of Your appointed times.
May we proclaim to others Your times appointed for them.
In Your name, Jesus~"

Please read Leviticus 24.

Meditate on verse 11a.

The son of the Israelite woman blasphemed the Name and cursed.

Leviticus reveals God's heart and expectations. His expectations from Leviticus 24 are:

- Provide oil, so the lamp burns continually (v. 2).
- Present the bread before the LORD continually (vs. 5-8).
- Protect the Name of the LORD and protect life (vs. 10-23).

Are you living up to God's expectations?

Jesus, the Light of the world, calls you "the light of the world" (John 9:5; Matthew 5:14). Jesus is the bread of life (John 6:35, 48, 51). His name is "above every name" (Philippians 2:9). Jesus gave up His life so you can have His eternal life (Matthew 20:28; John 10:28).

Ponder these truths and let your light shine before others, presenting the Bread of Life so they will want to consume rather than reject Him. Give life so others will become open to know the Giver of eternal life.

Pray Leviticus 24:2, 4, 9, 11, and 17-18 over yourself and those for whom you stand guard as a faithful, prayerful watchman (Isaiah 62:6-7).

> *"LORD, keep the lamps of _____ and me in*
> *order and let them burn continually before You.*
> *Thank You for letting us eat Your Bread.*
> *You are our portion forever!*
> *May we never curse and blaspheme Your Name.*
> *May we protect life rather than take it.*
> *In Your name, Jesus~"*

MARCH 5

Please read Leviticus 25.

Meditate on this phrase from verse 21.

I will so order My blessing for you …

The LORD knows the importance of rest. He created the heavens, earth, seas, and everything they contain in six days. On the seventh day He rested, making it a sabbath day (Exodus 20:11). God also made sabbath years. He commanded that after producing crops for six years, the land have a year of rest (vs. 1-7). The LORD also instituted the jubilee year. After seven sabbaths of years passed, that is 49 years, the fiftieth year was declared as a year of jubilee (v 8). During the year of jubilee, land was returned to its original owner and slaves were redeemed and set free.

As a Christian, you are always living in the year of jubilee. You were a slave to sin, and Christ redeemed you and set you free to live in Him.

> *In Him (Jesus), we have redemption through His*
> *blood, the forgiveness of our trespasses, according to*
> *the riches of His grace which He lavished on us.*
> —Ephesians 1:7-8a

Does your life reflect the LORD's jubilee? Live for others to want Christ's redemption of their lives so they can also enter their year of jubilee.

Pray Leviticus 25:21, 48, and 55 over yourself and those for whom you stand guard as a faithful, prayerful watchman (Isaiah 62:6-7).

> *"LORD, so order Your blessing for _____ and me.*
> *You redeemed us; thank You! Please redeem _____.*
> *We are Your servants, whom You brought out from the land of sin.*
> *You are the LORD our God, Jesus~"*

MARCH 6

Please read Leviticus 26.

Meditate on these phrases from verses 19 and 41.

> *I will also break down your pride of power ...*
> *If their uncircumcised heart becomes humbled ...*

God wanted there to be no doubt about His view of sin and disobedience. He called these things disobedience: rejecting His statutes, abhorring His ordinances, and acting with hostility against Him (vs. 15, 21, 23, 27). He also declared the consequences of disobeying Him: "I will act with wrathful hostility against you, and I, even I, will punish you seven times for your sins. My soul shall abhor you" (vs. 28, 30).

Amazingly, in the midst of His abhorrence for sin, God provided a way of escape for the sinner.

> *If they confess their iniquity and the iniquity of their forefathers,*
> *in their unfaithfulness which they committed against Me, and also*
> *in their acting with hostility against Me—If their uncircumcised*
> *heart becomes humbled so that they then make amends for their*
> *iniquity, then I will remember My covenant ... I will not reject*
> *them, nor will I so abhor them as to destroy them, breaking*
> *My covenant with them; for I am the LORD their God.*
> —Leviticus 26:40, 41b-42a, 44b

Do not be tempted to trivialize sin; instead confess it. Then pray Leviticus 26:3, 19, and 41 over yourself and those for whom you stand guard as a faithful, prayerful watchman (Isaiah 62:6-7).

> *"LORD, help _____ and me to walk in Your statutes*
> *and keep Your commandments so as to carry them out.*
> *Break down our pride of power and*
> *humble our uncircumcised hearts.*
> *For You are the LORD our God, Jesus~"*

Please read Leviticus 27.

*Notice the repeated words **value** and **valuation**. As you read, ask the LORD how much He values you.*

Meditate on verse 2b.

> *When a man makes a difficult vow, he shall be valued according to your valuation of persons belonging to the LORD.*

When a man made a vow to God beyond his power to keep, he could buy back what he had promised. The children of Israel promised to be obedient to do all God commanded (Exodus 19:8; 24:3, 7). This was an impossible vow to keep, and the LORD's sacrificial system was the required payment for those broken vows. *Leviticus* ends with the payment necessary to redeem human life.

No human vow can dedicate you to the LORD. Rash promises are vain attempts to get to God. What could even begin to redeem humanity?

> *You were not redeemed with perishable things like silver or gold from your futile way of life inherited from your forefathers, but with precious blood, as of a lamb unblemished and spotless, the blood of Christ.*
> —1 Peter 1:18-19

The blood of Jesus redeems your difficult vows, your disobedience, your uncleanness, everything that makes it impossible to be devoted to God. God values your life with the life of His Son. What an appropriate ending to this book fulfilled completely by Jesus Christ!

Pray Leviticus 27:29 in thanksgiving for what Jesus did for you and those for whom you stand guard as a faithful, prayerful watchman (Isaiah 62:6-7).

> *"LORD, You were set apart among men, not to be ransomed, but to be the ransom for many (Matthew 20:28). You were surely put to death for _____ and me. Thank You, Jesus~"*

MARCH 8

Please read Hebrews 1.

Meditate on verse 3.

> *And He is the radiance of His glory and the exact*
> *representation of His nature, and upholds all things by the*
> *word of His power. When He had made purification of sins,*
> *He sat down at the right hand of the Majesty on high.*

The complexity of the sacrificial system illustrates how much effort your holy God puts into helping you be in fellowship with Him. It is appropriate to look at *Hebrews* since it provides a New Testament completion to *Exodus* and *Leviticus*.

Hebrews carefully documents how Jesus fulfills God's requirements found in *Exodus* and *Leviticus*. Jesus purifies you with His blood. He is seated next to the Majesty on high; therefore, He is God's accepted sacrifice which covers your sins. The Holy Spirit leads you to God when you ask for and receive Jesus, the necessary sacrifice for the forgiveness of sins. Have you accepted Jesus as that sacrifice?

Pray Hebrews 1:3 over yourself and those for whom you stand guard as a faithful, prayerful watchman (Isaiah 62:6-7).

> *"LORD, You uphold all things by the word of Your power.*
> *Make purification of sins for _____ and me.*
> *In Your name, Jesus~"*

MARCH 9

Please read Hebrews 2.

Meditate on verses 9-10.

> *But we do see Him who was made for a little while lower than the angels, namely, Jesus, because of the suffering of death crowned with glory and honor, so that by the grace of God He might taste death for everyone. For it was fitting for Him, for whom are all things and through whom are all things, in bringing many sons to glory, to perfect the author of their salvation through sufferings.*

The book of *Hebrews* is a great gift because it helps you understand the superiority of Jesus over other revelations of God, angels, Moses, the Levitical priesthood, and previous sacrifices. The words superior and better are used 15 times in *Hebrews*. It is a book of better things.

Chapter 2 completes the argument of Jesus' superiority over angels started in Hebrews 1 and reveals the benefits of God's gift of Jesus. He overcomes death (vs. 9, 14-15), makes you His brethren (vs. 10-14, 17), and becomes your high priest taking away your sin (17-18).

As thankful children, pray Hebrews 2:12-13a over yourself and those for whom you stand guard as a faithful, prayerful watchman (Isaiah 62:6-7).

> *"LORD, _____ and I proclaim*
> *Your name to our brethren.*
> *In the midst of the congregation,*
> *we sing Your praise.*
> *We will put our trust in You.*
> *In Your name, Jesus~"*

MARCH 10

Please read Hebrews 3.

Meditate on verse 6.

But Christ was faithful as a Son over His house—whose we are, if we hold fast our confidence and the boast of our hope firm until the end.

This section of Scripture honors Moses' faithfulness. The writer of *Hebrews* used that faithfulness to compare the superiority of Jesus' faithfulness because Jesus is the builder of Moses' ministry (house). Jesus built a superior ministry (house) to the one founded in the Law through Moses. With this statement, the writer quoted from Psalm 95 and exhorted his readers not to behave like those who wandered in the wilderness and did not hear God's voice, hardened their hearts, tried and tested the LORD, went astray, and did not know His ways (vs. 7-11).

Ponder these exhortations in the positive: hear God's voice, soften your heart, see His works, trust Him, remain on His path, know Him, know His ways, and enter His rest.

Pray Hebrews 3:6-11 over yourself and those for whom you stand guard as a faithful, prayerful watchman (Isaiah 62:6-7).

"LORD, help _____ and me hold fast our hope until the end. Let us hear your voice. Please soften our hearts. Let us see Your works. Help us trust You and not go astray. Help us know You and Your ways. Let us enter Your rest. In Your name, Jesus~"

MARCH 11

Please read Hebrews 4.

Meditate on verse 16a.

Therefore, let us draw near with confidence to the throne of grace …

Hebrews 4 is a chapter of extraordinary encouragement for you. Christianity is a real-time journey with God. You have a history and a future with the God of the universe, and you have the ability to be with Him right now!

The Promised Land of Joshua's time was not the final spiritual rest for God's people (vs. 8-10); therefore, you are to fearfully remain faithful until you enter this last state of rest. You are not alone in this journey. You get to confidently approach the LORD for help. As you approach Him, think about these truths:

God already knows everything about you, and His Word helps you understand more about yourself (vs. 12-13).

Jesus, the Son of God, is your high priest and has passed through the heavens to enable you to come before God (vs. 14-16).

Jesus sympathetically helps you with your temptations so you can come near to God with confidence. This is a right-now benefit and a command to come to Him (vs. 14-16).

Pray Hebrews 4:16 over yourself and those for whom you stand guard as a faithful, prayerful watchman (Isaiah 62:6-7).

"LORD, help _____ and me draw near
to You with confidence and receive
Your mercy and grace.
In Your name, Jesus~"

MARCH 12

Please read Hebrews 5.

Meditate on verses 8-10.

> *Although He was a Son, He learned obedience from the things which*
> *He suffered. And having been made perfect, He became to all those*
> *who obey Him the source of eternal salvation, being designated*
> *by God as a high priest according to the order of Melchizedek.*

The author of *Hebrews* proved the superiority of Jesus as high priest by contrasting Him to earthly high priests in terms of human sinfulness and bloodlines.

An earthly high priest offered sacrifices for the people and himself since he also was sinful (vs. 1-3). Jesus was "without sin" (Hebrews 4:15) until He became sin for us and made the sacrifice of Himself (2 Corinthians 5:21).

Previous high priests were from the order and lineage of Levi, particularly of Aaron. Jesus was from the tribe of Judah; therefore, not eligible to be an earthly high priest. God appointed Jesus as high priest from the order of King Melchizedek who lived 400 years before Aaron. David, who lived 500 years after Aaron, wrote:

> *The LORD has sworn and will not change His mind,*
> *You are a priest forever according to the order of Melchizedek.*
> —Psalm 110:4

This prophecy is referenced multiple times in *Hebrews* and quoted in 5:6 and 7:17. Jesus is the superior high priest—being sinless and eternal—from the lineage of Melchizedek. Since Jesus was born of David's lineage, He is also the eternal King of Israel and your eternal High Priest and King!

Pray Hebrews 5:9 over yourself and those for whom you stand guard as a faithful, prayerful watchman (Isaiah 62:6-7).

> *"LORD, help _____ and me obey you.*
> *Help _____ come to know You*
> *as the source of eternal salvation.*
> *In Your name, Jesus~"*

MARCH 13

Please read Hebrews 6.

Meditate on verse 1a.

> *Therefore, leaving the elementary teaching about*
> *the Christ, let us press on to maturity...*

Reread Hebrews 5:11-14. Do you and your church make an intentional effort to feed your flock with spiritual food appropriate for their particular levels of growth?

Following the resurrection, Jesus restored Peter with three questions followed by three commands (John 21:15-19). Jesus asked, "Do you love me?" Peter's three responses were followed by Jesus's commands: "Tend my lambs." "Shepherd my sheep." "Tend my sheep." Decades later, Peter wrote to all Christian leadership for all time, "Shepherd the flock of God among you. And when the Chief Shepherd appears you will receive the unfading crown of glory" (I Peter 5:2a, 4).

The passage beginning in Hebrews 5:11 illustrates the need for teaching the truths of God at appropriate levels. The writer of Hebrews was frustrated with his readers' lack of maturity. Believers today, no matter their age, need to mature more in the LORD. Therefore, churches need to feed their flock with appropriate food for the individual member's growth. New believers need special care. The new lambs need to be tended from the moment they are born in the faith and cared for daily. They need the milk of the Word, the elementary things, in order to learn how to walk with Jesus, their Chief Shepherd. As they develop, they need the meat of the Word to build them up and make them strong in the Lord.

Pray Hebrews 5:11-12 and 6:2 over yourself and those for whom you stand guard as a faithful, prayerful watchman (Isaiah 62:6-7).

> *"LORD, help _____ and me not become*
> *dull of hearing. Let us press on maturity.*
> *LORD, send someone, or me, to teach _____ the*
> *elementary principles of Your Word.*
> *In Your name, Jesus–"*

MARCH 14

Please read Hebrews 7.

Meditate on verse 19b.

> *There is a bringing in of a better hope,*
> *through which we draw near to God.*

"Draw near to God" is used twice in this chapter (vs. 19, 25). Only the high priest was permitted to go behind the veil to meet God in the Holy of Holies. God's holiness could not be in the presence of man's sinfulness, and any man with sin present who stepped behind the veil was struck dead.

When you became a Christian, the new covenant in Jesus' blood made you holy. The Holy Spirit in you is proof of this change. Since you are now holy through Jesus, you can draw near to God. In fact, the Holy Spirit in you affirms you are one of God's children and lets your spirit call out to God, *"Abba"* (Romans 8:15), which means "Daddy!"

Jesus, the eternal High Priest, lives to make intercession for you, lets you draw near to God, and saves you forever (v. 25). Drawing near to God is such a big deal to Him. He has gone to all of this trouble just so you can have this eternal relationship with Him!

Pray Hebrews 7:19 and 25 over yourself and those for whom you stand guard as a faithful, prayerful watchman (Isaiah 62:6-7).

> *"LORD, help _____ and me live in the better hope of You.*
> *Let us draw near to You, God. Jesus, thank You for saving*
> *us forever and constantly making intercession for us.*
> *Let us draw near to You, God.*
> *In Your name, Jesus~"*

Please read Hebrews 8.

Meditate on verse 6.

But now He has obtained a more excellent ministry,
by as much as He is also the mediator of a better covenant,
which has been enacted on better promises.

Jesus is the superior High Priest, superior to all earthly priests. He works in a better sanctuary; He has obtained a better ministry, and He is the mediator of a better covenant with better promises (vs. 1-6).

A covenant is a binding agreement. Today, a marriage ceremony or purchase of a house are examples of serious covenants. God loves covenants and uses them to help us know His love, faithfulness, and desire to interact with us.

There are many covenants recorded in the Bible. The primary Old Testament covenant was the covenant of the Law, which contained the sacrificial and purity requirements for priests and worshippers.

Hebrews 8 describes a change in God's primary covenant with you. Jesus' life and ministry on earth culminated in Him being the perfect sacrifice for you. He is also the perfect priest who fulfills the sacrificial role of the Law and Temple. Therefore, the old covenant is no longer needed to become right with God (v. 13); it has been replaced by a new and better covenant (v. 6). Now you can know the merciful and forgiving God personally through the covenant relationship with Jesus Christ.

Pray Hebrews 8:11b-12 over yourself and those for whom you stand guard as a faithful, prayerful watchman (Isaiah 62:6-7).

"LORD, help _____ and me know You,
from the least to the greatest of us.
Be merciful to our iniquities and
remember our sins no more.
In Your name, Jesus~"

Please read Hebrews 9.

Meditate on verses 11-12.

> *But when Christ appeared as a high priest of the good things to come,*
> *He entered through the greater and more perfect tabernacle, not made*
> *with hands, that is to say, not of this creation; and not through the*
> *blood of goats and calves, but through His own blood, He entered*
> *the holy place once for all, having obtained eternal redemption.*

Hebrews 9 is a very powerful chapter. It teaches that the earthly tabernacle and temples were only models of the ones in heaven. As you read verse 24 again, catch the purpose of entering this higher tabernacle.

> *For Christ did not enter a holy place made with hands,*
> *a mere copy of the true one, but into heaven itself,*
> *now to appear in the presence of God for us.*

Jesus is seated with God in heaven, making intercession for you and all believers (Hebrews 7:25; 8:1). He is preparing to come get His children and bring you to your new home (v. 28).

Pray Hebrews 9:11-12, 24, and 28 in thankfulness for Jesus' loving work for you and those for whom you stand guard as a faithful, prayerful watchman (Isaiah 62:6-7).

> *"LORD, thank You for entering the more perfect tabernacle*
> *for _____ and me. Thank You for sacrificing Your*
> *blood, obtaining eternal redemption, and entering the*
> *holy place to appear in the presence of God for us.*
> *We eagerly await Your appearing*
> *a second time to take us home.*
> *In Your name, Jesus~"*

Please read Hebrews 10.

Meditate on verses 19-23.

> *Therefore, brethren, since we have confidence to enter the holy place by the blood of Jesus, by a new and living way which He inaugurated for us through the veil, that is, His flesh, and since we have a great priest over the house of God, let us draw near with a sincere heart in full assurance of faith, having our hearts sprinkled clean from an evil conscience and our bodies washed with pure water. Let us hold fast the confession of our hope without wavering, for He who promised is faithful.*

Here it is, the pinnacle of *Hebrews*! Ten chapters demonstrating that Jesus' life, death, and resurrection are the world's greatest act of love. They culminate in the most amazing invitation ever offered to a human—draw near, through the veil, into the holy place, to the presence of God. How? With confidence, a sincere heart, and full of faith because HE WHO PROMISED IS FAITHFUL!

This invitation is a command. Because of all that Jesus did for you to be righteous before God, you must honor the LORD by coming to Him to love and worship Him.

Pray Hebrews 10:19-23 over yourself and those for whom you stand guard as a faithful, prayerful watchman (Isaiah 62:6-7).

> *"LORD, give _____ and me confidence to enter the holy place through this new living way, Your flesh. Because You are our high priest, let us draw near, with sincere hearts, in full assurance of faith, with hearts sprinkled clean from an evil conscience and our bodies washed with pure water. Help us hold fast the confession of our hope without wavering, for You who promised are faithful. In Your name, Jesus~"*

MARCH 18

Please read Hebrews 11.

Meditate on verse 3.

> *By faith we understand that the worlds were*
> *prepared by the word of God, so that what is seen*
> *was not made out of things which are visible.*

Immediately after the great call to come to God in the spiritual realm, is the call for believers to work together to remain faithful to the LORD (Hebrews 10:19-23). God's call and encouragement to faithfulness continues to the end of *Hebrews* and includes the "Great Faith Chapter." Hebrews 11 lists 45 people who, prior to Jesus' time on earth, were honored by God because of their forward-looking faith in the Messiah.

This kind of faith believes without seeing (v. 1). It recognizes that God made the world you see out of the invisible (v. 3). Godly faith is required to please Him (v. 6). It is required to come to God since one must have faith to believe that God is and that He rewards those who seek Him (v. 6).

Faith builds on the Hebrews 10:19-23 challenge. With this kind of faith, you can come to God and abide with Him.

Pray Hebrews 11:1, 3, and 6 over yourself and those for whom you stand guard as a faithful, prayerful watchman (Isaiah 62:6-7).

> *"LORD, give _____ and me the faith to be assured*
> *of the things hoped for and convicted of the things not seen.*
> *LORD, thank You that You made the worlds by Your Word.*
> *Help us please You with our faith. We come to*
> *You because we know You are real,*
> *and we know that You reward us when we seek You.*
> *In Your name, Jesus~"*

Please read Hebrews 12.

Meditate on verses 1-2a.

> *Therefore, since we have so great a cloud of witnesses surrounding us,*
> *let us also lay aside every encumbrance and the sin which so easily*
> *entangles us, and let us run with endurance the race that is set before*
> *us, fixing our eyes on Jesus, the author and perfecter of faith ...*

Hebrews 12 starts and ends with *therefore* (vs. 1, 28). Observe why it is there.

Because of the resounding encouragement of the faithful, run this race well by setting your eyes on Jesus and obeying Him. Hebrews 12 is full of exhortations from God to help you as you run.

As you run with Jesus and enter the Holy Place of God, note who else is in heaven:

> *But you have come to Mount Zion and to the city of the*
> *living God, the heavenly Jerusalem, and to myriads of angels,*
> *to the general assembly and church of the firstborn who are*
> *enrolled in heaven, and to God, the Judge of all, and to*
> *the spirits of the righteous made perfect, and to Jesus, the*
> *mediator of a new covenant, and to the sprinkled blood ...*
> —Hebrews 12:22-24

Therefore, as you near the finish line, seeing who awaits you in Christ's kingdom, continue serving God with gratitude, reverence, and awe (v. 28).

Pray Hebrews 12:28 over yourself and those for whom you stand guard as a faithful, prayerful watchman (Isaiah 62:6-7).

> *"LORD, thank You for letting _____ and*
> *me be part of Your unshakable kingdom.*
> *Let us show our gratitude by offering You*
> *the acceptable service of our lives with reverence and awe.*
> *In Your name, Jesus~"*

Please read Hebrews 13.

Meditate on verses 15-16.

> *Through Him then, let us continually offer up a sacrifice of praise to God, that is, the fruit of lips that give thanks to His name. And do not neglect doing good and sharing, for with such sacrifices God is pleased.*

In light of the glorious work of the LORD in establishing the new covenant for you, how should you respond? God says that giving praise and thanks to Him through Jesus are spiritual sacrifices (v. 15). He also views doing the right things and living unselfishly with others the same way (v. 16). These are acceptable acts of service (Romans 12:1).

Note this list of holy actions that you can do as sacrifices to God:

- Love the brethren (v. 1)
- Show hospitality to strangers (v. 2)
- Remember the prisoners (v. 3)
- Honor the marriage bed (v. 4)
- Be content and trust God for the needs of life (v. 5)
- Fear the LORD, not man (v. 6)
- Remember and imitate those who brought you to faith (v. 7)
- Jesus is the same—do not be carried away by strange teaching (vs. 8-9)

Pray with excitement Hebrews 13:20-21 (in the Holy Place in heaven) over yourself and those for whom you stand guard as a faithful, prayerful watchman (Isaiah 62:6-7).

> *"LORD, You are the God of peace, who brought up from the dead the great Shepherd of the sheep through the blood of the eternal covenant, even Jesus our LORD. Equip _____ and me in every good thing to do Your will; work in us that which is pleasing in Your sight. Through Jesus Christ to whom be the glory forever and ever! Amen!"*

MARCH 21

Please read Mark 1.

Meditate on verses 2-3.

> *As it is written in Isaiah the prophet: "Behold, I send*
> *My messenger ahead of You, who will prepare Your way;*
> *The voice of one crying in the wilderness, 'Make ready*
> *the way of the LORD; make His paths straight.'"*

Mark quoted Isaiah to introduce Jesus Christ as LORD and John the Baptist as God's messenger. The last word Mark recorded from the prophecy is *straight* (v. 3). It comes from the Greek word *euthys*, meaning "immediately, straightforward, and forthwith."[1] Mark used the word *euthys* 43 times as he wrote about Jesus, and it is most often translated as "immediately."

For the next 16 days, you have the privilege of going down the straightforward path of God's Word and <u>immediately</u> seeing your Savior in action. As you marvel at Jesus' power and authority, immediately speak to Him about your concerns, falling on your knees and beseeching Him for the miraculous (vs. 30, 40).

Pray Mark 1:30 and 40-41 over yourself and those for whom you stand guard as a faithful, prayerful watchman (Isaiah 62:6-7).

> *"Jesus, I am immediately speaking to You about _____.*
> *Jesus, I come to You, beseeching You, and*
> *falling on my knees before You.*
> *If You are willing, You can _____.*
> *Jesus, please be moved with compassion, stretch*
> *out Your hand, and touch _____.*
> *Let us hear You say, 'I am willing; be cleansed.'*
> *In Your name, LORD Jesus~"*

---

1. Retrieved from: *www.blueletterbible.org/lang/lexicon/lexicon.cfm?Strongs=G2117&t=NASB*

MARCH 22

Please read Mark 2.

Meditate on this phrase from verse 5.

And Jesus seeing their faith …

There is much to *see* in Mark 2.

- Jesus *saw* four men's faith on behalf of a paralytic. Their faith resulted in forgiveness and healing (vs. 2-12).
- Everyone *saw* the paralytic healed and walking. They were amazed and glorified God (v. 12).
- Jesus *saw* Levi and invited him to follow. Levi immediately accepted the LORD's invitation (v. 14).
- The scribes of the Pharisees *saw* Jesus eating with sinners. They questioned Him accusingly (vs. 15-16).
- The Pharisees *saw* Jesus' disciples picking grain on the Sabbath. They continued with their skeptical, faultfinding questions (v. 23-24).

What do you see, and what does Jesus see when He looks at you? Do you see circumstances, others, and yourself with cynical negativity? Or do you see life through faith-filled eyes, proclaiming, "Ah LORD God! Behold You have made the heavens and the earth by Your great power and by Your outstretched arm! Nothing is too difficult for You!" (Jeremiah 32:17).

Ask the LORD for His perspective. Intentionally and faithfully follow Him. The LORD will be pleased with what He sees.

Pray Mark 2:5 and 14 over yourself and those for whom you stand guard as a faithful, prayerful watchman (Isaiah 62:6-7).

*"Jesus, see _____ and my faith and forgive
our sins. Help us to get up and follow You.
In Your name, Jesus~"*

MARCH 23

Please read Mark 3.

Meditate on verse 5a.

> *After looking around at them with anger,*
> *grieved at their hardness of heart …*

The Pharisees continued maliciously watching Jesus in order to bring accusations against Him. After healing a man's withered hand, Jesus asked the Pharisees a question about harming versus healing and saving versus killing. Their attitudes and refusal to answer made Jesus both very angry and deeply sad. How could people who claimed to love God care so little about others?

What does Jesus see and how does He feel when He looks around at you? How will you answer His questions about what you are doing to bring good to others instead of harm, saving their lives instead of killing them?

Let the LORD examine your heart for hardness. Ask Him to remove your hard heart and replace it with His compassionate heart.

Pray Mark 3:5 over yourself and those for whom you stand guard as a faithful, prayerful watchman (Isaiah 62:6-7).

> *"LORD, please forgive _____ and me for making*
> *You angry and grieved at our hardness of heart.*
> *We stretch our lives out to You.*
> *Restore us!*
> *In Your name, Jesus~"*

MARCH 24

Please read Mark 4.

Meditate on verses 9 and 39.

> *And He was saying, "He who has ears to hear, let him hear."*
> *And He got up and rebuked the wind and said to the sea,*
> *"Hush, be still." And the wind died down,*
> *and it became perfectly calm.*

Jesus taught a very large crowd with these opening words: "Listen to this!" (v. 3). He proceeded to tell a parable, a story that teaches truth. Afterwards, Jesus explained to His followers what the main elements of the story represented and that not everyone listening to the story actually heard Him.

Mark 4 ends with a vivid picture of really hearing Jesus. When Christ gave the wind and the sea the command to "hush, be still," they listened and obeyed Him; the wind died down, and the sea became perfectly calm (v. 39).

Do you have ears to hear Jesus? The proof will be your obedience to His Word.

Pray Mark 4:20 over yourself and those for whom you stand guard as a faithful, prayerful watchman (Isaiah 62:6-7).

> *"LORD, let _____ and me be good soil*
> *on whom Your seed is sown.*
> *Let us hear the Word, accept it,*
> *and bear fruit thirty, sixty, and a hundredfold.*
> *For the sake of Your Kingdom, Jesus~"*

Please read Mark 5.

Meditate on verse 17a.

And they began to implore Him …

There was a lot of begging in Mark 5. The demons begged Jesus not to send them out of the country; they begged Him to send them into a herd of swine instead (vs. 10-12). When the people in the region heard about the man delivered from the demons and about the drowned pigs, they begged Jesus to leave them (v. 17). The man, who had been demon-possessed, begged to go with Jesus (v. 18). And a synagogue official named Jairus begged Jesus to save his dying little girl (vs. 22-23).

Do you relate to anyone in this chapter? Do you want to be with Christ, excited about what He is doing in your life and the lives of others, or does the miraculous make you nervous, so you would rather not be around it? Are you seeking the LORD and asking Him to save those you love, knowing that simply touching the hem of His garment brings healing (v. 28)?

Pray Mark 5:33 and 36 over yourself and those for whom you stand guard as a faithful, prayerful watchman (Isaiah 62:6-7).

"LORD, I come and fall down before You.
I want to tell You the whole truth about _____.
Help _____ and me not be afraid any longer;
may we only believe.
In Your name, Jesus~"

Please read Mark 6.

Meditate on what Jesus said in verse 31.

"Come away by yourselves to a secluded place and rest a while."

In the midst of people taking offense, a cousin beheaded, and caring for thousands of people, Jesus gave the command to "come and rest." Christ knew the importance of quiet times. Several times, Scripture records the LORD being alone to pray (Matthew 14:23; Mark 6:46; Luke 6:12). Ponder the fact that God Himself took time to rest in prayer.

Jesus extends the same invitation to you, calling you to Himself to breathe deeply and exhale slowly, absorbing His peace and letting go of stress and worry. Your quiet times with the LORD can be your favorite time of day, your time to get away from the coming and going, being nourished by God and His Word (v. 31).

Pray Mark 6:31 and 51 over yourself and those for whom you stand guard as a faithful, prayerful watchman (Isaiah 62:6-7).

"LORD, I accept Your invitation
to come away to a secluded place and rest a while.
Help _____ to do the same.
As we do, let us be utterly astonished by You.
In Your name, Jesus~"

Please read Mark 7.

Meditate on verse 9.

> *He (Jesus) was saying to them, "You are experts at setting aside*
> *the commandment of God in order to keep your tradition."*

The Pharisees considered themselves experts in God's Law, and in their prideful zeal, they added to and changed God's Word to fit what they wanted to teach. Jesus sharply rebuked such arrogant behavior, calling them hypocrites whose hearts were far from the LORD because they neglected God's commandments and taught their manmade precepts as scriptural doctrine.

What about you? Have you compromised God's Word for the sake of the traditions of your family, friends, and the world? The Bible counters culture; do not be tempted to change Scripture to fit the culture.

> *The precepts of the LORD are right, rejoicing the heart;*
> *the commandment of the LORD is pure, enlightening the eyes.*
> —Psalm 19:8

Let God's Word change your mindset, enlighten your worldview, and create your traditions.

Pray Mark 7:14, 32, and 37 over yourself and those for whom you stand guard as a faithful, prayerful watchman (Isaiah 62:6-7).

> *"LORD, help _____ and me listen*
> *to You and understand.*
> *We implore You to lay Your hand on us.*
> *We will be utterly astonished and say,*
> *'You do all things well.'*
> *In Your name, Jesus~"*

MARCH 28

Please read Mark 8.

Meditate on verse 34.

> *And He (Jesus) summoned the crowd with His disciples,*
> *and said to them, "If anyone wishes to come after Me,*
> *he must deny himself, and take up his cross and follow Me."*

Peter knew Jesus was the Christ, the Messiah, and he wanted his Messiah to do things his way. So, Peter rebuked Jesus for talking about impending suffering and death. Jesus quickly responded by publicly rebuking Peter, calling him Satan because he set his mind on man's interests instead of God's. Jesus then gave the invitation to everyone listening to get behind Him, not as a self-serving Satan, but as a self-denying disciple (vs. 29-34).

Is Jesus telling you to stop being rebellious and line up behind Him as His faithful follower? Ask Him to reveal areas where you are more concerned about the things of the world instead of the things of God.

Pray Mark 8:34 and 38 over yourself and those for whom you stand guard as a faithful, prayerful watchman (Isaiah 62:6-7).

> *"LORD, help _____ and me to come after You,*
> *deny ourselves, and take up our cross and follow You.*
> *Let us not be ashamed of You and Your Words*
> *in this adulterous and sinful generation.*
> *In Your name, Jesus~"*

MARCH 29

Please read Mark 9.

Meditate on verse 29.

> *And He said to them, "This kind cannot*
> *come out by anything but prayer."*

Christ's disciples ineffectively tried, on their own power, to drive out a demon from a boy. When the father brought his still-possessed child to Jesus, the LORD was not pleased, describing his disciples and the crowd as unbelieving (v. 19). The LORD had compassion for this father, who must have many times pulled his convulsing little boy out of fire and water. Jesus said to him, "All things are possible to him who believes" (vs. 22-23). Jesus healed the boy because the father believed and brought him to the LORD.

Jesus is the "all things are possible" God (Matthew 19:26), and He says to you that all things are possible when you believe and trust Him. As you ponder this story, understand that your belief is made evident to the LORD when you prayerfully bring your loved ones to Him.

Pray Mark 9:22-24 over yourself and those for whom you stand guard as a faithful, prayerful watchman (Isaiah 62:6-7).

> *"LORD, You can do anything!*
> *Take pity on us and help us!*
> *Please make _____ possible for _____.*
> *I believe; help my unbelief!*
> *In Your name, Jesus~"*

Please read Mark 10.

Meditate on verse 47b.

"Jesus, Son of David, have mercy on me!"

Observe the various reactions of the people to Jesus.

- ✎ A man was saddened and grieved by Jesus' answer to his question (vs. 17-22).
- ✎ Jesus' disciples were amazed and astonished at His words (vs. 23-26).
- ✎ Some followed Jesus with fear (vs. 32).
- ✎ Bartimaeus courageously obeyed the LORD's command. This blind beggar jumped up, came to Christ, and boldly told Him what he wanted (vs. 46-52).

Picture blind Bartimaeus begging Jesus to have mercy on him. Stern reproaches to hush only made him beg louder. And when Jesus issued the command to come to Him, he jumped up and came to Christ, despite his inability to see where he was going. Bartimaeus knew what he needed, and he knew Jesus was the One who could meet his need. Jesus granted his request to see because of his faith.

How do you respond to Jesus? Are you more like the sad, fearful people or Bartimaeus, who faithfully came to Christ fearlessly asking for mercy to regain his sight?

Pray Mark 10:47 and 50-52 over yourself and those for whom you stand guard as a faithful, prayerful watchman (Isaiah 62:6-7).

"Jesus, Son of David, have mercy on _____ and me!
Help us throw aside any hindrance, jump up, and come to You.
We want You to do _____ for us! Let us hear You say,
'Your faith has made you well.' We will follow You.
In Your name, Jesus~"

Please read Mark 11.

Meditate on verse 22.

And Jesus answered saying to them,
"Have faith in God."

Mark 11 starts the week of Christ's crucifixion. It began on Sunday with Jesus riding into Jerusalem on an untamed donkey. When that colt was under the command and control of its Creator, it was able to do the impossible; maneuvering well through busy streets and shouting people. The LORD does the same in your life when you give Him the command and control of yourself and those you love.

As the story progresses into Monday, Jesus expected a fig tree to bear fruit, even out of season. The fig tree did not respond to its Creator like the donkey did, and Christ was not pleased. By Monday evening, it had withered. Do you relate more to the untamed donkey doing the impossible because you are Christ-controlled, or are you more like a withered fig tree?

Jesus gave the antidote to withering: "Have faith in God" (v. 22). Without faith in Almighty God, you are an untamed, out of control donkey. But when, by faith, you submit to Jesus Christ, your life will no longer be withered and out of control. Instead it will be purposeful, even producing fruit out of season.

Pray Mark 11:22-24 over yourself and those for whom you stand guard as a faithful, prayerful watchman (Isaiah 62:6-7).

"LORD, I have faith in You, God! Do not let _____ and me
doubt in our hearts, but believe that what we say will happen
and be granted to us. Jesus, I believe You when You say:
'All things for which you pray and ask, believe that you
have received them, and they will be granted you.'
In Your name, Jesus~"

APRIL

On your walls, O Jerusalem,
I have appointed watchmen;
All day and all night they
will never keep silent.
You who remind the LORD,
take no rest for yourselves;
And give Him no rest until He establishes
And makes Jerusalem a
praise in the earth.
Isaiah 62:6-7, NASB

APRIL 1

Please read Mark 12.

Meditate on verse 24.

> *Jesus said to them, "Is this not the reason you are mistaken,*
> *that you do not understand the Scriptures or the power of God?"*

Mark 12 is filled with rich doctrine. Ask God to help you understand these truths and His power.

- ஃ Jesus is the chief cornerstone (v. 10). Are you building your life on Him?
- ஃ Rising from the dead is a fact (v. 26). Are you confident about resurrection, or do you fear death?
- ஃ God is God of the living, not of the dead (v. 27). Is He your God; are you alive in Him?
- ஃ You shall love the LORD your God (v. 30). Is He your LORD, your Master, the One in charge of you? Do you love Him?
- ஃ The Holy Spirit, Christ, and God the Father are all in the Old Testament (vs. 35-36). Do you understand that Jesus is LORD and that Jesus, God, and the Holy Spirit are One?

Jesus admonished His listeners for not understanding the Scriptures or His power. Ask the LORD to give you insight with understanding into His Word, so you can walk by His power.

Pray Mark 12:30 over yourself and those for whom you stand guard as a faithful, prayerful watchman (Isaiah 62:6-7).

> *"LORD my God, help _____ and me*
> *to love You with all our heart, and with all our soul,*
> *and with all our mind,*
> *and with all our strength.*
> *In Your name, Jesus~"*

Please read Mark 13.

Meditate on verses 23 and 31b. Jesus is talking.

> *"But take heed; behold, I have told you everything*
> *in advance. My words will not pass away."*

Mark 13 contains fascinating end of time prophecies. Jesus introduced the prophecies by exhorting His listeners not to be misled by anyone (v. 5). In the middle of His teaching, Jesus reminded His listeners He was telling them everything in advance (v. 23). Then He ended His teaching with: "My words will not pass away. Take heed, keep on the alert" (vs. 31, 33).

Jesus issued the command to "be alert" four times (vs. 33-37). The command was given to all, so this includes you.

> *What I say to you I say to all,* ***"Be on the alert!"***
> —Mark 13:37

Well, if God says something one time, it is important; if He says it four times, He certainly wants you to take notice. God's Word is eternal, and He has told you everything in advance. Take heed and keep alert in what He says.

Pray Mark 13:5, 31, and 33 over yourself and those for whom you stand guard as a faithful, prayerful watchman (Isaiah 62:6-7).

> *"LORD, help _____ and me see to it that no one misleads us.*
> *Thank You that Your Words will not pass away.*
> *Help us to take heed and keep on the alert.*
> *For the sake of Your name, Jesus~"*

APRIL 3

Please read Mark 14.

Meditate on verse 38. Jesus is talking.

> *"Keep watching and praying that you may not come into temptation; the spirit is willing, but the flesh is weak."*

Two days after Jesus commanded His disciples to stay on the alert (Mark 13:33-37), He gave them the opportunity to obey. Jesus knew prayer was the only way to go through the most horrible day of His life, and He wanted His disciples empowered by prayer also as they faced the trying day ahead of them. In the midst of His own agonizing prayer time, the Master Teacher continued to instruct His sleepyhead students, waking them up and reminding them to pray. After doing this three times, He led them away to face the greatest trial of their lives. Peter failed the test; instead of heeding his LORD's admonishment to pray three times, he denied Him three times. Imagine what Peter might have said and done around the campfire if he had been armed with the power of prayer.

Take seriously Jesus' words to "keep watch; keep watch; keep watching and praying" (vs. 34, 37-38). Is He asking you this question: "Are you still sleeping and resting" (v. 41)? The LORD wants you to "get up and be going" (v. 42) in your prayer life.

Pray Mark 14:38 and 41 over yourself and those for whom you stand guard as a faithful, prayerful watchman (Isaiah 62:6-7).

> *"LORD, help _____ and me keep watching and*
> *praying that we will not come into temptation;*
> *the spirit is willing, but the flesh is weak.*
> *Let us stop sleeping and resting.*
> *It is enough; the hour has come!*
> *By Your power, Jesus~"*

Please read Mark 15.

Meditate on verse 38.

And the veil of the temple was torn in two from top to bottom.

The veil of the temple separated the holy place from the holy of holies, which contained the Ark of the Covenant and represented the presence of God (Exodus 26:33-34). The veil partitioned Holy God from sinful people. Only the high priest was permitted entry into that sacred place once a year by taking the blood of a sacrifice offered for the sins of himself and the people (Hebrews 9:7).

When Jesus Christ took your sins upon Himself, He was separated from God because Holy God cannot be in the presence of sin. The separation was so agonizing that Jesus cried out, "My God, My God, why have You forsaken Me?" (v. 34). The sacrifice of Jesus for your sins was enough to satisfy Holy God, so much so that He tore down the veil that separated Him from people. Now you have the joy and the privilege of boldly coming into God's presence by the blood and through the body of Jesus Christ (Hebrews 10:19-22).

Let the story of Christ's sacrifice and crucifixion penetrate your heart and mind like never before this Easter. May the agonizing death of your LORD not be in vain. Live so others can see the evidence of what Jesus did on that cross; He sprinkled your heart clean from an evil conscience and washed your body with pure water (Hebrews 10:22).

Use the words from Mark 15:34 and 38 in a prayer of thanksgiving and commitment to Jesus.

"LORD, thank You that I will never have to say,
"My God, My God, why have You forsaken me?"
The veil of the temple has been torn in two from top to bottom.
LORD, I come to You.
All because of You, Jesus~"

Please read Mark 16.

Meditate on verse 6.

> *And he said to them, "Do not be amazed; you are looking for*
> *Jesus the Nazarene, who has been crucified. He has risen;*
> *He is not here; behold, here is the place where they laid Him."*

Resurrection! It is what separates Christianity from every other religion. The resurrection of Jesus Christ is the crux and proof of everything a Christian believes. For the trembling, astonished, fearful, mourning, weeping, unbelieving, and hard-hearted disciples (vs. 8, 10, 14), a resurrected LORD so changed them that they lived the rest of their lives going everywhere with "the sacred and imperishable proclamation of eternal salvation" (v. 20).

Has the resurrection of the LORD Jesus Christ changed you from a trembling, fearful, hard-hearted unbeliever into a faithful follower? If you are a Christian, you have resurrection power in you because the same Holy Spirit who raised Christ from the dead also lives inside of you. Use His power to proclaim eternal salvation, so others will believe and not be condemned (v. 16).

Pray Mark 16:15 and 20 over yourself and those for whom you stand guard as a faithful, prayerful watchman (Isaiah 62:6-7).

> *"Resurrected LORD, let _____ and me obey Your command*
> *to go into all the world and preach the Gospel to all creation.*
> *LORD, work with us and confirm Your Word in us.*
> *Jesus, through us, send out the sacred and imperishable*
> *proclamation of eternal salvation.*
> *Because You are the living Savior, Jesus~"*

Please read 1 Corinthians 15.

Meditate on verses 13-14.

> *But if there is no resurrection of the dead, not even Christ*
> *has been raised, and if Christ has not been raised,*
> *then our preaching is vain; your faith also is vain.*

There were people in the Corinthian church who doubted the resurrection of Jesus. Without a resurrected Savior, there is no Christianity. This truth is so fundamental to the foundation of Christian faith that Paul devoted a portion of his letter to prove Jesus indeed rose from the dead.

At one point in the letter, Paul lost patience with the Corinthians for asking, "How are the dead raised? And with what kind of body do they come?" (vs. 35-36). Paul answered that a picture of resurrection happens every time a plant comes out of the ground looking nothing like the seed that went into the ground. Every tree, flower, fruit, vegetable, blade of grass, etc. comes from an individually buried seed, miraculously raised up by its Creator. The entire earth screams resurrection! Not coincidentally, the LORD crafted this beautiful resurrection picture on the third day of creation (Genesis 1:11-13). Ever since the third day of the world's existence, the LORD foreshadowed what would take place on that incredible third day, 4,000 years later.

As you enjoy fresh flowers, fruits, and vegetables this spring, thank your risen Savior for His daily gifts and His future gifts in the resurrection. Pray 1 Corinthians 15:58 over yourself and those for whom you stand guard as a faithful, prayerful watchman (Isaiah 62:6-7).

> *"LORD, make _____ and me steadfast,*
> *immovable, always abounding in Your work,*
> *knowing that our toil is not in vain in You,*
> *Our resurrected LORD Jesus~"*

APRIL 7

Please read Colossians 1.

Meditate on verse 18b.

> *He (Jesus) is the beginning, the firstborn from the dead, so*
> *that He Himself will come to have first place in everything.*

Jesus conquered death and is preeminent over it (v. 18). Jesus made Satan powerless over death, so you can live without fearing it (Hebrews 2:14-15).

Through Jesus, you are rescued from the domain of darkness and transferred to His Kingdom (v. 13). In Jesus, you are "holy, blameless, and beyond reproach" (v. 22).

If you are a follower of Jesus, He lives inside of you, and He is your hope of glory (v. 27). Because of Jesus, you can "continue in the faith firmly established and steadfast, and not moved away from the hope of the Gospel" (v. 23).

Jesus holds you together (v. 17). Jesus completes you (v. 28).

Thank Him for accomplishing everything for you through His death and resurrection. In dedication to His will, pray Colossians 1:9-14 over yourself and those for whom you stand guard as a faithful, prayerful watchman (Isaiah 62:6-7).

> *"LORD, fill _____ and me with the knowledge of Your*
> *will in all spiritual wisdom and understanding, so that we will*
> *walk in a manner worthy of You, to please You in all respects,*
> *bearing fruit in every good work and increasing in the knowledge*
> *of You, God. Strengthen us with all power, according to Your*
> *glorious might, for the attaining of all steadfastness and patience.*
> *We joyously give thanks to You, Father, for qualifying us*
> *to share in the inheritance of the saints in Light. Thank*
> *You for rescuing us from the domain of darkness, and*
> *transferring us to the Kingdom of Your beloved Son,*
> *in whom we have redemption, the forgiveness of sins.*
> *In Your name, Jesus~"*

Please read Colossians 2.

Meditate on verse 3.

> *In whom (Jesus) are hidden all the treasures*
> *of wisdom and knowledge.*

All the treasures of wisdom and knowledge are found in Jesus Christ (v. 3). Many are revealed in *Colossians.* Meditate on these treasures:

- Good discipline comes from Jesus (v. 5).
- Stability of faith and establishment in faith comes from Jesus (vs. 5, 7).
- All the fullness of God dwells in Jesus (v. 9).
- In Jesus, you are made complete (v. 10).
- Jesus is the head over all rule and authority (v. 10).
- With Jesus, you are alive, no longer dead in your sins (v. 13).
- In Jesus, all your sins are forgiven (v. 13).
- Jesus nailed your certificate of debt to the cross, and cancelled it (v. 14).

This wisdom keeps you from being taken "captive through philosophy and empty deception" (v. 8). Share this knowledge with others. Let it eternally change their lives just like it is changing yours.

Pray Colossians 2:2-3 over yourself and those for whom you stand guard as a faithful, prayerful watchman (Isaiah 62:6-7).

> *"LORD, encourage _____ and my hearts*
> *and knit us together in love. Let us attain to all the wealth*
> *that comes from the full assurance of understanding,*
> *resulting in a true knowledge of Your mystery,*
> *that is Christ Himself. In You, Jesus, are hidden*
> *all the treasures of wisdom and knowledge.*
> *Thank You for sharing them with us, Jesus~"*

Please read Colossians 3.

Meditate on verses 1-2.

> *Therefore if you have been raised up with Christ, keep seeking the things above, where Christ is, seated at the right hand of God. Set your mind on things above, not on the things that are on earth.*

Resurrection is the core of Christianity and the proof of your salvation. Colossians 3 lists the attributes of a person whose life is resurrected in Jesus Christ. Does this list describe you?

- You have died, and your life is hidden with Christ in God (v. 3).
- Jesus is your life (v. 4).
- You are dead to immorality, impurity, passion, evil desire, and greed (v. 5).
- You lay aside anger, wrath, malice, slander, and abusive speech (v. 8).
- You do not lie to others because you laid aside your old self with its evil practices (v. 9).
- You have put on the new self that is being renewed to the image of your Creator, Jesus Christ (v. 10).
- You are chosen of God, holy, and beloved (v. 12).

Pray the characteristics from Colossians 3:12-17 to be visible in you and those for whom you stand guard as a faithful, prayerful watchman (Isaiah 62:6-7).

> *"LORD, let _____ and me put on a heart of compassion, kindness, humility, gentleness, and patience. Let us bear with one another and forgive each other, whoever has a complaint against anyone, just as You forgave us. Beyond all these things, let us put on love, which is the perfect bond of unity. Let Your peace rule in our hearts, and let us be thankful. Let Your Word dwell within us richly with all wisdom, teaching and admonishing one another with psalms and hymns and spiritual songs, singing with thankfulness in our hearts to You. Whatever we do in word or deed, let us do all in Your name, LORD Jesus, giving thanks through You to God the Father."*

Please read Colossians 4.

Meditate on verse 17b.

Take heed to the ministry which you have received
in the LORD, that you may fulfill it.

Jesus Christ came to earth to die for your sins. He was resurrected to conquer death and become your living Savior. In Christ you are eternally alive. Christ lives inside you to give you glorious, eternal hope (Colossians 1:27). You are complete in Christ because Christ is your life (Colossians 2:10; 3:4). God chose you to live in Christ; you are His beloved, and you are holy (Colossians 3:12).

As you consider these amazing truths about who you are in Jesus, be mindful that the LORD has given you a ministry, and He wants you to fulfill it. Do you know what that ministry is? If not, ask Him to reveal it to you. If you know what the ministry is, are you paying attention to it and fulfilling it by the LORD's power? Living a resurrected life means living for the One who gave you that life.

Pray Colossians 4:12 and 17 over yourself and those for whom you stand guard as a faithful, prayerful watchman (Isaiah 62:6-7).

"LORD, may _____ and I stand perfect
and fully assured in all Your will.
Let us take heed to the ministry
which we have received in You, that we may fulfill it.
In Your name and by Your power, Jesus~"

Please read Jonah 1.

Meditate on verse 17.

> *And the LORD appointed a great fish to swallow Jonah, and Jonah was in the stomach of the fish three days and three nights.*

> *But He (Jesus) answered and said to them, "An evil and adulterous generation craves for a sign; and yet no sign will be given to it but the sign of Jonah the prophet; for just as Jonah was three days and three nights in the belly of the sea monster, so will the Son of Man be three days and three nights in the heart of the earth."*
> —Matthew 12:39-40

Jonah's story foreshadowed the life and death of Jesus Christ:

- The same LORD who hurled a great wind on the sea to break up Jonah's boat commanded the winds to hush and be still when He was awakened on a storm-tossed ship (v. 4; Mark 4:37-39).
- The sailors on Jonah's ship did not want innocent blood on their hands (v. 14). At the crucifixion, Pilate washed his hands of Jesus' blood; the crowd said Jesus' blood would be on them and their children (Matthew 27:24-25).
- Jonah's time in the belly of the great fish foreshadowed where Jesus went prior to His resurrection (Ephesians 4:9-10).

God's Word is amazing! Every page tells the story of Jesus. Be fascinated by your Savior as you ponder Him on the pages of Jonah.

Pray Jonah 1:9 and 14 over yourself and those for whom you stand guard as a faithful, prayerful watchman (Isaiah 62:6-7).

> *"LORD God of heaven who made the sea and the dry land, may _____ and I fear You.*
> *We earnestly pray, O LORD, do not let us perish on account of _____, and do not put innocent blood on us.*
> *O LORD, do as You please in the life of _____.*
> *For the sake of Your name, Jesus~"*

Please read Jonah 2.

Meditate on verses 3a and 4a.

> *For You had cast me into the deep, so I said,*
> *"I have been expelled from Your sight."*

> *Jesus cried out with a loud voice,*
> *"My God, My God, why have You forsaken Me?"*
> —Matthew 27:46; Mark 15:34

Jonah experienced the wrath of God because he was punished for his sins. Jesus experienced the wrath of God because He was punished for your sins.

Without Jesus, you are Jonah:

- In distress, in the depth of Sheol, the belly of hell (v. 2).
- Expelled from the sight of God (v. 4).
- Engulfed to the point of death (v. 5).

BUT with Jesus, God:

- Answers you and hears your voice (v. 2).
- Brings your life out of the pit (v. 6).
- Gives you His salvation (v. 9).

Pray the prayer of Jonah in recognition and thanksgiving for what Jesus Christ did for you when He died for your sins (Jonah 2:2-9).

> *"I called out of my distress to the LORD, and He answered me.*
> *I cried for help from the depth of Sheol; You heard my voice.*
> *For You had cast me into the deep, into the heart of the seas, and*
> *the current engulfed me. All Your breakers and billows passed over*
> *me. So I said, 'I have been expelled from Your sight. Nevertheless*
> *I will look again toward Your holy temple.' Water encompassed me*
> *to the point of death. The great deep engulfed me; I descended to*
> *the roots of the mountains, but You have brought my life up from*
> *the pit. While I was fainting away, I remembered the LORD, and*
> *my prayer came to You, into Your holy temple. Those who regard*
> *vain idols forsake their faithfulness, but I will sacrifice to You with*
> *the voice of thanksgiving. That which I have vowed I will pay.*
> *Salvation is from the LORD. Thank You! In Your name, Jesus~"*

Please read Jonah 3.

Meditate on verse 10.

> *When God saw their deeds, that they turned from their wicked way,*
> *then God relented concerning the calamity which He declared*
> *He would bring upon them. And He did not do it.*

The LORD gave Jonah a second chance to obey and give His message to the people of Nineveh. It was an eight-word sermon (four Hebrew words) that brought this great city to its knees in repentance and faith in God. The LORD was so moved by the people turning from their violent wickedness and earnestly calling on Him that He relented of the calamity He was about to bring on them. Amazing!

800 years after Jonah proclaimed the Word of the LORD, Christ preached a similar message, "Repent, for the kingdom of heaven is at hand" (Matthew 4:17). And as He died on the cross in the place of those who needed to repent, the same LORD who forgave the Ninevites cried out, "Father, forgive them, for they do not know what they are doing" (Luke 23:34).

Thankfully, your merciful Savior still turns to all who call on Him in repentance, relenting of the deserved calamity. Have you humbled yourself in repentance to Christ Jesus your LORD?

Pray Jonah 3:8-9 over yourself and those for whom you stand guard as a faithful, prayerful watchman (Isaiah 62:6-7).

> *"God, I am earnestly calling on You!*
> *May _____ and I turn from our wicked way*
> *and from the violence in our hands.*
> *God, please turn and relent and withdraw*
> *Your burning anger so that we will not perish.*
> *In Your name, Jesus~"*

Please read Jonah 4.

Meditate on verse 4.

The LORD said, "Do you have good reason to be angry?"

The Ninevites repented; God relented, and Jonah resented the entire situation. He was mad that God was true to His character: gracious, compassionate, slow to anger, abundant in lovingkindness, and relenting of calamity (v. 2). Ironically, Jonah did not complain when the LORD showed him those same qualities by not allowing him to perish in the belly of the fish, giving him a second chance, and growing a plant to give him shade. Jonah was extremely happy about that plant, yet he was not even a tiny bit happy for a repentant sinner. On the contrary, he was so mad when God spared the people and killed his plant that he wanted to die.

It is easy to judge Jonah for his merciless attitude, yet examine your own thoughts. Does a Jonah lurk inside you? Are there people you wish God would judge and condemn? Do you pout when He does not let you have your way? How much time do you spend begging God for things you want compared to the amount of time you pray for others to repent and come to Christ?

Pray for the LORD to make His characteristics (Jonah 4:2) evident in you and those for whom you stand guard as a faithful, prayerful watchman (Isaiah 62:6-7).

"LORD, make _____ and me like You:
gracious, compassionate, slow to anger, and
abundant in lovingkindness.
Thank You for the times You relent concerning
calamity. Because You desire all men to be saved
and come to the knowledge of the truth (1 Timothy 2:4), Jesus~"

APRIL 15

Please read Judges 1.

Meditate on this repeated phrase from verses 21 and 28-33.

... did not drive out ...

When God gave the land of Canaan to the Israelites, He commanded them to utterly destroy the inhabitants. This instruction was so they would not teach the Israelites all the detestable things they did with their idols (Deuteronomy 20:17-18). But the Israelites did not obey the LORD, and *Judges* records some of the consequences of their disobedience.

As you read this book, ask the LORD to teach you from their mistakes.

Israel sinned against God when they "did not drive out." Their sin resulted in "the Jebusites living with the sons of Benjamin in Jerusalem to this day" (v. 21). And "the Canaanites persisted in living in that land and lived among them" (vs. 27, 29). Heathen idolatry lived with, in, and among God's people because they refused to drive it out.

Can you imagine how different the world might be today if the children of Israel had completely driven out the idol worshippers occupying their land? Can you imagine how different you and your family might be if you completely drove out things in your life that displease the LORD?

Use the words from Judges 1:29 to pray over yourself and those for whom you stand guard as a faithful, prayerful watchman (Isaiah 62:6-7).

"LORD, help _____ and me drive out _____,
so it no longer lives among us.
In Your name, Jesus~"

APRIL 16

Please read Judges 2.

Meditate on verse 2.

> *And as for you, you shall make no covenant with the*
> *inhabitants of this land; you shall tear down their altars.*
> *But you have not obeyed Me; what is this you have done?*

Judges records vivid pictures of the consequences for refusing to drive out sin. Sin is a snare that provokes God to anger (vs. 3, 12). His burning anger results in:

- ✺ God giving sinners into the hands of plunderers and selling them to enemies (v. 14).
- ✺ God's hand being against sinners for evil, resulting in severe distress (v. 15).

In the midst of His anger, God is moved to pity by the groaning of the oppressed, and He delivers them from their enemies (v. 18). Yet, after being delivered, the people in *Judges* turned back and did not abandon their stubborn ways (v. 19). They were stuck in the sin cycle.

Are you caught in a sin cycle?

Sin—>Snared—>God's anger—>Oppression—>

Cry to God—>Delivered—>

Sin—>Snared—>And here you go again

As you continue to read *Judges*, ask God to use His Word to break the sin cycle and help you live victoriously in Him.

Pray to be the opposite of Judges 2:11-13 over yourself and those for whom you stand guard as a faithful, prayerful watchman (Isaiah 62:6-7).

> *"LORD, do not let _____ and me do evil in Your sight and*
> *forsake You. Do not let us follow the gods of the people around*
> *us, bowing down to them. LORD, we do not want to provoke*
> *You to anger. May we never forsake You and serve another.*
> *Because of our covenant with You, Jesus~"*

APRIL 17

Please read Judges 3.

Meditate on verse 7.

> *The sons of Israel did what was evil in the sight of the LORD and forgot the LORD their God and served the Baals and Asheroth.*

Israel was drowning in sin and experiencing the anger of God. In the midst of their distress, they cried to the LORD, who faithfully answered their cries with deliverers or judges to lead them back to Him. Three of Israel's judges are mentioned in this chapter. Learn from these men, making appropriate applications to your life.

- The Spirit of the LORD came upon Othniel, and he went out to war (v. 10).
    - Fight the spiritual battles by the power of God's Spirit.
- Ehud turned from the idols and delivered God's message to the king (v. 19).
    - Pass by the temptation to sin and be used as God's messenger.
- Ehud had the sword he needed to kill the king (v. 21).
    - God will give you the weapons you need to fight His battles.
- Moab was subdued and Israel was undisturbed under Ehud's leadership (vs. 26-30).
    - Your faithfulness can bring rest to those around you.
- Shamgar killed 600 Philistines and saved Israel (v. 31).
    - God will make you victorious.

Pray Judges 3:10, 26, and 28 over yourself and those for whom you stand guard as a faithful, prayerful watchman (Isaiah 62:6-7).

> *"Spirit of the LORD, come upon _____ and me.*
> *Let us prevail over the enemy.*
> *Let us pass by the idols and escape from evil.*
> *LORD, give the enemy into our hands.*
> *For the sake of Your name, Jesus~"*

APRIL 18

Please read Judges 4.

Meditate on verse 9.

> *She (Deborah) said, "I will surely go with you; nevertheless,*
> *the honor shall not be yours on the journey that you are about to take,*
> *for the LORD will sell Sisera into the hands of a woman."*
> *Then Deborah arose and went with Barak to Kedesh.*

The Israelites continued in their sin cycle, and the LORD continued to give them over to their enemies. When they cried out in their oppression, the LORD sent two women to bring deliverance, Deborah, a prophetess and a judge, and Jael, a cunning, brave, and strong wife (vs. 4, 17-21).

The LORD uses those who willingly follow and serve Him to be His leaders. Do not let your gender, age, occupation, nationality, etc. be an excuse not to lead. Deborah and Jael both accomplished tasks that would have typically been done by men, but the LORD chose them to lead an army and a nation and to kill a commander of 900 iron chariots who had terrorized Israel for 20 years (v. 3).

Are you willing to do whatever God asks you to do?

Pray Judges 4:14-15 over yourself and those for whom you stand guard as a faithful, prayerful watchman (Isaiah 62:6-7).

> *"LORD, let this be the day that*
> *You give _____ into our hands.*
> *LORD, go before us.*
> *Rout the enemy!*
> *For Your sake, Jesus~"*

APRIL 19

Please read Judges 5.

Meditate on verse 13b.

The people of the LORD came down to me as warriors.

Judges 5 gives you more information about this time in Israel's history. The roads were not safe (v. 6). The battles against the Canaanites were at the city gates, but the Israelite armies had no weapons to fight them (v. 8). Many of the men who should have been fighting were away, daydreaming in the fields, sitting on the seashore, and out at sea (vs. 16-17). They were so self-absorbed that some wanted to die (v. 18). Rather than focusing on God's purposes, they focused on themselves; the result was rampant sin, being overcome by the enemy, and the anger of God burning against them.

Thankfully, the LORD did not turn His back on His rebellious people; instead He raised up two women who led Israel and destroyed formidable opponents.

Take courage from the story of Deborah and Jael and aspire to be like them. The LORD will strengthen you for the battle; He needs you to be willing to fight.

Pray Judges 5:13, 21, and 31 over yourself and those for whom you stand guard as a faithful, prayerful watchman (Isaiah 62:6-7).

> *"LORD, let _____ and me come to You as warriors.*
> *Let our souls march on with strength.*
> *We love You; let us be like the rising of the sun in its might.*
> *For the sake of Your Kingdom, Jesus~"*

Please read Judges 6.

Meditate on verse 12b.

The LORD is with you, O valiant warrior.

God used Midian to punish Israel for doing evil (v. 1). The Midianites ravaged the Israelites, and they cried to God for help. God reminded them He rescued them from slavery to the Egyptians, brought them to the land of promise, and taught them how to live with Him. Yet they disobeyed, resulting in extreme oppression by their enemies. God sent them a deliverer named Gideon. Though he was a fearful man, God saw his destiny and called him "valiant warrior" (v. 12).

This story has many practical applications for you. The LORD delivered you from slavery to sin, brought you to the land of promises in Christ, and teaches you with His Word and His Spirit. When you obey Him, sin does not ravage your life. Listen for the name God has given you. It will describe how God sees you and who He is shaping you to be. Have the courage to cut down the idols in your home, church, city, etc. Experience the LORD's peace as you obey Him.

Pray Judges 6:12, 14, and 23-25 over yourself and those for whom you stand guard as a faithful, prayerful watchman (Isaiah 62:6-7).

"LORD, be with _____ and me and make us valiant warriors.
As You look at us, we go in Your strength to deliver
our people from the hand of the enemy.
Give us Your peace. Do not let us fear. Do not let us die.
Let us pull down and cut down all the idols.
By Your name, The LORD is Peace, Jesus~"

Please read Judges 7.

Meditate on verses 20b-21a.

> *A sword for the LORD and for Gideon!*
> *Each stood in his place around the camp.*

What a great story of victory with the LORD! After reducing Gideon's army from 32,000 to 300 men, God miraculously used them to conquer the Midianite and Amalekite armies, whose men and camels were too numerous to count.

This story is so typical of God. He puts you in an impossible situation (v. 12). He gives you signs of His presence (vs. 13-15), then He ensures that He will get the glory for the victory by removing what makes you prideful (vs. 2-8). He overcomes your fears (vs. 9-11). He sets the sword of the enemy against itself (v. 22), and He removes the enemies' heads (v.25).

Is this a typical story in your life? Obey God's Word, which is the sword of the LORD (Ephesians 6:17) and take a stand in the place He puts you. You will see His victory!

Pray Judges 7:7, 15, and 20-21 over yourself and those for whom you stand guard as a faithful, prayerful watchman (Isaiah 62:6-7).

> *"LORD, deliver _____ and me!*
> *We bow in worship of You; give _____ into our hands.*
> *With Your sword, LORD, we stand in the place You put us.*
> *For the glory of Your victory, Jesus~"*

APRIL 22

Please read Judges 8.

Meditate on verses 23-24a.

> *But Gideon said to them, "I will not rule over you, nor shall my son rule over you; the LORD shall rule over you." Yet Gideon said …*

Gideon went from a trembling man to become the valiant warrior the LORD said he would be (Judges 6:11-16). God raised him out of a wine press and used him to subdue the mighty Midianite and Amalekite armies (Judges 6:11; 7:12). He was courageous before his enemies and his bullying kinsmen, and he declared that God would rule over the people (vs. 8-23). His story should have stopped there, but instead it continued with "yet Gideon said …" (v. 24). When Gideon opened his mouth and asked for spoils for himself, the cycle of sin began again.

Can you relate to Gideon? You serve the LORD, fearfully believing God will do what He said He would do through you. The LORD gets the victory, and you get some courage, fighting spiritual battles. At some point in the victories, your Christ-confidence changes to self-confidence, and you get carried away with yourself, saying prideful, sinful things.

Learn from Gideon. Stop, if you are about to say or do something regrettable. Ask the LORD to keep you from sinning, then walk the rest of the day pleasing Him.

Use the words from Judges 8:23 and 27 to pray over yourself and those for whom you stand guard as a faithful, prayerful watchman (Isaiah 62:6-7).

> *"LORD, rule over _____ and me.*
> *Help us not say or do anything that would*
> *become a snare to our household.*
> *In Your name, Jesus~"*

Please read Judges 9.

Meditate on verses 8-9.

> *Once the trees went forth to anoint a king over them,*
> *and they said to the olive tree, "Reign over us!" But the olive*
> *tree said to them, "Shall I leave my fatness with which God*
> *and men are honored, and go to wave over the trees?"*

The LORD likes to teach with parables. Jotham told one of the first ones in this chapter (vs. 8-15).

After the massacre of Gideon's 70 sons, Jotham, a survivor, told this parable to the men of Shechem when they made Abimelech, the assassin, their king. In the story, the trees asked an olive tree, a fig tree, and a vine to rule over them. The olive, fig, and vine declined because they were fulfilling their purpose and had no desire to wave (rule) over the other trees. The trees resorted to asking the worthless bramble to be their ruler. He gladly accepted and invited the trees to sit in his shade. Of course brambles do not produce shade, only piercing, painful thorns.

God was to be Israel's only king, but in their sinful delusion, the people wanted a human king, even a worthless one like thorny, evil Abimelech.

As a Christian, Jesus is to be your King. Are there areas of your life being ruled by worthless brambles? Remove the brambles, like the woman removed Abimelech (v. 53), then stay focused on God's purpose for you.

Use the words from Judges 9:9, 11, and 13 to pray over yourself and those for whom you stand guard as a faithful, prayerful watchman (Isaiah 62:6-7).

> *"LORD, make _____ and me like an olive*
> *tree which brings honor to You and men.*
> *Make us like a fig tree producing sweet and good fruit.*
> *Make us like a vine which cheers You and men.*
> *For Your glory, King Jesus~"*

Please read Judges 10.

Meditate on verses 13-14.

> *Yet you have forsaken Me and served other gods;*
> *therefore I will no longer deliver you.*
> *Go and cry out to the gods which you have chosen;*
> *let them deliver you in the time of your distress.*

God's conversation with the children of Israel in this chapter is unlike any other recorded in *Judges*. Listen to it carefully and apply it to your life.

When the oppressed Israelites again cried to God, He reminded them of all the times He delivered them in the past, yet every time, they cycled back into forsaking Him and serving other gods (vs. 10-13). Enough was enough! This time, the LORD told them to cry out to those gods for help (v 14).

Are you caught in the sin cycle? Is the LORD saying, "Enough is enough! Let the gods you have forsaken Me for, take care of you"? Of course, the LORD knows those gods will never take care of you but will destroy you. He is waiting for you to come to your senses, confess your sins, and commit yourself wholeheartedly to Him. He is heartbroken over your misery and mercifully wants you to return to Him.

Pray Judges 10:15 over yourself and those for whom you stand guard as a faithful, prayerful watchman (Isaiah 62:6-7).

> *"LORD, _____ and I have sinned.*
> *Do to us whatever seems good to You;*
> *only please deliver us this day.*
> *In Your name, Jesus~"*

Please read Judges 11.

Meditate on verse 29a.

> *Now the Spirit of the LORD came upon Jephthah …*

Jephthah's is a story of a valiant warrior with the Spirit of the LORD who made serious mistakes. What is the LORD teaching you from Jephthah's life?

- Jephthah was a valiant warrior (v. 1). Let God make you a valiant warrior in His Kingdom.
- Jephthah was the son of a harlot and rejected by his half-brothers (vs. 1-2). Let God use you regardless of your family history.
- Jephthah was surrounded by worthless fellows (v. 3). Surround yourself with people who love the LORD and obey His Word.
- Jephthah had the Spirit of the LORD so that he covered a lot of ground (v. 29). Let God's Spirit lead you wherever He wants you to go.
- Jephthah made a foolish request of the LORD (v. 30). Do not let God's work in your life go to your head, so that you ask Him to put things into *your* hand instead of putting everything into *His* hand.
- Jephthah made a foolish vow to the LORD (v. 31). Jesus said, "Make no oath at all" (Matthew 5:34).

Use the words from Judges 11:1, 3, and 29-31 to pray over yourself and those for whom you stand guard as a faithful, prayerful watchman (Isaiah 62:6-7).

> *"LORD, make _____ and me Your valiant warriors.*
> *Do not let worthless fellows gather around us and go out with us.*
> *Spirit of the LORD, be upon us to lead us wherever You will.*
> *Let us make no foolish requests and vows.*
> *In Your name, Jesus~"*

APRIL 26

Please read Judges 12.

Meditate on verses 2-3a.

> *Jephthah said to them, "I and my people were at great strife*
> *with the sons of Ammon; when I called you, you did not deliver*
> *me from their hand. When I saw that you would not deliver*
> *me, I took my life in my hands and crossed over against the*
> *sons of Ammon, and the LORD gave them into my hand."*

Judges is about people who need deliverance from sin and its consequences. They looked to other people for deliverance, and they even tried to deliver themselves. Every effort proved futile. They needed a Savior; they needed the LORD.

The Hebrew word that is translated as *deliver* in *Judges* is also used in Isaiah 49:26 where it is translated as *Savior*[1].

> *And all flesh will know that I, the LORD, am your **Savior***
> *and your Redeemer, the Mighty One of Jacob.*
> —Isaiah 49:26b

> *Our great God and Savior, Christ Jesus, who gave Himself*
> *for us to redeem us from every lawless deed ...*
> —Titus 2:13b-14a

Jesus is the Deliverer, the Savior! Let Him deliver you from recycled sins, so you can live for Him.

Use the words from Judges 12:3 to pray over yourself and those for whom you stand guard as a faithful, prayerful watchman (Isaiah 62:6-7).

> *"LORD, I see that _____ will not deliver _____ and me.*
> *Let us stop taking our lives into our own hands.*
> *We give our lives to You. In Your name,*
> *Jesus, our Deliverer and Savior ~"*

---

1. Retrieved from: *www.blueletterbible.org/lang/lexicon/lexicon.cfm?Strongs=H3467&t=NASB*

APRIL 27

Please read Judges 13.

Meditate on verse 5.

> *For behold, you shall conceive and give birth to a son,*
> *and no razor shall come upon his head, for the boy shall*
> *be a Nazirite[1] to God from the womb, and he shall begin*
> *to deliver Israel from the hands of the Philistines.*

What an incredible encounter with God! Manoah and his wife were childless when God appeared to them and told them they would have a son (vs. 2-5, 22). Their boy, Samson, was set apart for God's purposes before he was even conceived (v. 7). Before his birth, the LORD taught Samson's father and mother how to parent him because Manoah asked God to teach them (vs. 8-14).

If you are a parent, have you given your children to the LORD to be used for His purposes? Have you asked the LORD to teach you how to parent your child? Have you given yourself to God to be used as He desires? Share these incredible insights from God's Word with other parents.

Pray Judges 13:7-8 and 24-25 over yourself and those for whom you stand guard as a faithful, prayerful watchman (Isaiah 62:6-7).

> *"LORD, make _____ and me like a Nazirite,*
> *devoted to You, from the womb to the day of our death.*
> *God, come and teach us what to do for the children in our lives.*
> *Let us and our children grow up and be blessed by You.*
> *Spirit of the LORD, begin to stir in us.*
> *For Your purposes, Jesus-"*

---

1. *Nazarite means "consecrated or devoted one." Retrieved from www.blueletterbible.org/lang/lexicon/lexicon.cfm?Strongs=H5139&t=NASB*

Please read Judges 14.

Meditate on verses 3b and 7.

> *But Samson said to his father, "Get her for me,*
> *for she looks good to me." So he went down and talked*
> *to the woman; and she looked good to Samson.*

These meditation verses introduce the theme of *Judges*: "Every man did what was right in his own eyes" (Judges 17:6). Contrary to God's law (Deuteronomy 7:3-4), Samson chose to marry an idol-worshipping Philistine simply because she looked good to him. In his eyes, it was the right thing to do.

King David lived with the consequences of seeing a woman who looked good to him, then doing to her "what was right in his own eyes" (2 Samuel 11). He wrote: "Transgression speaks to the ungodly within his heart; there is no fear of God before his eyes, for it flatters him in his own eyes" (Psalm 36:1-2a).

Ask the LORD to put "fear of God" glasses over your eyes; let them filter everything you see. Make decisions based on what is right in God's eyes, not what is right in your own eyes.

Use the words from Judges 14:3, 6, and 19 to pray over yourself and those for whom you stand guard as a faithful, prayerful watchman (Isaiah 62:6-7).

> *"Spirit of the LORD, come upon _____ and me*
> *mightily to do what looks good to You.*
> *Let us not get something (or someone) because it looks good to us.*
> *Keep our eyes on You, Jesus~"*

Please read Judges 15.

Meditate on verse 19a.

> *But God split the hollow place that is in Lehi so that water came out of it. When he drank, his strength returned and he revived.*

Recall God's purpose for Samson was to "begin to deliver Israel from the hands of the Philistines" (Judges 13:5). In the stories you have read so far, he has killed at least 1,030 of them (Judges 14:19; 15:15). After killing 1,000 Philistines he was very thirsty, so he called on the LORD for help (vs. 15-18). Samson was dependent on the Spirit of God for his extraordinary strength, and he needed the LORD for a drink of water (vs. 14, 19).

Jesus said, "If anyone is thirsty, let him come to Me and drink. He who believes in Me, as the Scripture said, 'From his innermost being will flow rivers of living water'" (John 7:37b-38). Jesus was talking about His Spirit (John 7:39).

If you are a Christian, the same Spirit of the LORD that gave Samson the power to tear a lion apart with his bare hands lives inside of you (Judges 14:6)! The same Spirit of the LORD that let Samson kill 30 Philistines lives inside of you (Judges 14:19)! The same Spirit of the LORD that removed the bonds from Samson and enabled him to kill 1,000 Philistines with a donkey's jawbone, lives inside of you (vs. 14-15)!

Drink deeply of His Spirit and use the words from Judges 15:18-19 to pray over yourself and those for whom you stand guard as a faithful, prayerful watchman (Isaiah 62:6-7).

> *"LORD, You have given great deliverance to _____ and me.*
> *Let us drink You, our Living Water.*
> *Let our strength return.*
> *Revive us! In Your name, Jesus~"*

Please read Judges 16.

Meditate on verse 21.

> *Then the Philistines seized him and gouged out his eyes,*
> *and they brought him down to Gaza and bound him with*
> *bronze chains, and he was a grinder in the prison.*

Samson had a problem with women, often succumbing to ones he saw and doing with them what was right in his own eyes. By the end of his life, his enticement by the visual became his undoing. His last woman, Delilah, betrayed him to the Philistines. These enemies seized him and gouged out his eyes (v. 21). He no longer sinned with that part of his body.

Jesus preached a lot about eyes. He said, "The eye is the lamp of the body; if your eye is bad, your whole body is full of darkness. Is your eye envious? Take the log out of your eye, and tear out your eye if it makes you stumble" (Matthew 5:29; 6:22-23; 7:5; 20:15). Jesus wanted his followers to understand that doing what was right in their own eyes was sinning.

God wants you to understand these truths. Seek to do what is right in His eyes rather than what is right in the eyes of the world.

Use the words from Judges 16:28 to pray over yourself and those for whom you stand guard as a faithful, prayerful watchman (Isaiah 62:6-7).

> *"O LORD God, please remember _____ and me,*
> *and please strengthen us again this time.*
> *O God, may our eyes not be the cause for vengeance.*
> *Let us see with Your eyes, LORD Jesus~"*

MAY

On your walls, O Jerusalem,
I have appointed watchmen;
All day and all night they
will never keep silent.
You who remind the LORD,
take no rest for yourselves;
And give Him no rest until He establishes
And makes Jerusalem a
praise in the earth.
ISAIAH 62:6-7, NASB

MAY 1

Please read Judges 17.

Meditate on verse 6.

> *In those days there was no king in Israel;*
> *every man did what was right in his own eyes.*

Observe every man doing what was right in his own eyes, yet evil in the eyes of God:

- ⚜ Micah's mother asked God to bless her son after he stole from her (v. 2).
- ⚜ She dedicated the stolen silver to the LORD then gave it back to Micah to make idols (v. 3).
- ⚜ Micah made a shrine for the idols and kept them in his home. He made one of his sons a priest to serve his idols (v. 5).
- ⚜ A Levite, willing to stay anywhere, lived in Micah's idolatrous home (vs. 9-11).
- ⚜ Micah thought the LORD would bless him because he made the Levite his personal priest (vs. 12-13).

There are staggering parallels from Micah's story with people today. Parents bless their disobedient, rebellious children with more and more toys and gadgets instead of disciplining them, admonishing them in the fear of God. Money is used to buy things that detract from time and devotion to the LORD. Children are encouraged to serve those idols instead of serving God. The LORD is not consulted about where to go and what to do. In the midst of their idolatry, people call on the name of the LORD to invoke His blessings on them. "LORD, convict us!"

Pray the opposite of Judges 17:6 over yourself and those for whom you stand guard as a faithful, prayerful watchman (Isaiah 62:6-7).

> *"LORD, be King in my family!*
> *Let us stop doing what is right in our own eyes*
> *and do what is right in Your eyes.*
> *In Your name, Jesus~"*

Please read Judges 18.

Meditate on verse 20.

> *The priest's heart was glad, and he took the ephod and household*
> *idols and the graven image and went among the people.*

Observe Micah's priest:

- He told the evil Danites what they wanted to hear, lying that God approved of the way they were going (vs. 5-6).
- He kept silent as the Danites stole from Micah (vs. 18-19).
- He was glad at the thought of being priest to the tribe of Dan instead of only one man (vs. 19-20).

Can you relate to this priest? Do you find yourself telling people what they want to hear instead of what God's Word says? Do you give others the false notion that their sin is okay with God? Do you keep quiet about sin instead of speaking up for righteousness? Are you willing to do sinful things in order to be popular? Are you so glad to be part of a group that you are willing to compromise your Christian integrity?

"Every man did what was right in his own eyes" (Judges 17:6). Ask God to give you His eyes to see sins' consequences and the courage to take His stand against it.

Use the words from Judges 18:5-6 to inquire of the LORD about the way you are going.

> *"God, let _____ and me know whether our way on which*
> *we are going is actually Your way, so it will be prosperous.*
> *Then, let us go in peace because Your way in*
> *which we are going has Your approval.*
> *In Your name, Jesus-"*

Please read Judges 19.

Meditate on verse 30.

> *All who saw it said, "Nothing like this has ever happened or been*
> *seen from the day when the sons of Israel came up from the land*
> *of Egypt to this day. Consider it, take counsel and speak up!"*

Sadly, the gruesome details of this chapter are not merely facts from over 3,000 years ago; they are eerily similar to today's disturbing local, national, and international news. The woman raped and ravaged by a gang of homosexuals, cut into twelve pieces, and her body parts sent throughout Israel was a sign for the people of the land to wake up. Enough was enough. Doing what is right in one's own eyes is disgustingly horrible! God gave the command. "Consider it, take counsel, and speak up!"

This is God's command to you. Consider what is going on around you. Take counsel from His Word and speak up about what God says.

Pray Judges 19:30 over yourself and those for whom you stand guard as a faithful, prayerful watchman (Isaiah 62:6-7).

> *"LORD, nothing like this has ever happened*
> *or been seen before in our land.*
> *Let _____ and me consider it,*
> *take counsel, and speak up!*
> *For the sake of Your Word, Jesus~"*

MAY 4

Please read Judges 20.

Meditate on verse 7.

> *Behold, all you sons of Israel, give your advice and counsel here.*

Israel was in the middle of sin, and the results were deadly. Shocked to their senses by a murdered woman's body parts, the men of Israel sought their own counsel and decided to punish the murderers. Only after making their plans, did they ask God for a little advice (v. 18). God was not pleased to be consulted after plans were made, and He allowed 22,000 men to be killed (vs. 18-21). The sons of Israel were dismayed and wept before the LORD (v. 23). Afterwards, 18,000 more men were killed (v. 25). "Then all the sons of Israel and all the people went up and came to Bethel and wept; thus they remained there before the LORD and fasted that day until evening. And they offered burnt offerings and peace offerings before the LORD. The sons of Israel inquired of the LORD …" (vs. 26-27).

God taught His people important lessons, and He wants you to learn them, too. Seeking human counsel before getting God's counsel displeases the LORD and results in defeat. Here are the steps that bring God's plans and blessings (vs. 26-28):

- Remain in God's presence
- Fast
- Confess sins
- Accept God's forgiveness
- Seek His advice
- Cease fighting
- Let God deliver you

Pray Judges 20:26-28 over yourself and those for whom you stand guard as a faithful, prayerful watchman (Isaiah 62:6-7).

> *"LORD, may _____ and I remain before You,*
> *fasting and offering _____ before You.*
> *We inquire of You concerning _____.*
> *Tell us if we should go out to battle or cease fighting.*
> *Deliver us, LORD. In Your name, Jesus~"*

MAY 5

Please read Judges 21.

Meditate on verse 25.

> *In those days there was no king in Israel; everyone*
> *did what was right in his own eyes.*

The Israelites made a rash vow not to let their daughters marry a Benjaminite. This created a problem. If no one would marry into the tribe of Benjamin, eventually the line would cease, and they would be missing from the twelve tribes of Israel. So they made a plan to kill the people in Jabesh-gilead for not coming to an impromptu sacrifice, allowing 400 of the Jabesh virgins to live and be given to the men of Benjamin. They executed the plan, but still needed more women. Blaming God for Benjamin's problems, they advised the men of Benjamin to kidnap the daughters of Shiloh after they danced at one of the LORD's feasts. The Benjaminites took the advice and carried off the women. Unbelievable! Sin takes people to such pathetic places!

Judges ends with the Israelites still not consulting God before making decisions, still doing what was right in their own eyes, making worse and worse decisions, and cycling deeper and deeper into sin's pit.

Ask the LORD to help you remember the lessons from *Judges*, and pray the opposite of Judges 21:25 over yourself and those for whom you stand guard as a faithful prayerful watchman (Isaiah 62:6-7).

> *"LORD, You are the King of _____ and me.*
> *We will do what is right in Your eyes.*
> *Because of You, King Jesus~"*

MAY 6

Please read Ezra 1.

Meditate on these phrases from verse 1.

*In order to fulfill the word of the LORD … the LORD
stirred up the spirit of Cyrus king of Persia …*

Nebuchadnezzar, king of Babylon, destroyed Jerusalem and the temple in 586 BC (2 Kings 25:8-9). In 539 BC, the LORD appointed King Cyrus of Persia to decree the rebuilding of God's house. Israelites exiled to Babylon were given permission to return to Jerusalem to do the work, and their non-Jewish neighbors were commanded to support them with silver, gold, and other valuables. King Cyrus even returned all of the temple articles that Nebuchadnezzar had taken and put in his temples for his idols.

Amazingly, Cyrus was a pagan who did not know the LORD. His role in God's plans was prophesied 175 years before he was born (Isaiah 45:1-7), and He was used by God to accomplish what God desired.

Be encouraged as you read *Ezra*. The LORD will accomplish His plans, and He will use whomever and whatever He chooses. Despite what is happening in your world, the LORD is in charge; His desires cannot be thwarted.

Pray Ezra 1:2-3 and 5 over yourself and those for whom you stand guard as a faithful, prayerful watchman (Isaiah 62:6-7).

*"LORD, the God of heaven,
_____ and I are Your people;
God be with us!
Stir our spirits to go up and rebuild Your house.
In Your name, Jesus~"*

MAY 7

Please read Ezra 2.

Meditate on verse 68.

> *Some of the heads of fathers' households, when they arrived*
> *at the house of the LORD which is in Jerusalem, offered*
> *willingly for the house of God to restore it on its foundation.*

There were 42,360 people who returned to Jerusalem from Babylon (v. 64). When they saw the desolation of the temple, some of them offered *"to restore it on its foundation"* (v. 68).

Foundation is used six times in Ezra 2 and 3. It is the groundwork on which something stands. Jesus said, "Everyone who comes to Me and hears My words and acts on them ... is like a man building a house, who dug deep and laid a foundation on the rock; and when a flood occurred, the torrent burst against that house and could not shake it, because it had been well built" (Luke 6:47-48).

The LORD wants to restore people and their desolate situations on the rock solid foundation of Himself and His Word. Without Christ, life has no foundation (1 Corinthians 3:11). Pray for and share Jesus with those who need Him.

Use the words from Ezra 2:68 over yourself and those for whom you stand guard as a faithful, prayerful watchman (Isaiah 62:6-7).

> *"LORD, _____ needs to be restored*
> *with You as their foundation.*
> *I offer myself willingly to help restore them.*
> *Because You are the foundation, Jesus~"*

MAY 8

Please read Ezra 3.

Meditate on verse 12.

> *Yet many of the priests and Levites and heads of fathers'*
> *households, the old men who had seen the first temple,*
> *wept with a loud voice when the foundation of this house was*
> *laid before their eyes, while many shouted aloud for joy.*

What a relief to the Israelites when "the builders had laid the foundation of the temple of the LORD" (Ezra 3:10)! The solid foundation gave the people hope that the LORD's temple would be rebuilt.

You live in an age when the foundation of Christ's church is being attacked. False teachers change God's Word and ignore sound doctrine to justify fleshly desires.

Do not be deceived. Build your life on the Rock solid foundation of Christ and His Word (Deuteronomy 32:4; Luke 6:47-48).

Here are truths from God's Word to stand firm on:

> *The sum of Your Word is truth, and every one of*
> *Your righteous ordinances is everlasting.*
> —Psalm 119:160

> *Truth is according to Godliness, and God cannot lie.*
> —Titus 1:1-2

Pray Ezra 3:11 over yourself and those for whom you stand guard as a faithful, prayerful watchman (Isaiah 62:6-7).

> *"LORD, You are good, for Your*
> *lovingkindness is upon _____ and me forever.*
> *May we shout with a great shout as we praise You*
> *because You are the foundation of Your church.*
> *In Your strong name, Jesus~"*

Please read Ezra 4.

Meditate on verses 3b and 4.

*"You have nothing in common with us in building a house
to our God ..." Then the people of the land discouraged the
people of Judah, and frightened them from building.*

The Israelites were rebuilding the LORD's temple, and their enemies did
not like it. The builders faced bullying threats, frustrating legal actions,
and even an executive order from the king, which was carried out by armed
force (Ezra 4:4-5, 21-23). This discouraging and frightening situation
happened more than 2,500 years ago, yet it sounds like a news article
about attacks against Christ's church today.

Be encouraged by God's Word! Ever since sin entered the world, there have
been people who try to discourage, frustrate, and threaten God's people;
however, "the people who know their God will display strength and take
action" (Daniel 11:32).

The LORD declares, "No weapon that is formed against you will prosper;
and every tongue that accuses you in judgment you will condemn. This
is the heritage of the servants of the LORD, and their vindication is from
Me" (Isaiah 54:17).

Pray Ezra 4:3 over yourself and those for whom you stand guard as a
faithful, prayerful watchman (Isaiah 62:6-7).

*"LORD God, help _____ and me
not build Your church with people
who have nothing in common with us.
Let us build together with people
who hold to Your Word as You command.
For the sake of Your name, Jesus~"*

MAY 10

Please read Ezra 5.

Meditate on verse 11a.

> *Thus they answered us, saying, "We are the servants
> of the God of heaven and earth and are rebuilding
> the temple that was built many years ago ..."*

Work on the temple stopped for 14 years because of King Artaxerxes' executive order (Ezra 4:23-24). Then two preachers, Haggai and Zechariah, prophesied to the Jews and reminded them who was in control. The God of Israel was over them, and He wanted His temple rebuilt (Ezra 5:1; Haggai 1:14).

The people took courage from the prophets' messages and began rebuilding the house of God. Questioning authorities did not detract the Jews from their work; they pressed on, confidently obeying God's commands rather than crumbling in fear under man's decrees.

Be confident in the LORD and His Word. Be taught by pastors and teachers who know the Bible and refuse to crumble under the decrees of man that attempt to compromise and change the Word of God.

Pray Ezra 5:5, 8, and 11 over yourself and those for whom you stand guard as a faithful, prayerful watchman (Isaiah 62:6-7).

> *"God, keep Your eye on _____ and me.
> Help us do Your work with great care;
> let it succeed in our hands.
> God of heaven and earth, we are Your servants.
> Because of Your name, Jesus–"*

Please read Ezra 6.

Meditate on verse 7.

*Leave this work on the house of God alone; let the governor of the
Jews and the elders of the Jews rebuild this house of God on its site.*

King Cyrus issued a decree to rebuild the temple in Jerusalem (Ezra 1:2-4).
King Artaxerxes issued a decree to stop rebuilding the temple (Ezra 4:21-
24). King Darius issued a decree for a search to be made for King Cyrus'
decree (v. 1). After finding it, Darius issued another decree for the builders
of the temple to be left alone (vs. 6-10). King Darius then issued a third
decree that any man hindering work on the temple, thus violating Darius'
second decree, be impaled on a timber taken from his own house, and his
house "made a refuse heap" (v. 11).

Darius' decrees changed Tattenai, Shethar-bozenai, and their colleagues
from tattle-telling bullies into submissive pawns in the hand of Almighty
God (Ezra 5:3, 6-17; 6:13). The Jewish people finished rebuilding the
temple according to God's command (v. 14).

Are you and your nation under executive decrees that hurt Christ's church?
Appeal to the King of kings and LORD of lords, Jesus Christ, who is in
charge of kings and kingdoms. His enduring Kingdom will crush and put
an end to all other kingdoms (Daniel 2:44).

Use the words from Ezra 6:7, 12, and 22 to appeal to the LORD of lords,
as a faithful, prayerful watchman (Isaiah 62:6-7).

> *"LORD, issue the decree for work in Your church to be left
> alone. God, You cause Your name to dwell in Your church.
> Overthrow any king or people who attempts to destroy Your church.
> LORD, cause us to rejoice. Turn the hearts of leaders toward
> Christians to encourage us in the work of Your house, God.
> For the sake of Your name, Jesus~"*

MAY 12

Please read Ezra 7.

Meditate on verses 9b – 10.

> *The good hand of his God was upon him. For Ezra had*
> *set his heart to study the law of the LORD and to practice*
> *it, and to teach His statutes and ordinances in Israel.*

Approximately 60 years passed between chapters six and seven of *Ezra*, and for the first time, Ezra's name is mentioned. Observe him carefully, for he is a man to be emulated. Ezra was a priest and a scribe skilled in God's Word, with the good hand of his God upon him (vs. 6, 9-12). *Hand* is a repeated word in this chapter. Three times, Ezra is described as having the hand of God on him, and twice he is described as having God's Word in his hand (vs. 6, 9, 14, 25, 28). It is no coincidence that the hand of God touches this man of God, who holds onto His Word.

The last of the seven executive orders in the book of Ezra was decreed in this chapter, giving Ezra, the priest, permission to do everything according to the will of God, even allowing him to teach anyone who was ignorant of the laws of God (vs. 18, 25). Boldly ask the LORD to move the leadership of your country to grant the same favor to Christians (vs. 11-26).

This chapter is a treasure chest of verses to pray. Here is a prayer to get you started using Ezra 7:6, 9-11, and 28.

> *"LORD, may _____ and I be skilled*
> *in the Word You have given.*
> *Let Your good hand be upon us.*
> *Let us set our hearts to study Your Law and to practice it,*
> *and to teach Your statutes and ordinances.*
> *Make us learned in the Words of Your commandments and statutes.*
> *Strengthen us according to Your hand being upon us.*
> *In Your name, LORD our God, Jesus~"*

Please read Ezra 8.

Meditate on verse 31b.

> *The hand of our God was over us, and He delivered us from*
> *the hand of the enemy and the ambushes by the way.*

Ezra led a group of Israelite exiles out of Babylon and back to Jerusalem. As they journeyed, Ezra discovered there were no ministers and teachers among the group to serve in the temple and to instruct the people in the things of the LORD. Thankfully the good hand of God was upon them, and He brought men of insight to minister to the people.

Before they journeyed another step, Ezra proclaimed a fast, so the people could humble themselves before God and ask Him for a safe journey. The LORD heard their prayers and put His hand over them, delivering them safely to Jerusalem.

This is another treasure chapter for prayerful watchmen. It continues the theme of God's hand being upon those who seek Him. It affirms that God really does hear and answer prayers, and one should not take a step without seeking the LORD's guidance and protection.

With these truths in mind, pray Ezra 8:18, 21-23, and 31 over yourself and those for whom you stand guard as a faithful, prayerful watchman (Isaiah 62:6-7).

> *"LORD, according to Your good hand being upon us,*
> *make _____ and me people of insight.*
> *We humbly come before You, God, to seek safety from You.*
> *As we seek You, let Your hand be favorably disposed to us.*
> *As we fast and seek You, please listen to our entreaties.*
> *Keep Your hand over us, and deliver us from the hand*
> *of the enemy and any ambushes along the way.*
> *In Your name, Jesus~"*

MAY 14

Please read Ezra 9.

Meditate on verse 8.

> *But now for a brief moment grace has been shown from*
> *the LORD our God, to leave us an escaped remnant and to*
> *give us a peg in His holy place, that our God may enlighten*
> *our eyes and grant us a little reviving in our bondage.*

God extended mercy to the exiled Israelites, allowing them to leave Babylon and return to their homeland. Many of them showed their gratitude by being unfaithful to the LORD and engaging in the abominations of the pagans in the land. Ezra was appalled by their behavior! He sat in shock and disgust until evening, then he fell to his knees and poured out his heart to the LORD.

You live in a world of shocking and disgusting news. It fills your news apps and your social media. You get it in your texts and phone calls from family and friends. What is your first course of action when you hear appalling news? Learn from Ezra, a man of God, who loved the LORD and His Word. Fall on your knees and confess everything to God, asking Him to intervene. Ezra's prayer is recorded in verses 6-15. Use his words to start your conversation with God.

Pray Ezra 9:4-5 and 8-9 over yourself and those for whom you stand guard as a faithful, prayerful watchman (Isaiah 62:6-7).

> *"LORD, may _____ and I tremble at Your Words*
> *on account of the unfaithfulness of our nation.*
> *We fall on our knees and stretch out our hands to You,*
> *LORD our God. For a brief moment,*
> *let Your grace be shown, and give us a peg in Your holy place.*
> *Enlighten our eyes and grant us a little reviving in our bondage.*
> *Extend lovingkindness to us and give us*
> *reviving to raise up Your house, God.*
> *In Your name, Jesus-"*

Please read Ezra 10.

Meditate on verse 4.

> *Arise! For this matter is your responsibility, but we*
> *will be with you; be courageous and act.*

The returning exiles committed the heinous sin of marrying pagan women who occupied Israeli land. The command to divorce these foreigners appears contrary to God's Word; however, it is important to know the rest of the story. Malachi 2:10-16 gives the additional insight that these Jewish men divorced their Jewish wives in order to marry the daughters of foreign gods. God described such actions as "profaning the covenant" and "committing abominations" (Malachi 2:10-11). The people had to separate themselves "from the peoples of the land and from the foreign wives" in order to do God's will (v. 11).

The main point of Ezra 10 is that true confession of sin results in action taken to stop sinning and to start obeying the LORD. Repentance requires a change in behavior.

How would God describe your times of confession? Does unfaithfulness grieve you? Do you have the courage to take action and live faithfully according the Word of God? Satan wants you to marry yourself to sin and the ways of this world. What does God want you to separate from in order to be wholly His and holy to Him?

Pray Ezra 10:4, 6, and 11 over yourself and those for whom you stand guard as a faithful, prayerful watchman (Isaiah 62:6-7).

> *"LORD, this matter is _____ and my responsibility.*
> *Help us to be courageous and act. May we mourn over*
> *unfaithfulness. We make confession to You, LORD God.*
> *Help us to do Your will and separate ourselves from the*
> *foreign things in our land that are contrary to Your will.*
> *For Your name's sake, Jesus~"*

Please read Haggai 1.

Meditate on verses 5 and 7.

> *Now therefore, thus says the LORD of hosts, "Consider your ways!"*
> *Thus says the LORD of hosts, "Consider your ways!"*

Haggai was one of the prophets God sent to rally the Jews to finish rebuilding His temple in spite of executive orders, threats, and negativity from others (Ezra 5:1-2). The book of *Haggai* records the sermon he preached.

Twice the LORD commanded the people to consider their ways. God wanted them to think about what they were doing and how He was responding to their choices. The LORD was not pleased the people neglected rebuilding His temple, and He was punishing them for disobeying Him (vs. 5-11).

God wants you to consider your ways. Think about what you are doing. Do you obey the LORD and His Word? Are you pleasing Him, or are you more concerned about pleasing the world? Is the LORD punishing you for disobedience?

Consider your ways! And pray Haggai 1:12-14 over yourself and those for whom you stand guard as a faithful, prayerful watchman (Isaiah 62:6-7).

> *"LORD, may _____ and I*
> *obey Your voice and Your Words.*
> *May we show reverence for You.*
> *LORD, thank You that You are with us.*
> *Stir up our spirits to work on Your house, LORD*
> *of hosts, our God, Jesus Christ~"*

MAY 17

Please read Haggai 2.

Meditate on verses 4 and 5b.

> *"But now take courage, Zerubbabel," declares the LORD,*
> *"take courage also, Joshua son of Jehozadak, the high priest,*
> *and all you people of the land take courage," declares the*
> *LORD, "and work; for I am with you," declares the LORD*
> *of hosts. "My Spirit is abiding in your midst; do not fear!"*

Zerubbabel, the governor of Judah, Joshua, the high priest, and the people helping rebuild the LORD's house needed an encouraging word from the LORD because there were people in the land discouraging and frightening them from building (Ezra 4:4-5). The LORD sent His prophet Haggai to tell the people to take courage; take courage; take courage and get to work because God was with them. His Spirit abided in their midst; they were not to fear! The message concluded with a prophecy; the LORD of hosts will shake the heavens, the earth, the sea, the land, and all the nations, and the LORD will fill His house with His glory (vs. 4-7).

What a timely message for Christians, today! The LORD wants you to take courage; take courage and get to work because He is with you. His Spirit abides in you, and you are not to be afraid because as His church, you are His house (Hebrews 3:6), and the LORD is going to shake all created things and fill His house with His glory. Despite what is happening in the world around you, take courage and be encouraged by God's Word.

Pray Haggai 2:4-5 over yourself and those for whom you stand guard as a faithful, prayerful watchman (Isaiah 62:6-7).

> *"LORD of hosts, help _____ and me to take courage,*
> *take courage and do Your work because you are with us.*
> *Thank You that Your Spirit is abiding in*
> *our midst. Help us not to fear!*
> *In Your name, Jesus~"*

Please read Zechariah 1.

Meditate on verse 4.

> *"Do not be like your fathers, to whom the former prophets*
> *proclaimed, saying, 'Thus says the LORD of hosts,*
> *"Return now from your evil ways and from your evil deeds."'*
> *But they did not listen or give heed to Me," declares the LORD.*

Zechariah was another prophet sent by the LORD to preach to the Israelites and encourage them in the task of rebuilding His temple (Ezra 5:1-2). Zechariah's first sermon was simple; the LORD wanted this remnant of Jews to return to Him and not be like their fathers who refused to return to the LORD and continued in their evil ways and deeds. The LORD was very angry with these fathers who refused to repent until they were overtaken by God's Words and dealt with by God.

Listen and give heed to Zechariah's message. Refusing God's gracious offer to return to Him will meet with His wrath.

> *But because of your stubbornness and unrepentant heart you*
> *are storing up wrath for yourself in the day of wrath.*
> —Romans 2:5a

Pray Zechariah 1:3-4 over yourself and those for whom you stand guard as a faithful, prayerful watchman (Isaiah 62:6-7).

> *"LORD, let _____ and me be obedient to return*
> *to You, that You may return to us.*
> *Let us listen and give heed to Your command*
> *to return now from our evil ways and from our evil deeds.*
> *In Your name, Jesus~"*

MAY 19

Please read Zechariah 1:7-2:13, asking the LORD to give you insight with understanding as you read the visions the LORD gave Zechariah.

Meditate on Zechariah 2:8.

> *For thus says the LORD of hosts, "After glory, He has sent Me against the nations which plunder you, for he who touches you, touches the apple of His eye."*

The temple rebuilders needed encouragement to finish building (Ezra 5:1-2). God sent Zechariah to tell the people, "Thus says the LORD, 'I will return to Jerusalem with compassion; My house will be built in it'" (Zechariah 1:16). God's people were the apple of His eye, so they could build with confidence because the eye of their God was on them (Zechariah 2:8; Ezra 5:5).

If the LORD Jesus is your Savior, you, too, are precious to God. You are the apple of His eye, and He does not take His eye off of you.

> *Wondrously show Your lovingkindness, O Savior of those who take refuge at Your right hand from those who rise up against them. Keep me as the apple of the eye; hide me in the shadow of Your wings.*
> —Psalm 17:7-8

> *"I will counsel you with My eye upon you."*
> —Psalm 32:8b

Ponder these truths in awe-filled silence before the LORD (Zechariah 2:13). Then pray Zechariah 2:5 over yourself and those for whom you stand guard as a faithful, prayerful watchman (Isaiah 62:6-7).

> *"LORD, be a wall of fire around _____ and me, and be the glory in our midst. In Your name, Jesus~"*

MAY 20

Please read Zechariah 3.

Meditate on verses 3-4.

> *Now Joshua was clothed with filthy garments and standing*
> *before the angel. He spoke and said to those who were standing*
> *before him, saying, "Remove the filthy garments from him."*
> *Again he said to him, "See, I have taken your iniquity*
> *away from you and will clothe you with festal robes."*

Joshua was the high priest working with Zerubbabel to rebuild the temple at Jerusalem (Haggai 2:2-4; Ezra 5:1-2). Before Joshua could do the LORD's work, God had to remove his filthy, sinful garments and give him clean, festive robes.

This vision of Joshua's wardrobe change is the picture of what it means to become a Christian. Before Christ, you wore foul, polluted rags representing the sin that consumed your life. "But the LORD caused the iniquity of us all to fall on Him" (Isaiah 53:6). God put your disgusting garment of sin on Jesus and gave you His garment of salvation and righteousness (Isaiah 61:10). Amazing!

Are you trying to do the LORD's work by your own righteousness? God says we are all "unclean, and all our righteous deeds are like a filthy garment" (Isaiah 64:6). Unless you are wearing the saving righteousness of Jesus Christ, your work is vain. "LORD, take away my iniquity and clothe me with festal robes" (v. 4).

When you are dressed in the righteousness of Christ, you have confidence in Him to complete the tasks He calls you to do.

Pray Zechariah 3:7 over yourself and those for whom you stand guard as a faithful, prayerful watchman (Isaiah 62:6-7).

> *"LORD, help _____ and me to walk in Your*
> *ways and perform Your service.*
> *Let us govern and have charge in Your house and courts.*
> *Grant us free access among those standing here.*
> *In Your name, Jesus~"*

Please read Zechariah 4.

Meditate on verse 6.

> *Then he said to me, "This is the word of the LORD*
> *to Zerubbabel saying, 'Not by might nor by power,*
> *but by My Spirit,' says the LORD of hosts."*

Zerubbabel, Judah's governor, started rebuilding the temple then stopped for 14 years because of threats and executive decrees (Ezra 3:8; 4:4, 21-24). The LORD sent the prophets Haggai and Zechariah to encourage Zerubbabel and the other builders to press on in God's work and not fear men (Ezra 5:1-2). The LORD wanted Zerubbabel to know the temple would be rebuilt by the power of His Spirit, not by Zerubbabel's power or the might of his building crew (v. 6). This mountain of a project would become a plain by God's grace (v. 7). Zerubbabel laid the foundation of the temple, and by the Spirit's strength, he would lay its capstone 22 years later (Zechariah 4:7, 9; Ezra 6:14-16).

What mountain are you facing that seems insurmountable? Bring it to the LORD and seek His power and grace. Nothing is too difficult for Him (Jeremiah 32:17).

Pray Zechariah 4:6 over a difficult situation in your life and the life of those for whom you stand guard as a faithful, prayerful watchman (Isaiah 62:6-7).

> *"Not by might nor by power,*
> *but by Your Spirit, LORD,*
> *work in _____.*
> *In Your name, Jesus~"*

Please read Zechariah 5.

Meditate on verse 8a.

Then he said, "This is Wickedness!"

Zechariah preached a sermon to the builders of the temple emphasizing God's Word. He had a vision of a scroll, 30 feet by 15 feet in size, which contained in writing God's law and the curse for not obeying. As the builders concerned themselves with the exact measurements for building the temple structure, the LORD wanted them to focus on His Word.

God then gave Zechariah a vision of evil personified: a woman sitting in a bushel basket with a lead weight on top of her; her name was Wickedness. God's Word clearly defines sin and the punishment that results from it. Sin is wickedness, and every human will be held accountable to the LORD and His Word.

What projects are you and your church doing? Is your focus on teaching and learning God's Word? The world describes behavior contrary to the Bible as a "personal choice." God calls it "wickedness." Ask the LORD to give you His courage to speak His Truth.

Pray Zechariah 5:4 and 8 over yourself and those for whom you stand guard as a faithful, prayerful watchman (Isaiah 62:6-7).

"LORD, You will make Your Word go forth
into every house to consume it.
May _____ and I take Your Word
to every house before it is too late.
Keep us from Wickedness!
In Your name, Jesus~"

Please read Zechariah 6.

Meditate on verse 12.

> *Then say to him, "Thus says the LORD of hosts, 'Behold, a man whose name is Branch, for He will branch out from where He is; and He will build the temple of the LORD.'"*

Zechariah wasn't the only prophet who preached about Branch. Isaiah said Branch would be "beautiful and glorious" (Isaiah 4:2). Jeremiah declared Branch would "reign as king and be called the LORD our righteousness" (Jeremiah 23:5-6). Branch is Jesus; He is the builder of the temple of the LORD, and He sits on His throne as king and priest (vs. 12-13). Joshua, the high priest, and those who worked on and in the temple needed a reminder that they were not ruling over the temple; it was under the reign of the LORD (vs. 11-14).

If you are a follower of the Branch, the LORD Jesus Christ, you are His temple and under His reign and authority (1 Corinthians 6:19). Ask Him to branch out and take over every part of you (v. 12). Let Him build your life.

Pray Zechariah 6:12-13 and 15 over yourself and those for whom you stand guard as a faithful, prayerful watchman (Isaiah 62:6-7).

> *"LORD, Branch out in _____ and me.*
> *Build us into Your temple, LORD.*
> *Bear the honor and sit and rule on Your throne.*
> *Be priest on Your throne and counsel peace in us.*
> *Let us completely obey You, LORD our God.*
> *In Your name, Jesus~"*

MAY 24

Please read Zechariah 7.

Meditate on verse 12.

> *They made their hearts like flint so that they could not*
> *hear the law and the words which the LORD of hosts*
> *had sent by His Spirit through the former prophets;*
> *therefore, great wrath came from the LORD of hosts.*

When the temple of the LORD was in its final two years of rebuilding, some men from Bethel came to Jerusalem to ask the priests and the prophets about seeking the favor of the LORD. The LORD told Zechariah to ask them their real motivation behind fasting for God's favor. Were they seeking God or were they seeking what God could give them? The LORD knew their selfish desires, so He reminded them of past admonishments to practice kindness and compassion instead of oppression and evil when fasting (vs.9-10; Isaiah 58). The people "refused to pay attention and turned a stubborn shoulder and stopped their ears from hearing" (v. 11). The LORD refused to listen to them because they refused to listen to Him.

Do you have a tender heart towards the LORD, desiring to know Him and His Word? Or do you have a hard heart that refuses to hear God and only seeks Him when you need something?

Pray to be the opposite of Zechariah 7:12 for yourself and those for whom you stand guard as a faithful, prayerful watchman (Isaiah 62:6-7).

> *"LORD, do not let _____ and me*
> *make our hearts like flint.*
> *Let us hear Your Law and the Words*
> *which You have sent by Your Spirit through the prophets*
> *so that we do not experience Your wrath.*
> *In Your name, Jesus~"*

Please read Zechariah 8.

Meditate on verses 17 and 19b.

> *"Also let none of you devise evil in your heart against another, and do not love perjury; for all these are what I hate," declares the LORD. "Love truth and peace."*

Zechariah 8 contains exciting end-time prophecies. The day will come when Jerusalem will be called the City of Truth. The LORD will bring His people there to "be their God in truth and righteousness" (v. 8). He will save a remnant of Judah and Israel to be a blessing.

This chapter also contains a list of four things God says you should do (vs. 16-17):

1. Speak truth to one another.
2. Judge with truth to bring peace.
3. Do not devise evil in your heart against another.
4. Do not love perjury.

The LORD hates evil and lies; He loves peace and truth. Do you hate the same things the LORD hates? Do you love what He loves? The world wants you to love what God hates. Ask the LORD to give you His heart and desire to obey His Word.

Pray Zechariah 8:16-17, 19, and 21 over yourself and those for whom you stand guard as a faithful, prayerful watchman (Isaiah 62:6-7).

> *"LORD, may _____ and I speak the truth to one another.*
> *Let us judge with truth for peace in our gates.*
> *Do not let us devise evil in our hearts against another.*
> *Let us not love perjury; for all these are what You hate.*
> *Let us love truth and peace. I entreat Your favor,*
> *LORD, and I seek You, LORD of hosts.*
> *In Your name, Jesus~"*

MAY 26

Please read Zechariah 9.

Meditate on verse 9.

> *Rejoice greatly, O daughter of Zion! Shout in triumph, O*
> *daughter of Jerusalem! Behold, your king is coming to you;*
> *He is just and endowed with salvation; humble and mounted*
> *on a donkey, even on a colt, the foal of a donkey.*

You may recognize the meditation verse as a prophecy about Jesus, which He fulfilled the week of His crucifixion when He rode into Jerusalem on a young donkey (Luke 19:30-40). The thousands of Jews in Jerusalem that week had this Word from the LORD for 500 years prior to seeing it actually happen. Yet, most of them rejected Jesus as their king, and by the end of the week, they were crying out, "Crucify, crucify Him!" (Luke 23:21). They rejected the Word of the LORD and gave into mob mentality.

As you hold God's Word in your hand, commit to keeping God's truths. Do not be tempted to give into mob mentality that wants to change the Word of the LORD to accommodate the sins of society. Be encouraged by Zechariah 9. The LORD is destroying His enemies and saving those who are in a covenant relationship with Him. Let Him defend you!

Pray Zechariah 9:11-12 and 15a over yourself and those for whom you stand guard as a faithful, prayerful watchman (Isaiah 62:6-7).

> *"LORD, because of the blood of Your covenant*
> *with _____ and me, set us free from the waterless pit.*
> *We have the hope, so we return to You, our stronghold.*
> *Restore double to us. LORD of hosts, defend us.*
> *In Your name, Jesus~"*

MAY 27

Please read Zechariah 10.

Meditate on verses 11a and 12.

> *"And they will pass through the sea of distress, and
> I will strengthen them in the LORD, and in His
> name they will walk," declares the LORD.*

Zechariah 10 is full of promises from the LORD for His flock, the house of Judah (vs. 5-8):

- ❧ He will be with them.
- ❧ He will strengthen them.
- ❧ He will save them.
- ❧ He will bring them back.
- ❧ He has compassion on them.
- ❧ They will be as though He had not rejected them.
- ❧ He will answer them.
- ❧ Their heart will rejoice in the LORD.
- ❧ He will gather them, for He has redeemed them.

The LORD has not forgotten His flock of Israel, and if you are a follower of Christ, He has not forgotten you, either; for you are part of His flock.

> *I have other sheep, which are not of this fold; I must
> bring them also, and they will hear My voice; and
> they will become one flock with one shepherd.*
> —John 10:16

Pray Zechariah 10:11a and 12 over yourself and those for whom you stand guard as a faithful, prayerful watchman (Isaiah 62:6-7).

> *"LORD, when _____ and I pass through
> the sea of distress, strengthen us.
> Let us walk in Your name, LORD Jesus."*

Please read Zechariah 11.

Meditate on verse 4.

> *Thus says the LORD my God, "Pasture the flock doomed to slaughter."*

The LORD was angry with the shepherds whose job was to care for His people. The people perished for lack of Godly leadership. The LORD told Zechariah to shepherd this pathetic flock. As he pastured, Zechariah became a sermon illustration and a prophecy. Zechariah broke his staff named Favor. Those watching knew it was the Word of the LORD; they no longer had His favor. When Zechariah asked to be paid for shepherding, he was given a measly 30 pieces of silver. Jesus, the Good Shepherd, was betrayed for the same amount. And unlike the worthless shepherds, Jesus laid down His life for the sheep that were doomed to death and annihilation without Him (v. 9; Matthew 26:15; John 10:11).

Who does the LORD expect you to shepherd? If you are a Christian, there is at least one person in your realm of influence you can pasture to Christlikeness. Shepherd well the flock God has given you, and heed His warning:

> *Woe to the worthless shepherd who leaves the flock! A sword*
> *will be on his arm and on his right eye! His arm will be*
> *totally withered, and his right eye will be blind.*
> — Zechariah 11:17

Pray Zechariah 11:7 over yourself and those for whom you stand guard as a faithful, prayerful watchman (Isaiah 62:6-7).

> *"LORD, help _____ and me pasture the flock*
> *doomed to slaughter apart from You,*
> *hence the afflicted of the flock.*
> *Help us pasture with Favor and Union.*
> *In Your name, Great Shepherd, Jesus~"*

MAY 29

Please read Zechariah 12.

Meditate on verse 1.

> *The burden of the Word of the LORD concerning Israel.*
> *Thus declares the LORD who stretches out the heavens, lays the*
> *foundation of the earth, and forms the spirit of man within him.*

Before the LORD told Zechariah amazing end time prophecies concerning Israel, He reminded him about who He is. The LORD, who miraculously stretched out the heavens, laid the earth's foundation, and forms the spirit of every human will save and defend Jerusalem and Judah. He will destroy all the nations that come against her. In that day, the LORD will pour out His Spirit of grace on the inhabitants of Jerusalem, and they will see and recognize the LORD Jesus, whom they pierced (v. 10).

Know with certainty the LORD has not rejected Israel; His miraculous plans for her will stand. Do not doubt God's Word or attempt to change it to fit false teaching. The LORD God made the heavens and the earth by His great power and outstretched arm; nothing is too difficult for Him (Jeremiah 32:17)!

As you wait for the LORD to fulfill His Word for Israel, pray for Him to do the same for you and those you love. Pray Zechariah 12:10 over yourself and those for whom you stand guard as a faithful, prayerful watchman (Isaiah 62:6-7).

> *"LORD, pour out Your Spirit of grace and*
> *supplication on _____ and me.*
> *Let us always look on You, Jesus,*
> *who was pierced because of us.*
> *Thank You, LORD Jesus~"*

MAY 30

Please read Zechariah 13.

Meditate on verse 1.

In that day a fountain will be opened for the house of David
and for the inhabitants of Jerusalem, for sin and for impurity.

In that day is an important repeated phrase in *Zechariah*. It is used 16 times in the last three chapters of this book you are praying, and it describes the time when God focuses His attention on Israel for their salvation. The LORD declares that one third of the Jews left in the land will say the LORD is their God, and He will declare them His people (vs. 8-9). It is exciting to know how the story ends!

As a child of God, you called on the name of the LORD to be saved (Romans 10:13). The fountain of salvation, the blood of Christ, was opened to cleanse you of all sin and impurity (Hebrews 9:14). Let the LORD of hosts remove any remaining idols and false prophets in your life (v. 2). Ask Him to keep you and those you love away from unclean spirits (v. 2). And pray for the salvation of Israel and those you love who need the Shepherd (v. 7).

Pray Zechariah 13:1-2 and 9 over yourself and those for whom you stand guard as a faithful, prayerful watchman (Isaiah 62:6-7).

"LORD, let Your fountain be opened for Israel and
for _____, for removing sin and impurity.
Cut off the names of the idols from _____ and me;
let them no longer be remembered.
Remove the false prophets and the unclean spirits from the
land. Refine us as silver is refined. Test us as gold is tested.
We call on Your name; answer us. Let us hear You say,
'You are My people.' We say, 'LORD, You are our God.'
Because of Your name, LORD Jesus~"

MAY 31

Please read Zechariah 14.

Meditate on verse 9.

> *And the LORD will be king over all the earth; in that day the*
> *LORD will be the only one, and His name the only one.*

Zechariah 14 describes the time when Christ returns with His holy ones, Christians, to rule the earth. It gives added details to the events recorded in Revelation 19-20:1-6. It is exciting to know that a day is coming when "Jerusalem will dwell in security" (v. 11). It is also sobering to know a day is coming when the enemies of God will experience their flesh "rot while they stand on their feet, and their eyes will rot in their sockets, and their tongue will rot in their mouth" (v. 12).

Now that you have read Zechariah, you know what God has declared will happen. This is not a fictional scene from a movie; this is not man's imagination. This is the Word of God, and this is the Truth (Psalm 119:160). Whom will you tell before it is too late?

Pray Zechariah 14:9 and 11 as a faithful, prayerful watchman (Isaiah 62:6-7).

> *"LORD, _____ and I look forward to the day*
> *when You are King over all the earth,*
> *the day when You, LORD, are the only one*
> *and Your name is the only one.*
> *We look forward to the day when people will live in Jerusalem,*
> *and there will no longer be a curse,*
> *for Jerusalem will dwell in security.*
> *Because of Your name, Jesus~"*

SUMMER OF PSALMS

It was 2005. Ron received orders to Iraq; he would be gone for many months, including most of summer. I dreaded the thought of him being away for so long. Prior to his departure, many of my days were filled with heart pounding, paralyzing anxiety. Thankfully, the LORD gave me Psalm 73:26: "My flesh and my heart may fail, but God is the strength of my heart and my portion forever." Every time I started to have a panic attack, I said that verse over and over and over … miraculously, my heart rate would return to normal, and I could breathe again.

When the day came for Ron to get on the plane to leave, I had the peace from God that surpasses comprehension (Philippians 4:7). And I had a plan for how to thrive (not merely survive) the days while he was gone. My countdown chain for Ron's return was to read one psalm a day. In my Bible, each psalm is dated with those days he was gone. It is a precious reminder of the LORD's faithfulness and how He used His Word to turn dreaded days into a savory season with Him.

For the next 100 days of summer, you will read 100 psalms. Summer can be a time for refreshing. It can be used for relaxation and vacation, a carefree departure from the normal. Let these daily doses of prayers and praises from *Psalms* keep you focused on God. We hope that as you read and pray *Psalms*, this will be a summer to savor with your Savior.

JUNE

On your walls, O Jerusalem,
I have appointed watchmen;
All day and all night they
will never keep silent.
You who remind the LORD,
take no rest for yourselves;
And give Him no rest until He establishes
And makes Jerusalem a
praise in the earth.
ISAIAH 62:6-7, NASB

JUNE 1

Please read Psalm 1.

Meditate on verses 4a and 6b.

The wicked are not so; the way of the wicked will perish.

In Psalm 1, the way of the righteous person is contrasted with the way of the wicked person. The wicked are hostile toward God. They have a path they want others to walk with them, and they have a seat where they sit and scoff at God (v.1). A righteous person refuses to partake in their evil ways or listen to their counsel; instead, they delight in and meditate on God's Word all the time. The result is a person who thrives and lives a prosperous and fruitful life, knowing and being known by the LORD (vs. 2-3, 6). Extermination and destruction are the result of the wicked person's choice to rebel against God and His Word (v. 6).

Who do you choose to be? Pray Psalm 1 over yourself and those for whom you stand guard as a faithful, prayerful watchman (Isaiah 62:6-7).

"LORD, I want my family to be blessed by You.
Please do not let _____ and me walk in the counsel of the wicked,
nor stand in the path of sinners, nor sit in the seat of scoffers.
Let us delight in Your Law, LORD, and
meditate on it day and night.
Let us be like a tree firmly planted by streams of water which
yields its fruit in its season and whose leaf does not whither.
Let us prosper in whatever we do. Do not let us be wicked.
We do not want to be like chaff which the wind drives away.
We want to stand in the judgment and be
in the assembly of the righteous.
LORD, You know the way of the righteous.
Make us Your righteous people.
Do not let us perish.
In Your name, Jesus~"

JUNE 2

Please read Psalm 2.

Meditate on verse 11.

Worship the LORD with reverence and rejoice with trembling.

Psalm 2 is a Messianic psalm. Notice the references to Jesus: His Anointed (v. 2), My King (v. 6), and My Son (v. 7, 12). Notice the contrasts in this psalm between the kings of the earth and the LORD's King. The LORD laughs and scoffs at earthly kings who plot against Him (vs. 1-4).

Take comfort from this psalm. The world around you may be in an uproar, and the kings and rulers of the earth may think they are in charge, but the LORD has already installed King Jesus on His holy mountain (v. 6). The nations are His inheritance, and the earth is His possession.

The LORD warns kings and judges (v. 10) to show discernment and worship Him. It is a warning for all to heed accompanied by verses to pray.

Pray Psalm 2:10-12 over yourself and those for whom you stand guard as a faithful, prayerful watchman (Isaiah 62:6-7).

"LORD, let _____ and me show discernment
and pay attention to Your warning.
Help us worship You with reverence and rejoice with trembling.
We give homage to You, Jesus.
We do not want You to become angry with us.
Do not let us perish in the way of Your
wrath that will soon be kindled.
Bless us as we take refuge in You.
In Your name, Jesus~"

JUNE 3

Please read Psalm 3.

Meditate on verses 2-3.

> *Many are saying of my soul, "There is no deliverance for*
> *him in God." But You, O LORD, are a shield about*
> *me, my glory and the One who lifts my head.*

King David wrote Psalm 3 when his son Absalom turned the people against him and attempted to make himself the king of Israel (2 Samuel 15). God used the situation to make David humble and contrite, and when he climbed the Mount of Olives, David was a broken, weeping man. He spent the night there and awoke knowing the LORD would sustain him. David no longer feared the ten thousands of people who set themselves against him (vs. 3-6; 2 Samuel 15:25-30).

Perhaps this psalm describes a daunting situation you face. Trust the LORD to deliver you. Even if everyone and everything around you says the situation is hopeless, declare with confidence, "But You, O LORD, are a shield about me, my glory and the One who lifts my head" (v. 3).

Come humbly before the LORD and pray Psalm 3:7-8 over yourself and those for whom you stand guard as a faithful, prayerful watchman (Isaiah 62:6-7).

> *"Arise, O LORD; save _____ and me, O my God!*
> *Smite all our enemies on the cheek;*
> *shatter the teeth of the wicked.*
> *Salvation belongs to You, LORD.*
> *Let Your blessing be upon us, Your people.*
> *For the sake of Your name, Jesus~"*

JUNE 4

Please read Psalm 4.

Meditate on verse 3.

> *But know that the LORD has set apart the Godly man*
> *for Himself; the LORD hears when I call to Him.*

Psalm 4 is another psalm of David, and there is much to learn from this man after God's own heart (1 Samuel 13:14). When David was upset, he appealed to his righteous God, and God relieved him in the midst of his distress (v. 1). David knew the LORD heard him when he called (v. 3).

Through David, God gives you six steps for handling times of adversity (vs. 4-5):

1. Tremble in awe of God, not in fear of your situation.
2. Do not sin.
3. Meditate in your heart upon your bed. When you lay awake at night, replace worries with the Word of God, perhaps speak a verse over yourself that you memorized as a child.
4. Be still.
5. Offer righteous sacrifices, such as the sacrifice of praise, even when times are tough (Hebrews 13:15).
6. Trust in the LORD.

Pray Psalm 4:6-8 over yourself and those for whom you stand guard as a faithful, prayerful watchman (Isaiah 62:6-7).

> *"LORD, many are saying, 'Who will show them any good?'*
> *Lift up the light of Your countenance upon _____ and me!*
> *Put gladness in our hearts, more than when*
> *their grain and new wine abound.*
> *In peace, let us both lie down and sleep,*
> *for You alone, O LORD, make us to dwell in safety.*
> *In Your name, Jesus~"*

JUNE 5

Please read Psalm 5.

Meditate on verse 3.

> *In the morning, O LORD, You will hear my voice; in the*
> *morning, I will order my prayer to You and eagerly watch.*

David had an intimate relationship with the LORD, so he talked to God and confidently waited for His response to troubling issues.

As you read through *Psalms*, you may want to make a list of what you learn about God. Knowing God increases your faith and makes you like David, able to talk to Him about everything.

Notice God's attitude toward wickedness in Psalm 5:4-6:

1. God does not take pleasure in wickedness.
2. No evil dwells with the LORD.
3. The boastful will not stand before God's eyes.
4. The LORD hates all who do iniquity.
5. God destroys those who speak falsehood.
6. The LORD abhors the man of bloodshed and deceit.

Do any of these attributes and actions of God surprise you? What is your response to Him? Notice how David responded—he came into God's presence and bowed in reverence to Him (v. 7). He knew God hated evil, so David asked the LORD to lead him in righteousness (v. 8).

Pray Psalm 5:11-12 over yourself and those for whom you stand guard as a faithful, prayerful watchman (Isaiah 62:6-7).

> *"LORD, _____ and I take refuge in You; let us be glad.*
> *Let us ever sing for joy. Shelter us, LORD! We love Your*
> *name; may we exult in You. You bless the righteous person,*
> *O LORD. Surround us with Your favor as with a shield.*
> *In Your name, Jesus~"*

JUNE 6

Please read Psalm 6.

Meditate on verse 9.

The LORD has heard my supplication. The LORD receives my prayer.

David was having a difficult time when he wrote Psalm 6. He admitted that the LORD was rebuking and chastening him. His soul and body were dismayed. He was deeply grieved. Adversaries and enemies were bothering him.

In the midst of his distress, David called on God to save him because of His lovingkindness. David knew his own merits could not save him. Only if God chose to give David His unmerited lovingkindness and grace, would David be saved from his distressful situation exacerbated by sin.

What is happening in your life? Is the LORD reprimanding and correcting you? Come humbly to the LORD in repentance; you can be confident that He hears and receives your prayers.

Pray Psalm 6:2 and 4 over yourself and those for whom you stand guard as a faithful, prayerful watchman (Isaiah 62:6-7).

> *"LORD, be gracious to _____ and me, for we are pining away.*
> *Heal us, O LORD, for our bones are dismayed.*
> *Return, O LORD, rescue our soul;*
> *save us because of Your lovingkindness.*
> *For the sake of Your name, Jesus~"*

JUNE 7

Please read Psalm 7.

Meditate on verse 9a.

O let the evil of the wicked come to an end,
but establish the righteous...

Before David appealed to God for justice, he asked Him if there was any injustice within his own heart. David wanted the LORD to reveal sin in his own life first, then he requested God to judge his adversaries.

David knew this truth about God:

If a man does not repent, He will sharpen His sword;
He has bent His bow and made it ready. He has also prepared
for Himself deadly weapons; He makes His arrows fiery shafts.
—Psalm 7:12-13

David found refuge in God because he had a repentant heart.

God is a righteous judge and a saving shield (vs. 10-11). Come to the LORD in repentance and ask Him to show you unconfessed sin. Ask Him to forgive you then pray Psalm 7:1, 10, and 17 over yourself and those for whom you stand guard as a faithful, prayerful watchman (Isaiah 62:6-7).

"O LORD my God, in You _____ and I have taken refuge.
Please save us from all those who pursue us, and deliver us.
Our shield is with You, God. Make us upright in heart and save us.
We give thanks to You, LORD, according to Your righteousness.
We will sing praise to Your name, LORD Most High.
Because Your name is Jesus~"

JUNE 8

Please read Psalm 8.

Meditate on verse 1.

*O LORD, our Lord, how majestic is Your name in all the
earth, who have displayed Your splendor above the heavens!*

Psalm 8 is a beautiful praise written by David. You may have even sung some of the words of this psalm in hymns or other worship songs. David began and ended this song of praise by acknowledging who God is. The LORD, the self-existent and eternal One, was David's master and superior; He was LORD of David.

The LORD displayed His splendor, and David took notice. As he considered God's creation, he was humble before the LORD. It amazed David that the LORD would take thought of him and care for him. Yet God not only cared for David and all humans, He even put people in charge of His creation. The LORD is indeed excellent, powerful, and majestic in all the earth!

Perceive and consider the LORD and what He is doing in your life and the lives of those you love. Pray Psalm 8:3-4 and 9 over yourself and them as a faithful, prayerful watchman (Isaiah 62:6-7).

*"LORD, help _____ and me to consider Your heavens,
the work of Your fingers, the moon and the
stars, which You have ordained.
Thank You for taking thought of us.
Thank You for taking care of us.
Oh LORD, our LORD,
how majestic is Your name in all the earth!
In Your name, LORD Jesus~"*

JUNE 9

Please read Psalm 9.

Meditate on verses 9-10.

> *The LORD also will be a stronghold for the oppressed, a stronghold in times of trouble. And those who know Your name will put their trust in You, for You, O LORD, have not forsaken those who seek You.*

As you read this psalm, notice what David says **he will** do in the first two verses:

- ✺ I will give thanks to the LORD with all my heart.
- ✺ I will tell of all Your wonders.
- ✺ I will be glad and exult in You.
- ✺ I will sing praise to Your name, O Most High.

There are days when doing these things comes naturally; there are other days when you must choose to do them. Practice these four things today.

Notice that David remembered things God had done. He listed at least ten of them in this psalm. What do you recall God doing in your life? Recount those things. Remember them often, because meditating on God's faithfulness in the past helps you be thankful in the present and confident of God's faithfulness for the future.

David prayed throughout this psalm. Use his words from Psalm 9:13-14 and 19-20 to pray over yourself and those for whom you stand guard as a faithful, prayerful watchman (Isaiah 62:6-7).

> *"Be gracious to _____ and me, O LORD.*
> *See our affliction from those who hate us.*
> *Lift us up from the gates of death, that we may tell of all Your praises.*
> *We will rejoice in Your salvation.*
> *Arise, O LORD, do not let man prevail;*
> *let the nations be judged before You.*
> *Put them in fear, O LORD; let the nations*
> *know that they are but men.*
> *Because of Your name, Jesus~"*

JUNE 10

Please read Psalm 10.

Meditate on verse 4.

The wicked, in the haughtiness of his countenance,
does not seek Him. All his thoughts are "There is no God."

Psalm 10 contains a list describing the wicked. In arrogance they:

- ⚬ boast of their heart's desire (v. 3).
- ⚬ curse and spurn God (v. 3).
- ⚬ think there is no God (v. 4).
- ⚬ think they will not be in adversity (v. 6).
- ⚬ have mouths full of curses, deceit, oppression, mischief, and wickedness (v. 7).
- ⚬ think God will never see their evil deeds (v. 11).

God's Word says, "The fool has said in his heart, 'there is no God'" (Psalm 14:1). The wicked are fools in God's eyes.

Wicked people have not changed in 3,000 years. The list in Psalm 10 could have been just as easily written today to describe evil people. The writer of this psalm appealed to God on behalf of the afflicted and the oppressed.

The LORD is the same yesterday, today, and forever (Hebrews 13:8). Appeal to Him with Psalm 10:16-18, as a faithful, prayerful watchman (Isaiah 62:6-7).

"LORD, You are King forever and ever.
Nations have perished from Your land.
O LORD, hear the desire of _____ and me.
We come to You in humility. Strengthen our hearts;
incline Your ear to vindicate the orphan and the oppressed,
so that man who is of the earth will no longer cause terror.
In Your name, Jesus~"

JUNE 11

Please read Psalm 11.

Meditate on verse 7.

> *For the LORD is righteous; He loves righteousness.*
> *The upright will behold His face.*

Observe the contrasts between the righteous and the wicked in this psalm, and observe actions and attributes of God. God hates the person who loves violence (v. 5). This truth about God may surprise you, but it is an important doctrine to remember and to teach others who may think that God's love is not capable of reproach or hate. There are things and people God hates; you do not want to do or be one of them.

David knew that God loves righteousness and hates evil. These foundational truths cannot be destroyed, so David took refuge in the LORD from the attacks of the wicked. The LORD was his foundation; there was no need to fear the attacks of the wicked blindly shooting arrows in the dark (vs. 1-3).

God is testing you (vs. 4-5), so you must examine yourself. In whom or what do you take refuge? Are you a person who loves violence, or do you love righteousness? Are you upright because you have a relationship with Jesus?

Pray Psalm 11:1 and 7 over yourself and those for whom you stand guard as a faithful, prayerful watchman (Isaiah 62:6-7).

> *"In You, LORD, _____ and I take refuge.*
> *We will flee to You! LORD, You are righteous;*
> *You love righteousness.*
> *Make us upright; we want to behold Your face!*
> *In Your name, Jesus~"*

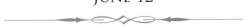

Please read Psalm 12.

Meditate on verse 6a.

The Words of the LORD are pure words.

David cried out to the LORD because the Godly and the faithful were disappearing from among the people. He observed that the words of men were lies, but the Words of God are pure.

The world today is similar to David's world 3,000 years ago. Be warned and encouraged by these pure Words of God:

- When vileness and worthlessness are exalted, make sure you not part of such wickedness (v. 8).
- As the Godly and the faithful cease to exist, make sure you do not disappear with them (v 1). Stay faithful in the LORD!
- Notice the words of the arrogant in verse 4: "With our tongue we will prevail; our lips are our own; who is lord over us?" Ask God to search your heart. Is there a similar attitude lurking inside you?

In humility, pray Psalm 12:5-7 over yourself and those for whom you stand guard as a faithful, prayerful watchman (Isaiah 62:6-7).

> *"LORD, _____ and I are afflicted and needy.*
> *Arise, LORD, set us in the safety for which we long!*
> *LORD, Your Words are pure Words;*
> *as silver tried in a furnace on the earth, refined seven times.*
> *Keep us, O LORD! Preserve us from this generation forever!*
> *In Your strong name, Jesus~"*

JUNE 13

Please read Psalm 13.
Meditate on verse 1.

> *How long, O LORD? Will You forget me forever?*
> *How long will You hide Your face from me?*

David was in a low place when he wrote this psalm, so low that he thought he might die. Have you or someone you love ever been overcome with sorrow and depression? This short psalm can be a big help. Notice how David handled his distress.

David addressed his questions to God. He was honest with the LORD. If he had expressed some of the same thoughts to a friend or counselor, he might have been thought of as histrionic. But God did not accuse him for being dramatic. God can handle raw emotion; He understands.

After pouring his heart out to the LORD, David recalled God's lovingkindness in the past. Because of God's faithfulness to him in previous situations, David knew he could trust God in this present situation. He remembered the LORD had dealt bountifully with him, so he chose to sing and rejoice in God's salvation.

Pray Psalm 13:3 and 5-6 over yourself and those for whom you stand guard as a faithful, prayerful watchman (Isaiah 62:6-7).

> *"Consider and answer _____ and me, O LORD my God.*
> *Enlighten our eyes, or we will sleep the sleep of death.*
> *We are trusting in Your lovingkindness.*
> *Our hearts will rejoice in Your salvation.*
> *We will sing to You, LORD, because You*
> *have dealt bountifully with us.*
> *In Your name, Jesus~"*

Please read Psalm 14.

Meditate on verse 1a.

> *The fool has said in his heart, "There is no God."*

Psalm 14:1-5 contains a list of actions and attributes of fools. They:

- say there is no God.
- are corrupt.
- commit abominable deeds.
- turn aside from God's way.
- have become corrupt with other fools.
- are workers of wickedness.
- devour others.
- do not call upon the LORD.
- are in great dread **because**:
  - God is with the righteous generation.
  - God is the refuge for the afflicted.
  - God restores His captive people (vs. 5-7).

The LORD is looking for people who understand these truths and seek after Him (Psalm 14:2). If you are one of the righteous who desire to know the LORD, be encouraged that He is with you to restore you and be your refuge.

Pray Psalm 14:2 and 5-7 over yourself and those for whom you stand guard as a faithful, prayerful watchman (Isaiah 62:6-7).

> *"LORD, as You look down from heaven, see _____ and me!*
> *We understand; we seek after You. God, we*
> *want to be Your righteous generation.*
> *Be our refuge when we are afflicted. Restore us, LORD.*
> *We will rejoice and be glad in You.*
> *In Your name, Jesus~"*

June 15

Please read Psalm 15.

Meditate on verse 5b.

He who does these things will never be shaken.

The LORD loves to teach with lists. As you read the Bible, notice lists, observing what God wants you to know.

There is a list in Psalm 15 of the characteristics of a person who abides with God and as a result of dwelling with the LORD, will never be shaken. Does this list describe you?

- walks with integrity
- works righteousness
- speaks truth in their heart
- does not slander with their tongue
- does no evil to their neighbor
- does not take up a reproach against their friend
- despises a reprobate
- honors those who fear the LORD
- keeps their promise even if it hurts
- does not change their mind
- lends money without charging interest
- does not take a bribe against the innocent

Pray Psalm 15 over yourself and those for whom you stand guard as a faithful, prayerful watchman (Isaiah 62:6-7).

> *"LORD, _____ and I want to abide in*
> *Your tent and dwell on Your holy hill.*
> *Help us walk with integrity and work righteousness.*
> *Let us speak truth in our hearts and not slander with*
> *our tongues. Do not let us do evil to our neighbors*
> *or take up a reproach against our friends.*
> *In our eyes, may a reprobate be despised, but let*
> *us honor those who fear You, LORD.*
> *May we swear to our own hurt and not change.*
> *May we not put out our money at interest, and let*
> *us not take a bribe against the innocent.*
> *LORD, let us never be shaken. Because of You, Jesus~"*

Please read Psalm 16.

Observe God's actions and attributes.

Meditate on verse 8.

> *I have set the LORD continually before me;*
> *because He is at my right hand, I will not be shaken.*

David took refuge in God instead of humans because David intimately knew the truth about God. In order not to be shaken, David set the LORD continually before him. Is God continually before you; is He foremost in your thoughts, plans, and decision-making processes?

David's relationship with God brought not only stability to his life, but also joy and gladness. Ask the LORD to give you that kind of relationship with Him.

Pray Psalm 16:1-2, 5-9, and 11 over yourself and those for whom you stand guard as a faithful, prayerful watchman (Isaiah 62:6-7).

> *"O God, preserve _____ and me, for we take refuge in*
> *You. You are our LORD; we have no good besides You.*
> *LORD, You are the portion of our inheritance and our cup;*
> *You support our lot. The lines have fallen to us*
> *in pleasant places; indeed our heritage is beautiful to us.*
> *We bless you, LORD! Counsel us; instruct our minds in*
> *the night. We set You, LORD, continually before us;*
> *because You are at our right hand, we will not be shaken.*
> *Therefore, our hearts are glad, and our glory rejoices;*
> *our flesh also will dwell securely. Make known to us the*
> *path of life. In Your presence is fullness of joy;*
> *in Your right hand are pleasures forever.*
> *Thank You, Jesus~"*

JUNE 17

Please read Psalm 17.

Meditate on verses 3b and 4b-5.

> *I have purposed that my mouth will not transgress.*
> *I have kept from the paths of the violent. My steps have*
> *held fast to Your paths. My feet have not slipped.*

David made decisions based on facts he knew about God. Because the LORD visited, tried, and tested him, David purposed (planned) not to sin by things he said (v. 3). Because David knew words from God's lips like, "The soul of the LORD hates the one who loves violence" (Psalm 11:5b), he chose to keep away from the paths of violent people (v. 4). Staying on God's paths, kept David's feet from slipping.

Ask the LORD to help you make decisions based on His Word.

This entire psalm is a prayer David said to God. As you reread it, say it to the LORD.

Pray Psalm 17:6-8 over yourself and those for whom you stand guard as a faithful, prayerful watchman (Isaiah 62:6-7).

> *"I have called upon You, for You will answer me, O*
> *God. Please incline Your ear to me; hear my speech.*
> *Wondrously show Your lovingkindness*
> *to _____ and me. O Savior, we take refuge at*
> *Your right hand from those who rise up against us.*
> *Keep us as the apple of Your eye[1];*
> *hide us in the shadow of Your wings.*
> *For the sake of Your name, Jesus~"*

---

1. *The apple of the eye refers to the pupil, the part of the eye that focuses on an object.*
   You are the apple of God's eye; He is focused on you because He loves you.

Please read Psalm 18.

Meditate on verse 6.

> *In my distress I called upon the LORD and cried to my*
> *God for help; He heard my voice out of His temple,*
> *and my cry for help before Him came into His ears.*

David had a personal, intimate relationship with the LORD. Notice the list from verses 1-2 of who God was to David:

- my strength
- my rock
- my fortress
- my deliverer
- my God
- my rock of refuge
- my shield
- my salvation
- my stronghold

David knew these truths about God, so he cried out to the LORD in his distress. God heard him and came to his rescue. David's list about God can also become your list. Reread this psalm and cry out to God to uphold and save you.

Pray Psalm 18:1 and 30-32 over yourself and those for whom you stand guard as a faithful, prayerful watchman (Isaiah 62:6-7).

> *"I love You, O LORD, my strength!*
> *God, Your way is blameless; Your Word is tried. Be a*
> *shield to _____ and me; we take refuge in You.*
> *There is no God but You, LORD! You are our Rock!*
> *Gird us with strength and make our way blameless.*
> *Because of You, Jesus~"*

JUNE 19

Please read Psalm 19.

Meditate on verses 1 and 14a.

> *The heavens are telling of the glory of God, and their expanse is declaring the work of His hands. Let the words of my mouth and the meditation of my heart be acceptable in Your sight …*

David acknowledged that the heavens are telling about God's glory and revealing His knowledge day and night (vs. 1-2). He asked God to make his thoughts and words pleasing to Him (v. 14). Sandwiched between the heavens declaring the work of God's hands and the request for you to do the same is a list about God's Word (vs. 7-11). The Testimony of the LORD is:

- perfect
- sure
- right
- pure
- clean

- true
- altogether righteous
- more desirable than gold
- sweeter than honey

The results of keeping God's Testimony are:

- restoring the soul
- making wise the simple
- rejoicing the heart
- enlightening the eyes

- enduring forever
- being warned
- receiving great reward

Meditate on these truths and pray Psalm 19:12-14 over yourself and those for whom you stand guard as a faithful, prayerful watchman (Isaiah 62:6-7).

> *"LORD, help _____ and me discern our errors.*
> *Acquit us of hidden faults. Keep us from presumptuous sins;*
> *let them not rule over us. Make us blameless and acquitted*
> *of great transgression. Let the words of our mouths and the*
> *meditations of our hearts be acceptable in Your sight.*
> *O LORD, our rock and our Redeemer, Jesus Christ~"*

JUNE 20

Please read Psalm 20.

Meditate on verse 9.

Save, O LORD; may the King answer us in the day we call.

This is an interesting prayer psalm. In the first five verses, the prayer requests are told to the person for whom prayer is being said. These are fervent prayers asking the LORD for help. Some of the requests are:

- ❧ May the LORD answer you in the day of trouble.
- ❧ May the name of God set you securely on high.
- ❧ May the LORD send you help.
- ❧ May God grant you your heart's desire.
- ❧ May the LORD fulfill all your petitions.

The one offering the prayer on behalf of another then confidently states truths about God:

- ❧ I know the LORD saves His anointed (v. 6).
- ❧ The LORD will answer with the saving strength of His right hand (v. 6).

Based on knowing those facts, the one praying says what they will do: "We will boast in the name of the LORD our God" (v. 7). And, what they are already doing: "We have risen and stood upright" (v. 8).

The psalm ends with a simple prayer of faith. Pray the prayer (Psalm 20:9) over yourself and those for whom you stand guard as a faithful, prayerful watchman (Isaiah 62:6-7). You can use this pattern for prayer and share it with someone you love.

"Save _____ and me, O LORD!
May You, King Jesus, answer us in the day we call."

JUNE 21

Please read Psalm 21.

Meditate on verse 7.

> *For the king trusts in the LORD, and through the*
> *lovingkindness of the Most High, he will not be shaken.*

Read Psalm 20:9-21:1 to understand the relationship King David had with the King:

> *Save, O LORD; may the King answer us in the day we*
> *call. Oh LORD, in Your strength the king will be glad,*
> *and in Your salvation, how greatly he will rejoice.*

Even though David was king of Israel, he knew who the real King was. He humbly acknowledged his dependence on that King's strength and salvation instead of his own. Notice the results of trusting in the King:

- ☙ The LORD gave him his heart's desire and the request of his lips (v. 2).
- ☙ The LORD met him with the blessings of good things and set a crown on his head (v. 3).
- ☙ The LORD gave him life and length of days forever and ever (v. 4).
- ☙ The LORD gave him glory, salvation, splendor, and majesty (v. 5).
- ☙ The LORD made him most blessed forever (v. 6).

David experienced such blessing because he simply trusted in the LORD (v. 7). Do you simply trust the LORD with every aspect of your life?

Pray Psalm 21:1, 7, and 13 over yourself and those for whom you stand guard as a faithful, prayerful watchman (Isaiah 62:6-7).

> *"O LORD, in Your strength, _____ and I will be glad,*
> *and in Your salvation, we will greatly rejoice!*
> *LORD, we trust in You, and through Your lovingkindness,*
> *Most High, we will not be shaken. Be exalted, O LORD,*
> *in Your strength; we will sing and praise Your power.*
> *In Your name, King Jesus~"*

———— ◆ ————

Please read Psalm 22.

Meditate on verse 19.

> *But You, O LORD, be not far off;*
> *O You my help, hasten to my assistance.*

As you read Psalm 22, you may hear words that are part of the crucifixion story. These words were spoken by David when he was in a distressful situation. These very same words were lived and spoken by Jesus 1,000 years after David when He was in the most distressful situation to occur in the history of mankind. Psalm 22 prophesies the crucifixion of Jesus Christ.

David and Jesus both lived these words, and they each experienced the promises contained in them. This can become your personal psalm as well. Reread it and look for promises for yourself and those you love.

Pray Psalm 22:3-5 and 19 over yourself and those for whom you stand guard as a faithful, prayerful watchman (Isaiah 62:6-7).

> *"LORD, You are holy. You are enthroned upon our praises.*
> *_____ and I trust You; please deliver us!*
> *We cry out to You to be delivered.*
> *In You we trust; we will not be disappointed.*
> *You, O LORD, be not far off.*
> *You are our help; hasten to our assistance!*
> *In Your name, Jesus~"*

Now read Matthew 27:38-46; Mark 15:22-37; Luke 23:33-46; and John 19:17-37. Do you see parallels with Psalm 22?

Please read Psalm 23.

Meditate on this phrase from verse 4.

I fear no evil, for You are with me.

There was evil around David, but he was not afraid because God was with him. Evil is still all around, but you do not need to fear if you belong to the LORD.

Psalm 23 tells you what God does for the sake of His name:

- ❧ He makes you lie down in green pastures (v. 2).
- ❧ He leads you beside quiet waters (v. 2).
- ❧ He restores your soul (v. 3).
- ❧ He guides you in the paths of righteousness (v. 3).

If you are in relationship with Jesus Christ, you do not need to be afraid. God is true to His name, which is now part of your name: *Christian.* Be confident in Christ that His goodness and lovingkindness will follow you all the days of your life.

Pray Psalm 23 over yourself and those for whom you stand guard as a faithful, prayerful watchman (Isaiah 62:6-7).

"LORD, You are _____ and my shepherd. Do not
let us be in want. Make us lie down in green pastures.
Lead us beside quiet waters. Restore our souls. Guide us
in the path of righteousness for Your name's sake.
Even though we walk through the valley of the shadow of
death, help us not fear evil because You are with us.
Let Your rod and staff comfort us. Prepare a table
before us in the presence of our enemies.
Anoint our heads with oil; let our cups overflow.
Surely Your goodness and lovingkindness will
follow us all the days of our lives!
Let us dwell in Your house, LORD, forever.
Because of You, Jesus~"

JUNE 24

Please read Psalm 24.

Meditate on verse 8.

> *Who is the King of glory? The LORD strong and*
> *mighty, the LORD mighty in battle.*

"The King of glory" is a repeated phrase in Psalm 24. When God repeats Himself in His Word, pay attention and observe what He is saying. What does God want you to notice in this psalm?

The LORD is the strong and mighty King of glory who invites you into His presence. There are qualifications to come before the King (vs. 3-4):

- clean hands
- a pure heart
- a soul not lifted up to falsehood
- one who does not swear deceitfully

The rewards for being with the King of glory are blessing and righteousness from the God of your salvation (v. 5). So examine your heart and life. Are you worthy to be in the presence of the King of glory? The God of your salvation, Jesus Christ, cleanses you from all sin and makes you worthy when you confess your sins and make Him your LORD (1 John 1:6-9; Romans 10:9-10).

Pray Psalm 24:3-6 over yourself and those for whom you stand guard as a faithful, prayerful watchman (Isaiah 62:6-7).

> *"LORD, _____ and I want to ascend into*
> *Your hill and stand in Your holy place.*
> *Give us clean hands and pure hearts.*
> *Do not let us lift up our souls to falsehood!*
> *Do not let us swear deceitfully.*
> *We want to receive Your blessing, LORD, and the*
> *righteousness that comes from You, God of our salvation.*
> *Make us the generation who seeks You, who seeks Your face.*
> *Let even Jacob (Israel) seek Your face. In Your name, Jesus~"*

JUNE 25

Please read Psalm 25.

Meditate on verse 14.

> *The secret of the LORD is for those who fear Him,*
> *and He will make them know His covenant.*

This is the first time *covenant* is used in *Psalms*. In Hebrew, the language of the Old Testament, *beriyth* is the word for covenant. *Beriyth* is the ancient practice of solemnifying a promise between two people by passing between an animal that has been cut in half and saying these words: "If I break the promise I am making with you, may what happened to this animal or worse happen to me" (*The Covenant Maker*, pgs. 6-8, Harvell).

Covenants are serious. If you are in a covenant relationship with God through Jesus Christ (John 14:6), then God takes His relationship with you very seriously, and He keeps His covenant promises; therefore:

- ❧ God remembers His compassion and lovingkindness toward you (v. 6).
- ❧ God pardons your iniquity (v. 11).
- ❧ God is intimate with you (v.14).
- ❧ God protects you (v.15).

Pray Psalm 25:4-7 over yourself and those for whom you stand guard as a faithful, prayerful watchman (Isaiah 62:6-7).

> *"Make _____ and me know Your ways, O LORD;*
> *teach us Your paths. Lead us in Your truth and teach us.*
> *For You are the God of our salvation; for You we wait*
> *all the day. Remember, O LORD, Your compassion and*
> *Your lovingkindness, for they have been from of old.*
> *Do not remember the sins of our youth or our transgressions;*
> *according to Your lovingkindness, remember us.*
> *For Your goodness' sake, LORD Jesus~"*

JUNE 26

Please read Psalm 26.

Meditate on verse 1.

> *Vindicate me, O LORD, for I have walked in my integrity,*
> *and I have trusted in the LORD without wavering.*

There are many self-help books for how to become a whole person. If you have access to a Bible, you do not need to waste a cent on one of those books. Psalm 26 tells you how to be a complete and whole person of integrity:

- Trust in the LORD without wavering (v.1).
- Walk in God's truth (v. 3).
- Do not sit with deceitful, wicked people (v. 4-5).
- Do not go with dishonest people (v. 4).
- Hate being with evildoers (v. 5).
- With thanksgiving, declare the wonders of God (v. 7).
- Love being in the LORD's house (v. 8).
- Love the presence of the glory of God (v. 8).

Examine your mind and your heart. Are you a whole person, a person of integrity?

Pray Psalm 26:9-12 over yourself and those for whom you stand guard as a faithful, prayerful watchman (Isaiah 62:6-7).

> *"LORD, do not take _____ and my life away with*
> *sinners; keep our lives away from men of bloodshed.*
> *Keep us from people in whose hands is a wicked*
> *scheme and whose right hand is full of bribes.*
> *LORD, let us walk in integrity.*
> *Redeem us and be gracious to us.*
> *Let our feet stand on a level place.*
> *In the congregation, let us bless You, LORD.*
> *In Your name, Jesus~"*

Please read Psalm 27.

Meditate on verses 1 and 3.

> *The LORD is my light and my salvation; whom shall I fear?*
> *The LORD is the defense of my life; whom shall I dread?*
> *Though a host encamp against me, my heart will not fear;*
> *though war arise against me, in spite of this, I shall be confident.*

David was a warrior. In one of the wars, he killed a total of 69,000 Arameans (Syrians) (1 Chronicles 18:5; 19:18). You might think someone that victorious would trust in himself, yet David trusted in the LORD and asked God not to deliver him over to the desire of his enemies.

The greatest joy in David's life was not bragging about his battle victories; it was being in God's presence, praising Him (v. 6).

Examine your life. Are you afraid? Let your heart take courage in God. Are you in despair? Believe that you will see the goodness of the LORD. What is your greatest desire? Desire to be in God's presence all the days of your life.

Pray Psalm 27:7-9 and 11 over yourself and those for whom you stand guard as a faithful, prayerful watchman (Isaiah 62:6-7).

> *"Hear, O LORD, when _____ and I cry with our voices,*
> *be gracious to us and answer us. You call us to seek Your face.*
> *O LORD, Your face we shall seek! Do not hide Your face from us.*
> *We are Your servants; do not turn us away in anger.*
> *You have been our help; do not abandon us nor forsake us,*
> *O God of our salvation! Teach us Your way, O LORD,*
> *and lead us in a level path because of our foes.*
> *In Your name, Jesus~"*

JUNE 28

Please read Psalm 28.

Meditate on verses 6-7.

> *Blessed be the LORD because He has heard the voice of*
> *my supplication. The LORD is my strength and my shield;*
> *my heart trusts in Him, and I am helped; therefore,*
> *my heart exults, and with my song, I shall thank Him.*

David so loved conversation with the LORD that the thought of God not talking to him, made David want to die (v. 1). David and the LORD had an intimate relationship. They discussed everything. David asked God questions and listened for His answers. David communicated with the LORD.

What about you? Do you and the LORD talk to each other all day long? Would the thought of not being able to communicate with your Savior make you cringe? Thankfully, if you are a Christian, you and God can talk to each other every moment of every day because His Spirit lives inside of you. What an amazing privilege you have! Don't ever take it for granted and always take advantage of it.

Pray Psalm 28:1-2 and 9 over yourself and those for whom you stand guard as a faithful, prayerful watchman (Isaiah 62:6-7).

> *"To You, O LORD, _____ and I call;*
> *Our Rock, do not be deaf to us, for if You are silent to us,*
> *we will become like those who go down to the pit.*
> *Hear the voice of our supplications when we cry to You for help,*
> *when we lift our hands toward Your holy sanctuary.*
> *Save us and bless us as Your inheritance.*
> *Be our shepherd and carry us forever.*
> *In Your name, Jesus~"*

JUNE 29

Please read Psalm 29.

Observe this repeated phrase: *The voice of the LORD…*

Meditate on verse 9b.

> *And in His temple everything says, "Glory!"*

David loved listening to God, and because he listened, he knew the sound of God's voice. Here are some things David knew:

- The voice of the LORD is upon the waters (v. 3).
- The voice of the LORD is powerful (v. 4).
- The voice of the LORD is majestic (v. 4).
- The voice of the LORD breaks the cedars (v. 5).
- The voice of the LORD hews out flames of fire (v. 7).
- The voice of the LORD shakes the wilderness (v. 8).
- The voice of the LORD makes the deer to calve and strips the forests bare (v. 9).

The response to God's voice from everything in His temple was: "Glory!"

Do the words of your mouth, the thoughts of your mind, and the actions of your life say "Glory!" to your LORD? Listen to God with everything you do, today. Let your response to Him be, "Glory!"

Pray Psalm 29:1-2 and 10-11 over yourself and those for whom you stand guard as a faithful, prayerful watchman (Isaiah 62:6-7).

> *"LORD, _____ and I ascribe to You glory and strength.*
> *We ascribe to You the glory due to Your name.*
> *We worship You in holy array. LORD, You sat as King at the flood.*
> *LORD, You sit as King forever! LORD, give*
> *strength to us; LORD, bless us with peace.*
> *For the glory of Your name, Jesus~"*

Please read Psalm 30.

Meditate on verses 4-5.

> *Sing praise to the LORD, you His Godly ones, and give thanks to His holy name. For His anger is but for a moment; His favor is for a lifetime; weeping may last for the night, but a shout of joy comes in the morning.*

David wrote a thank you list to God in Psalm 30:1-3. David exalted the LORD for doing these things:

- You have lifted me up.
- You have not let my enemies rejoice over me.
- You healed me.
- You have brought up my soul from Sheol (the place of no return, hell).
- You have kept me alive.

Could this be the start of your thank you list to God? David and the LORD do not mind sharing it with you.

Write out a thank you list to your LORD Jesus Christ. Make it personal like David did by talking to God and saying, "You have …"

Pray Psalm 30:10-12 over yourself and those for whom you stand guard as a faithful, prayerful watchman (Isaiah 62:6-7).

> *"Hear, O LORD, and be gracious to _____ and me.*
> *O LORD, be our helper! Turn our mourning into dancing.*
> *Loose our sackcloth and gird us with gladness.*
> *Let our souls sing praise to You and not be silent.*
> *O LORD our God, we will give thanks to You forever.*
> *In Your name, Jesus~"*

JULY

On your walls, O Jerusalem,
I have appointed watchmen;
All day and all night they
will never keep silent.
You who remind the LORD,
take no rest for yourselves;
And give Him no rest until He establishes
And makes Jerusalem a
praise in the earth.
ISAIAH 62:6-7, NASB

Please read Psalm 31.

Meditate on verse 24.

> *Be strong and let your heart take courage,*
> *all you who hope in the LORD.*

David had a personal relationship with God. The LORD was David's:

- ✤ Rock,
- ✤ Fortress,
- ✤ Strength (vs. 3-4).

Because David intimately knew the God of Truth and took refuge in Him, he boldly asked God to do things for him. Some of David's requests were:

- ✤ "Let me never be ashamed" (v.1).
- ✤ "In Your righteousness deliver me" (v. 1).
- ✤ "Incline Your ear to me" (v. 2).
- ✤ "Rescue me quickly" (v.2).
- ✤ "Be to me a rock of strength" (v.2).
- ✤ "Be a stronghold to save me" (v.2).
- ✤ "Be gracious to me" (v.9).

Have you committed your spirit to the God of Truth and let Him ransom you (v. 5)? If you have, reread Psalm 31 aloud, praying it with confidence to **your** Rock, **your** Fortress, and **your** Strength.

Pray Psalm 31:14-16 over yourself and those for whom you stand guard as a faithful, prayerful watchman (Isaiah 62:6-7).

> *"As for _____ and me, we trust in You, O LORD;*
> *we say, 'You are our God.' Our times are in Your hand;*
> *deliver us from the hand of our enemies*
> *and from those who persecute us.*
> *Make Your face to shine upon us, Your servants.*
> *Save us in Your lovingkindness.*
> *For the sake of Your name, Jesus~"*

JULY 2

Please read Psalm 32.

Meditate on verses 1 and 2.

> *How blessed is he whose transgression is forgiven, whose sin*
> *is covered! How blessed is the man to whom the LORD does*
> *not impute iniquity and in whose spirit there is no deceit!*

David wrote this psalm because he knew the misery of living in unconfessed sin: body wasting away, groaning all day long, the LORD's hand heavy upon him, and his vitality drained (vs. 3-4).

David wrote this psalm because he knew the reward of confession: the LORD forgave the guilt of his sin (v. 5).

David wrote this psalm because he knew the LORD promised to instruct and teach him the way he should go (v. 8). He knew the LORD would counsel him with His eye upon him (v. 8).

This is a psalm for the conviction of sin, what to do with sin, and the results of repentance. Ask the LORD to search your life for anything that displeases Him.

After you repent, pray Psalm 32:7-8 and 10-11 over yourself and those for whom you stand guard as a faithful, prayerful watchman (Isaiah 62:6-7).

> *"LORD, You are _____ and my hiding place.*
> *Preserve us from trouble; surround us with songs of deliverance.*
> *Please instruct us and teach in the way we should go.*
> *Counsel us with Your eye upon us. We trust in You,*
> *LORD; surround us with Your lovingkindness.*
> *Because of You, we are righteous and upright in heart.*
> *We will be glad and rejoice in You, LORD.*
> *We shout for joy.*
> *Because of You, Jesus~"*

JULY 3

Please read Psalm 33.

Meditate on verse 1b.

Praise is becoming to the upright.

It is appropriate to praise the LORD. The psalmist gave a list of reasons to thank and praise God. Some of them are:

- ✺ The Word of the LORD is upright (v. 4).
- ✺ All of God's work is done in faithfulness (v.4).
- ✺ The earth is full of the LORD's lovingkindness (v. 5).
- ✺ The Word of the LORD made the heavens (v. 6).
- ✺ The breath of God's mouth made everything in the heavens (v. 6).
- ✺ The LORD nullifies the counsel of the nations, but His counsel stands forever (vs. 10-11).
- ✺ The LORD frustrates the plans of the people, but the plans of His heart last from generation to generation (vs. 10-11).

Meditate on at least one of these truths about the LORD. Praise and thank Him all day long; it is appropriate.

Pray Psalm 33:18-22 over yourself and those for whom you stand guard as a faithful, prayerful watchman (Isaiah 62:6-7).

*"LORD, keep Your eye on _____ and me as we fear
You. LORD, we hope in Your lovingkindness to deliver
our souls from death and to keep us alive in famine.
Our souls wait for You, LORD;
You are our help and our shield.
Our heart rejoices in You because we trust in Your holy name.
Let Your lovingkindness, O LORD,
be upon us according as we have hoped in You.
Because of Your name, Jesus~"*

Please read Psalm 34.

Meditate on verses 4, 7, and 11.

> *I sought the LORD, and He answered me and delivered me*
> *from all my fears. The angel of the LORD encamps around*
> *those who fear Him and rescues them. Come, you children,*
> *listen to me; I will teach you the fear of the LORD.*

Years ago we counted how many times the word fear was in the Bible and how it was used. Eighty-eight times God said, "Fear not." However, 122 times He said, "Fear God."

People often do the opposite, fearing any and everything except Almighty God. God does not want you to be afraid, but He does expect you to fear Him—to have a healthy understanding of and respect for His authority, His power, and His majesty. Fearing God—standing before Him in total reverence, awe, and wonder, fully aware of His greatness and His overwhelming love for you—keeps you from sinning. He is your Sovereign.

Exodus 20:20 explains well what God is teaching you about *fear.*

> *Moses said to the people, "Do not be afraid; for God has*
> *come in order to test you, and in order that the fear of*
> *Him may remain with you, so that you may not sin."*

Pray Psalm 34:11-14 over yourself and those for whom you stand guard as a faithful, prayerful watchman (Isaiah 62:6-7).

> *"LORD, teach _____ and me the fear of You.*
> *We desire life and love to see what is good,*
> *so keep our tongues from evil and our lips from speaking deceit.*
> *Help us depart from evil and do good.*
> *Let us seek peace and pursue it.*
> *Because we fear Your name, LORD Jesus~"*

Please read Psalm 35.

Meditate on verse 1.

> *Contend, O LORD, with those who contend with me;*
> *fight against those who fight against me.*

Are you or someone you love being treated unjustly? Psalm 35 gives you a Godly way to handle the situation.

1. Give the person who is wronging you to the LORD.
   Let those be turned back and humiliated who devise evil against me.
   —Psalm 35:4b

2. Pray for the person who is mistreating you when they are in difficulty.
   But as for me, when they were sick, my clothing was sackcloth …
   I went about as though it were my friend and brother …
   —Psalm 35:13a, 14a

3. Worship the LORD with other believers.
   I will give You thanks in the great congregation …
   —Psalm 35:18a

4. Fellowship with Godly people who will pray and rejoice with you.
   Let them shout for joy and rejoice, who favor my vindication …
   —Psalm 35:27a

5. Continually thank and praise the LORD.
   And my soul shall rejoice in the LORD; it shall exult in His salvation.
   —Psalm 35:9

Pray Psalm 35:22-24 over an unjust situation.

> *"You have seen it, O LORD, do not keep silent; O LORD,*
> *do not be far from _____ and me. Stir up Yourself and awake*
> *to our right and to our cause, our God and our LORD.*
> *Judge us, O LORD, our God, according to Your righteousness, and*
> *do not let them rejoice over us. For the sake of Your name, Jesus~"*

JULY 6

Please read Psalm 36.

Meditate on verse 5.

> *Your lovingkindness, O LORD, extends to the*
> *heavens; Your faithfulness reaches to the skies.*

David contrasted the ungodly with the LORD in this psalm. Some of the characteristics of an ungodly person are (vs. 1-4):

- ◈ has no fear of God
- ◈ flatters himself
- ◈ speaks deceit and wickedness
- ◈ plans wickedness upon his bed
- ◈ sets himself on a path that is not good
- ◈ does not despise evil

Some of God's characteristics are (vs. 5-9):

- ◈ His lovingkindness extends to the heavens
- ◈ His faithfulness reaches to the skies
- ◈ His righteousness is like the mountains of God
- ◈ His judgments are like a great deep
- ◈ He preserves man and beast
- ◈ He has the fountain of life

Would the LORD describe you as Godly or ungodly?

Repent of any ungodliness and pray Psalm 36:7-11 over yourself and those for whom you stand guard as a faithful, prayerful watchman (Isaiah 62:6-7).

> *"How precious is Your lovingkindness, O God!*
> _____ *and I take refuge in the shadow of Your wings.*
> *Let us drink our fill of the abundance of Your house,*
> *and give us to drink of the river of Your delights.*
> *For with You is the fountain of life; in Your light we see light.*
> *O continue Your lovingkindness to us; let us know You.*
> *Continue Your righteousness to us; make us upright in*
> *heart. Do not let the foot of pride come upon us,*
> *and let not the hand of the wicked drive us away.*
> *In Your name, Jesus~"*

July 7

Please read Psalm 37.

Meditate on verses 7a and 8.

> *Rest in the LORD and wait patiently for Him...Cease from*
> *anger and forsake wrath; do not fret; it leads only to evildoing.*

"Do not fret" is a repeated command in Psalm 37. Are you a "fretter"? Do you allow people and situations to gnaw at you, corroding your thoughts and consequently your entire day? God's Word tells you why you should not fret. Observe these contrasts:

- Evildoers will be cut off, but those who wait for the LORD, they will inherit the land (v. 9).
- The arms of the wicked will be broken, but the LORD sustains the righteous (v. 17).
- The man of peace will have a posterity, but transgressors will be altogether destroyed (vs. 37-38).
- The posterity of the wicked will be cut off, but the salvation of the righteous is from the LORD; He is their strength in time of trouble (vs. 38-39).

Do not let people and situations cause you to take your focus off of the LORD. Fix your eyes on Jesus; trust Him! The LORD wants to keep you from fretting.

Pray Psalm 37:3-6 over yourself and those for whom you stand guard as a faithful, prayerful watchman (Isaiah 62:6-7).

> *"LORD, help _____ and me to trust in You and do good.*
> *Let us dwell in the land and cultivate faithfulness.*
> *As we delight ourselves in You, give us the desires of our heart.*
> *We commit our way to You, LORD. We trust in You to do it.*
> *Bring forth our righteousness as the light and*
> *our judgment as the noonday.*
> *For the sake of Your name, Jesus~"*

Please read Psalm 38.

Meditate on verse 9.

> *LORD, all my desire is before You,*
> *and my sighing is not hidden from You.*

Psalm 38 is a cry for help to God. David was in misery from his sins; he was doubled over in the pain of iniquity (v. 6). God's hand was heavy upon David as He chastened and rebuked him (vs. 1-2). Instead of continuing in sin and rebellion, David confessed his iniquity and gave all his desires to God (vs. 9, 18). David's family and friends were avoiding him; he knew his only hope was to hope in the LORD (vs. 11, 15).

Are you in over your head in sin; is the burden of your iniquity too much for you to bear (v. 4)? Humble yourself before the LORD, confess your sin, and give Him all your desire and sighing (vs. 9, 18).

Pray Psalm 38:15 and 21-22 over yourself and those for whom you stand guard as a faithful, prayerful watchman (Isaiah 62:6-7).

> *"O LORD, _____ and I hope in You;*
> *You will answer, O LORD, our God.*
> *Do not forsake us, O LORD;*
> *O our God, do not be far from us!*
> *Make haste to help us, O LORD, our salvation!*
> *Because of Your name, LORD Jesus~"*

July 9

Please read Psalm 39.

Meditate on verses 1-2.

> *I said, "I will guard my ways that I may not sin with my*
> *tongue; I will guard my mouth as with a muzzle while*
> *the wicked are in my presence." I was mute and silent; I*
> *refrained even from good, and my sorrow grew worse.*

Have you ever been in a situation where the conversation was ungodly, and lies were spoken as if they were truths, and you said not a word? David was in that situation in Psalm 39. He was with some wicked people, and he determined not to sin with his tongue, so he didn't say anything, not even anything good; he was miserable! David eventually spoke, and when he did, he talked to his LORD, confessing his sins, putting his hope in God, and asking Him not to make him the reproach of the foolish (vs. 7-8).

What do you fear, the reproach of people or the reproach of the LORD? Are you more concerned about pleasing others when you speak, or do you want the words of your mouth to please Jesus? Commit to speak the truth of God's Word to everyone around you.

Pray Psalm 39:4, 7-8, and 12a over yourself and those for whom you stand guard as a faithful, prayerful watchman (Isaiah 62:6-7).

> *"LORD, make _____ and me to know our*
> *end and what is the extent of our days;*
> *let us know how transient we are.*
> *And now, LORD, for what do we wait?*
> *Our hope is in You. Deliver us from all our transgressions;*
> *make us not the reproach of the foolish.*
> *Hear our prayer, O LORD, and give ear to our cry.*
> *For Your name's sake, Jesus~"*

JULY 10

Please read Psalm 40.

Meditate on verses 8 and 14.

> *I delight to do Your will, O God; Your Law is within my heart. Let those be ashamed and humiliated together who seek my life to destroy it; let those be turned back and dishonored who delight in my hurt.*

Observe the word *delight* in this psalm. David delighted to do the will of God. There were people in David's life who delighted in him being hurt. How did David handle that kind of evil?

- David waited patiently for God, asking Him for help and deliverance (vs. 1, 13).
- The LORD heard David's cry and brought him out of the pit of destruction and set his feet firmly on a rock (vs. 1-2).
- God put a song of praise in David's mouth (v. 3).
- David sang that song and spoke of God's faithfulness, lovingkindness, and truth. Many feared and trusted in the LORD (vs. 3, 10).

Reread Psalm 40 and find the treasures God wants to show you for handling difficult situations.

Pray Psalm 40:11, 13, and 17 over yourself and those for whom you stand guard as a faithful, prayerful watchman (Isaiah 62:6-7).

> *"O LORD, do not withhold Your compassion from _____ and me.*
> *Let Your lovingkindness and Your truth continually preserve us.*
> *Be pleased, O LORD, to deliver us;*
> *make haste, O LORD, to help us.*
> *We are afflicted and needy; LORD, be mindful of us;*
> *You are our help and our deliverer.*
> *Do not delay, O our God.*
> *For the sake of Your name, LORD Jesus~"*

Please read Psalm 41.

Meditate on verse 1.

> *How blessed is he who considers the helpless;*
> *the LORD will deliver him in a day of trouble.*

David had problems with enemies: they spoke evil against him; they wanted him dead, and they poured out wickedness upon him (vs. 5, 8). Despite such wicked opposition, David helped others less fortunate than himself (v. 1). He gave a list of benefits that come from caring for the helpless:

- The LORD will deliver him in a day of trouble (v. 1).
- The LORD will protect him and keep him alive (v. 2).
- He will be called blessed upon the earth (v. 2).
- The LORD will not give him over to the desire of his enemies (v. 2).
- The LORD will sustain him upon his sickbed and restore him to health (v.3).

What an amazing protection plan David had with the LORD! He could have easily felt sorry for himself and been the helpless one; instead he helped others, and God delivered Him from his enemies.

Are you in the midst of a difficult situation? Care for the needs of others. As you do, God will miraculously take care of you.

Pray Psalm 41:1 and 11-13 over yourself and those for whom you stand guard as a faithful, prayerful watchman (Isaiah 62:6-7).

> *"LORD, bless _____ and me as we consider the helpless.*
> *Deliver us in the day of trouble. Make us pleasing to You;*
> *do not let our enemy shout in triumph over us.*
> *Uphold us in our integrity and set us in Your presence forever.*
> *We will bless You, LORD, from everlasting*
> *to everlasting. Amen and Amen."*

JULY 12

Please read Psalm 42.

Meditate on verse 5.

> *Why are you in despair, O my soul? And why have you*
> *become disturbed within me? Hope in God, for I shall*
> *again praise Him, for the help of His presence.*

The psalmist was desperate. God brought him to a seemingly hopeless place, so he could only be brought out of his despair by the LORD.

Just as the refreshing stream satisfies a parched and panting deer, God would quench his desperate thirst (vs. 1-2). He put his hope in God (v. 11).

What situation threatens to roll over you and those you love? Has the LORD allowed it so your only hope is to hope in Him?

Pray Psalm 42:1-2, 5-6, 8, and 11 over yourself and those for whom you stand guard as a faithful, prayerful watchman (Isaiah 62:6-7).

> *"As the dear pants for the water brooks,*
> *so _____ and my soul pants for You, O God.*
> *Our souls thirst for God, for You, the living God;*
> *we come and appear before You.*
> *Our souls are in despair; they are disturbed within us, LORD.*
> *We hope in You, God, for we shall again praise*
> *You for the help of Your presence.*
> *O my God, our souls are in despair within us;*
> *therefore, we remember You!*
> *LORD, command Your lovingkindness in the daytime!*
> *Let Your song be with us in the night.*
> *This is our prayer to You, the God of our lives!*
> *LORD, our souls are in despair and disturbed within us!*
> *We choose to hope in You, God, for we will yet praise You.*
> *You are the help of our countenance and our God.*
> *Because of You, Jesus~"*

July 13

Please read Psalm 43.

Meditate on verse 2.

> *For You are the God of my strength; why have You rejected me?*
> *Why do I go mourning because of the oppression of the enemy?*

The psalmist was still in despair when he penned the words of Psalm 43. In the midst of oppression, he remembered God was his strength and his exceeding joy (vs. 2, 4). His soul was disturbed, yet he hoped in the LORD.

Are you oppressed and disturbed by the enemy? God uses times of despair to solidify in you who He really is. Cry out, "You are the God of my strength; You are God, my exceeding joy!" (vs. 2, 4). Say it hundreds of times today; then say it hundreds of times tomorrow. The enemy cannot stand to be in the hearing of that truth.

Pray Psalm 43 over yourself and those for whom you stand guard as a faithful, prayerful watchman (Isaiah 62:6-7).

> *"Vindicate _____ and me, O God,*
> *and plead our case against the ungodly.*
> *O deliver us from the deceitful and unjust man!*
> *You are the God of our strength; do not reject us!*
> *Let us stop mourning because of the oppression of the enemy.*
> *O send out Your light and Your truth; let them lead us;*
> *let them bring us to Your holy hill and to Your dwelling places.*
> *We will go to Your altar, God. God, You are our exceeding joy!*
> *Upon the lyre, we shall praise You, O God, our God!*
> *Let our souls no longer be in despair and disturbed within us.*
> *We hope in You, God, for we shall again praise You.*
> *You are the help of our countenance and our God.*
> *In Your name, Jesus~"*

Please read Psalm 44.

Meditate on verse 8.

> *In God we have boasted all day long, and we*
> *will give thanks to Your name forever.*

Have you ever felt rejected by God? Observe this psalm carefully; it can be helpful in life's difficult seasons.

Psalm 44:1-8 recalls God's faithfulness in the past and expresses confidence in God's faithfulness in the future. Verses 9-16 describe the psalmist's present situation as one of dishonor, reproach, scoffing, and derision. Notice his honesty with the LORD as he tells God what is happening to him. The psalm ends with the declaration of one who refuses to forget God or deviate from His way. The psalmist appeals to the lovingkindness of the LORD and cries out to Him for help.

Pray Psalm 44:17-20 and 23-26 over a difficult situation as a faithful, prayerful watchman (Isaiah 62:6-7).

> *"LORD, all of this has come upon _____ and me,*
> *but we have not forgotten You, and we have*
> *not dealt falsely with Your covenant.*
> *Our heart has not turned back, and our steps*
> *have not deviated from Your way.*
> *Yet You have crushed us in a place of jackals and*
> *covered us with the shadow of death.*
> *God, we have not forgotten Your name or*
> *extended our hands to a strange god.*
> *Arouse Yourself; do not sleep, O LORD!*
> *Awake; do not reject us forever!*
> *Do not hide Your face and forget our affliction and our oppression!*
> *Our soul has sunk down into the dust; our body cleaves to the earth.*
> *Rise up; be our help, and redeem us for the*
> *sake of Your lovingkindness.*
> *And the sake of Your name, Jesus~"*

Please read Psalm 45.

Meditate on verse 1.

> *My heart overflows with a good theme; I address my verses*
> *to the King; my tongue is the pen of a ready writer.*

Reading Psalm 45 is like eavesdropping on an intimate conversation. An enthralled psalmist spoke adoring words to his King.

> *You are fairer than the sons of men; grace is poured upon*
> *Your lips; therefore, God has blessed You forever.*
> —Psalm 45:2

He calls the King, "Mighty One" and "God" (vs. 3, 6). He speaks of His splendor and describes His scepter as "a scepter of uprightness" (vs. 3, 6).

Psalm 45 was written at least 1,000 years before the birth of Christ. Reading it more than 2,000 years after the coming of Messiah, it is obvious the psalmist was talking to King Jesus.

Use the psalmist's words to begin adoring your King; then continue praising Him for eternity. Pray Psalm 45:3-4, 11, and 17 as a faithful, prayerful watchman (Isaiah 62:6-7).

> *"Gird Your sword on Your thigh, O Mighty One,*
> *in Your splendor and Your majesty!*
> *And in Your majesty ride on victoriously, for the*
> *cause of truth and meekness and righteousness;*
> *let Your right hand teach _____ and me awesome things.*
> *We bow down to You because You are our LORD.*
> *We want to cause Your name to be remembered in all generations.*
> *May we and all peoples give You thanks forever and ever, King Jesus~"*

JULY 16

Please read Psalm 46.

Meditate on verse 1.

> *God is our refuge and strength, a very present help in trouble.*

Observe the tumultuous words and phrases in Psalm 46.

- ◈ The earth changes (v. 2).
- ◈ The mountains slip into the heart of the sea (v. 2).
- ◈ Waters roar and foam (v. 3).
- ◈ The mountains quake (v. 3).
- ◈ The nations made an uproar (v. 6).
- ◈ The kingdoms tottered (v. 6).
- ◈ The earth melted (v. 6).

In the midst of apparent chaos, "the LORD of hosts is with us; the God of Jacob is our stronghold. He makes wars to cease … He breaks the bow and cuts the spear in two; He burns the chariots with fire" (vs. 7, 9). No wonder the LORD gave the command to be still and know that He is God (v. 10). The LORD is in control; the appropriate response is to relinquish control, relax, and trust in Him.

Pray Psalm 46:10-11 over yourself and those for whom you stand guard as a faithful, prayerful watchman (Isaiah 62:6-7).

> *"LORD, help _____ and me to cease*
> *striving and know that You are God.*
> *You will be exalted among the nations;*
> *You will be exalted in the earth.*
> *LORD of hosts, be with us;*
> *God of Jacob, be our stronghold.*
> *In Your name, Jesus~"*

Please read Psalm 47.

Meditate on verses 6-7a.

> *Sing praises to God, sing praises; sing praises to our King,*
> *sing praises. For God is the King of all the earth...*

God alone is worthy of all praise. Paul wisely quoted from Jeremiah, "Let him who boasts, boast in the LORD" (1 Corinthians 1:31; Jeremiah 9:23-24).

Paul, like the psalmist, bragged about the LORD. Other bragging is haughty and prideful, but glorying in Christ is not arrogant. In fact, singing the praises of God and His ways is the appropriate thing to do.

Pray Psalm 47 as a faithful, prayerful watchman (Isaiah 62:6-7).

> *"LORD, _____ and I clap our hands for You.*
> *We shout to You with the voice of joy!*
> *For You, LORD Most High, are to be feared.*
> *You are the great King over all the earth.*
> *LORD, subdue peoples under us and nations under*
> *our feet. Choose our inheritance for us.*
> *God, You have ascended with a shout,*
> *O LORD, with the sound of a trumpet.*
> *We sing praises to You, God! We sing praises to You, our King!*
> *For God, You are the King of all the earth.*
> *We sing praises to You with a skillful psalm.*
> *God, You reign over the nations. You sit on Your holy throne.*
> *We assemble as Your people.*
> *The shields of the earth belong to You, God.*
> *You are highly exalted.*
> *Because of Your name, King Jesus~"*

JULY 18

Please read Psalm 48.

Meditate on verse 1.

> *Great is the LORD and greatly to be praised, in*
> *the city of our God, His holy mountain.*

Observe Mount Zion (vs. 1-2). It is:

- God's holy mountain and beautiful in elevation.
- the joy of the whole earth and the city of the great King.

Observe how the kings of the earth responded to Zion (vs. 5-6). They:

- were amazed and terrified
- fled in alarm
- were seized with panic and anguish

Observe how the people of God responded (vs. 8-10, 13). They:

- know God will establish His city forever
- think about the LORD's lovingkindness
- know God's right hand is full of righteousness
- consider the LORD and His city, so they can tell it to the next generation

If you are a Christian, then "you have come to Mount Zion and to the city of the living God, the heavenly Jerusalem …" (Hebrews 12:22). You can pray Psalm 48:3, 8b-10, and 14 over yourself and those for whom you stand guard as a faithful, prayerful watchman (Isaiah 62:6-7).

> *"God, make Yourself known as a stronghold to _____ and me.*
> *God, establish us forever. Let us think on Your lovingkindness,*
> *O God, in the midst of Your temple. As is Your name,*
> *O God, so is Your praise to the ends of the earth;*
> *Your right hand is full of righteousness.*
> *For such are You, God. You are our God forever*
> *and ever. Guide us until death.*
> *For the sake of Your name, Jesus~"*

Please read Psalm 49.

Meditate on verses 1 and 7-8a.

> *Hear this, all peoples: give ear, all inhabitants of the world.*
> *No man can by any means redeem his brother or give to God a*
> *ransom for him—for the redemption of his soul is costly...*

God wants every person on earth to hear this psalm.

The psalmist was surrounded by sin and adversity, poverty and wealth, but he knew death puts an end to all those things, but death cannot put an end to a person's soul. The soul of every human lives forever, either with God or separated from God. The cost to redeem a soul was expensive; it cost God His life. Every human must know and believe the story of redemption to live forever with God.

Do not let Satan distract you with his evil. Do not be consumed by the news of the day; be consumed by the love of your Savior who died, so you can live. That is the news that must be told. Ask your LORD to remove your fears and help you tell others the story of Jesus Christ.

Pray Psalm 49:3 and 15 over yourself and those for whom you stand guard as a faithful, prayerful watchman (Isaiah 62:6-7).

> *"LORD, let _____ and my mouth speak wisdom and*
> *the meditation of our hearts be understanding.*
> *God, redeem the soul of _____ from the power of Sheol (hell).*
> *Let them choose You, so You will receive them.*
> *In Your name, Jesus~"*

July 20

Please read Psalm 50.

Meditate on verses 22-23. God is talking.

> *"Now consider this, you who forget God, or I will tear you in pieces, and there will be none to deliver. He who offers a sacrifice of thanksgiving honors Me; and to him who orders his way aright, I shall show the salvation of God."*

God addressed every human in this psalm. He first spoke to those who are His people in verses 1-15. He gave them a command, an invitation, and a promise in verses 14-15:

> *Offer to God a sacrifice of thanksgiving and pay your vows to the Most High; call upon Me in the day of trouble; I shall rescue you, and you will honor Me.*

The LORD then admonished the wicked in verses 16-22. The contrast is obvious. Notice how God described wicked people (vs. 17-20):

- They hate discipline and cast God's Words behind them.
- They see a thief and are pleased with him; they associate with adulterers.
- They let their mouth loose in evil; their tongue frames deceit.
- They speak against their brother and slander their own mother's son.

How is the LORD speaking to you through this psalm? Are there areas of your life you need to humble before the LORD, confessing and asking forgiveness? Repent then offer a sacrifice of thanksgiving to your God and Savior Jesus Christ.

Pray Psalm 50:23 over yourself and those for whom you stand guard as a faithful, prayerful watchman (Isaiah 62:6-7).

> *"LORD, teach _______ and me how to offer a sacrifice of thanksgiving that honors You. Help us order our way aright. God, show us Your salvation! In Your name, Jesus~"*

JULY 21

Please read Psalm 51.

Meditate on verse 17.

> *The sacrifices of God are a broken spirit: a broken and*
> *a contrite heart, O God, You will not despise.*

Psalm 51 is David's prayer of confession after committing adultery with Bathsheba and attempting to cover his sins by having her husband killed (2 Samuel 11-12:23). Only the blood of Jesus and His righteousness covers sins. Be quick to confess yours; do not be tempted to ignore and downplay sin.

Pray Psalm 51:1-17 over yourself, so you can be a faithful, prayerful watchman for others (Isaiah 62:6-7).

> *"Be gracious to me, O God, according to Your lovingkindness;*
> *according to the greatness of Your compassion, blot out my*
> *transgressions. Wash me thoroughly from my iniquity and cleanse*
> *me from my sin. For I know my transgressions, and my sin is ever*
> *before me. Against You, You only, I have sinned and done what*
> *is evil in Your sight, so that You are justified when You speak and*
> *blameless when You judge. Behold, I was brought forth in iniquity,*
> *and in sin my mother conceived me. Behold, You desire truth in the*
> *innermost being, and in the hidden part You will make me know*
> *wisdom. Purify me with hyssop, and I shall be clean; wash me, and*
> *I shall be whiter than snow. Make me to hear joy and gladness;*
> *let the bones which You have broken rejoice. Hide Your face from*
> *my sins and blot out all my iniquities. Create in me a clean heart,*
> *O God, and renew a steadfast spirit within me. Do not cast me*
> *away from Your presence and do not take Your Holy Spirit from*
> *me. Restore to me the joy of Your salvation and sustain me with a*
> *willing spirit. Then I will teach transgressors Your ways, and sinners*
> *will be converted to You. Deliver me from bloodguiltiness, O God,*
> *the God of my salvation; then my tongue will joyfully sing of Your*
> *righteousness. O LORD, open my lips that my mouth may declare*
> *Your praise. For You do not delight in sacrifice, otherwise I would*
> *give it; You are not pleased with burnt offering. The sacrifices of*
> *God are a broken spirit; a broken and a contrite heart, O God, You*
> *will not despise. Because of Your sacrifice, LORD Jesus Christ~"*

JULY 22

Please read Psalm 52.

1 Samuel 21 and 22 tell about the events surrounding this Psalm of David. Meditate on verse 1.

> *Why do you boast in evil, O mighty man? The*
> *lovingkindness of God endures all day long.*

David was in the midst of wicked people. They were workers of deceit who loved evil and falsehood (vs. 2-3). David could have been describing people you hear about in the news today. Notice how David hunkered down in the Truth of God in the midst of the evil around him.

> *But God will break you down forever; He will snatch you up and*
> *tear you away from your tent, and uproot you from the land of the*
> *living. The righteous will see and fear, and will laugh at him, saying,*
> *"Behold, the man who would not make God his refuge, but trusted*
> *in the abundance of his riches and was strong in his evil desire."*
> —Psalm 52:5-7

As wickedness whirls around the world today, it is more important than ever to know God and His Word. Say, like David did, "I trust in the lovingkindness of God forever and ever" (v. 8b).

Pray Psalm 52:8-9 over yourself and those for whom you stand guard as a faithful, prayerful watchman (Isaiah 62:6-7).

> *"God, make _____ and me a green olive tree in Your house.*
> *We trust in Your lovingkindness forever and ever.*
> *We will give You thanks forever because You have done it.*
> *We will wait on Your name, for it is good,*
> *in the presence of Your Godly ones.*
> *In Your name, Jesus~"*

Please read Psalm 53.

Meditate on verse 1a.

> *The fool has said in his heart, "There is no God."*

God is not what the world would call "politically correct." God cannot lie (Titus 1:2), so He calls a person who thinks He does not exist a fool, someone who is senseless and stupid.

Amazingly, God even saves fools.

> *And you were dead in your trespasses and sins, in which you formerly walked ... Among them we, too, all formerly lived in the lusts of our flesh, indulging the desires of the flesh and of the mind, and were by nature children of wrath, even as the rest, but God, being rich in mercy, because of His great love with which He loved us, even when we were dead in our transgressions, made us alive together with Christ (by grace you have been saved).*
> —Ephesians 2:1-5

Apart from Jesus Christ, everyone is a fool. Thank your Savior for saving you from your foolish self. As a faithful, prayerful watchman (Isaiah 62:6-7), pray Psalm 53:2 and 6 over those you know who need God's salvation.

> *"God, look down from heaven upon _____.*
> *Let them understand and seek after You.*
> *Bring them Your salvation; rescue Your captive people.*
> *Let them rejoice and be glad.*
> *Because of Your name, Jesus~"*

Please read Psalm 54.

Meditate on verse 4.

> *Behold, God is my helper; the LORD is the sustainer of my soul.*

Psalms 52-55 are introduced as Maskils of David. They are psalms to be contemplated with lessons to be learned.

1 Samuel 26 gives the historical context for Psalm 54. David was hiding in the wilderness of Ziph from an angry King Saul who was pursuing him with 3,000 men. The Ziphites told Saul that David was hiding in their midst. Read 1 Samuel 26 to learn what God wants to teach you about trusting Him in impossible situations. You will discover verses to pray in that chapter; for example, "May the LORD deliver me from all distress" (1 Samuel 26:24).

Now, pray Psalm 54 as a faithful, prayerful watchman (Isaiah 62:6-7). Hear the LORD teaching you as you talk to Him.

> *"Save _____ and me, O God, by Your name,*
> *and vindicate us by Your power.*
> *Hear our prayer, O God; give ear to the words of our mouths.*
> *For strangers have risen against us, and violent men have*
> *sought our lives; they have not set You before them.*
> *Behold, God, You are our helper; LORD,*
> *You are the sustainer of our souls.*
> *Recompense the evil to our foes; destroy them in Your faithfulness.*
> *Willingly we will sacrifice to You; we will give thanks*
> *to Your name, O LORD, for it is good.*
> *LORD, deliver us from all trouble; let our eyes*
> *look with satisfaction upon our enemies.*
> *Because of Your name, Jesus~"*

Please read Psalm 55.

Meditate on verses 1-2.

> *Give ear to my prayer, O God, and do not hide Yourself*
> *from my supplication. Give heed to me and answer me; I*
> *am restless in my complaint and am surely distracted.*

Psalm 55 is another Maskil of David, a thought-provoking psalm. The words of the distracted psalmist bring comfort to those of us in similar situations.

Someone who had been David's friend became his enemy. David used words like: anguish, fear, trembling, and horror to describe his feelings (vs. 4-5). He took his anguished, fearful, trembling, horrified self to his LORD.

> *As for me, I shall call upon God, and the LORD will save*
> *me. Evening and morning and at noon, I will complain*
> *and murmur, and He will hear my voice. He will redeem*
> *my soul in peace from the battle which is against me ...*
> —Psalm 55:16-18a

Contemplate the fact that you can take any situation, any complaint to your LORD. You can talk to Him all day long about what is happening to you and those you love. In fact, He wants you to bring Him all your needs. If you are in the midst of a restless, distracted time of life, use the words of Psalm 55 to voice the cries of your heart.

Pray Psalm 55:1 and 22-23b over yourself and those for whom you stand guard as a faithful, prayerful watchman (Isaiah 62:6-7).

> *"Give ear to _____ and my prayer, O God,*
> *and do not hide Yourself from our supplication.*
> *We cast our burden upon You, LORD.*
> *Please sustain us!*
> *Make us righteous and do not allow us to be shaken.*
> *We will trust in You! In Your name, Jesus~"*

JULY 26

Please read Psalm 56.

Meditate on verse 3.

> *When I am afraid, I will put my trust in You.*

It was the summer of 1969 in Amarillo, Texas; I (Marsha) was eight years old. Several life changing things happened that summer. The most important was on June 8; I invited Jesus to live in my life as my Savior and LORD. I was baptized on June 22.

We moved to a different house that summer. I did not like change, and I missed my old house; I dreaded going to a new school to start third grade.

And there was the week I attended Vacation Bible School at my church. Each morning there was a Bible verse to memorize, and on one particular day, the verse was Psalm 56:3. I memorized it in the King James Version:

> *What time I am afraid, I will trust in Thee.*

Now, summertime in Amarillo can bring significant thunderstorms, which often contain very large hail and even tornadoes. As a little girl, I was terribly afraid of tornadoes.

This particular summer night, my parents had already tucked me into bed. As I lay there trying to fall asleep, I overheard them talking, and the tone of their voices told me something bad was about to happen. Being eight years old, I reasoned that I needed to be a "big girl" and not add to their concerns, so I decided to stay in bed even though I was honestly scared to death. I started saying the Bible verse I had memorized that morning over and over.

> *"What time I am afraid, I will trust in Thee. What time I am afraid, I will trust in Thee. What time I am afraid, I will trust in Thee …"*

And I fell asleep.

The next morning I awoke to learn that half the windows in our house were broken, and our entire roof needed to be replaced because of the destructive hailstorm. Miraculously, I heard none of it because the LORD caused me to sleep through the night.

The LORD laid a significant foundation stone for my walk of faith. I knew that I knew that I did not need to be afraid. I could trust in the LORD.

Psalm 56:3 became my "forever verse," a Bible verse tucked forever into my memory to be said the moment I need it. Do you have a forever verse, a Biblical truth that comes to mind quickly in difficult circumstances?

Trusting God was a forever theme of David's life. In Psalm 56, he was scared, yet he chose to put his trust in the LORD and not be afraid (v. 11).

As a faithful, prayerful watchman (Isaiah 62:6-7), pray Psalm 56:8-13 over a situation where you and someone you love need to trust God.

"LORD, take account of _____ and my wanderings.
Put our tears in Your bottle and in Your book.
Turn back our enemies in the day when we call on You.
This we know, that You are for us, God!
God, we praise Your Word. LORD, we praise Your Word.
God, we put our trust in You; we will not be afraid.
What can man do to us? Your vows are binding upon us,
O God. We will give You thank offerings, for You have delivered
our souls from death, indeed our feet from stumbling.
LORD, let us walk before You in the light of the living.
In Your name, Jesus~"

JULY 27

Please read Psalm 57.

Meditate on verse 7.

> *My heart is steadfast, O God; my heart is steadfast;*
> *I will sing, yes, I will sing praises!*

When David wrote this psalm, his life was not going smoothly. Nothing was quite working out as he had hoped. It was a season of living in caves, hiding from King Saul who wanted him dead (1 Samuel 22; 24). When David's family heard where he was living, they even visited him in his cave (1 Samuel 22:1).

Sometimes life is like David's, things are not going as you may have hoped. This is an encouraging psalm because it gives you words to pray confidently on days, weeks, months ... even during years when life is hard.

Pray Psalm 57:1-3 and 7 over yourself and those for whom you stand guard as a faithful, prayerful watchman (Isaiah 62:6-7).

> *"Be gracious to _____ and me, O LORD,*
> *be gracious to us, for our souls take refuge in You;*
> *and in the shadow of Your wings,*
> *we will take refuge until destruction passes by.*
> *We will cry to God Most High, to You, God,*
> *who accomplishes all things for us.*
> *You will send from heaven and save us.*
> *You reproach him who tramples upon us.*
> *LORD, You will send forth Your lovingkindness and Your truth.*
> *Our hearts are steadfast, O God; our hearts are steadfast;*
> *we will sing, yes, we will sing praises.*
> *In Your name, Jesus~"*

JULY 28

Please read Psalm 58.

Meditate on verses 10-11.

> *The righteous will rejoice when he sees the vengeance; he will wash his feet in the blood of the wicked. And men will say, "Surely there is reward for the righteous; surely there is a God who judges on earth!"*

Psalm 58 is a disturbing, violent psalm. As you read it, you may have questions to ask your LORD about wicked people and the nature of God. You may want to read more about the coming wrath and judgment of God on sinful, evil people. Revelation 14 is a good cross-reference to Psalm 58.

> *So the angel swung his sickle to the earth and gathered the clusters from the vine of the earth and threw them into the great wine press of the wrath of God. And the wine press was trodden outside the city, and blood came out from the wine press, up to the horses' bridles, for a distance of two hundred miles.*
> —Revelation 14:19-20

Psalm 58 is also a great reminder to pray for those you know who do not have a relationship with the LORD Jesus Christ and to beg God to choose them for the sake of His salvation.

David asked God to shatter the teeth of the evil people around him (v. 6). There are wicked people in the world right now that you may want to ask God to make them "like the miscarriages of a woman which never see the sun" (v. 8).

You may want to ask God to make those evil people righteous people. As a faithful, prayerful watchman (Isaiah 62:6-7), pray Psalm 58:11 over them.

> *"Surely You are the God who judges the earth!*
> *Make _____ righteous, so there will be a reward for them.*
> *You are the reward, Jesus, in whose name I pray~"*

JULY 29

Please read Psalm 59.

Meditate on verse 17b.

> *God is my stronghold, the God who shows me lovingkindness.*

David repeated the words *stronghold* and *lovingkindness* in this psalm (vs. 9-10, 16-17). He was in a desperate situation, literally surrounded by men commanded to kill him (1 Samuel 19:11). David reminded himself about who God is and appealed to Him for help (vs. 4-5).

What evil surrounds you or someone you love? Is there a stronghold in your family that needs to be replaced by the stronghold of God? Reread Psalm 59 and find a phrase or verse about who God is. Meditate on and memorize it. Share it with someone who needs to know about the strength and lovingkindness of the LORD.

Pray Psalm 59:4b, 9-11, and 16-17 over yourself and those for whom you stand guard as a faithful, prayerful watchman (Isaiah 62:6-7).

> *"LORD, arouse Yourself to help _____ and me,*
> *and see us and this situation!*
> *Because of the strength of this situation, we will*
> *watch for You, for You are our stronghold.*
> *My God, in Your lovingkindness, meet us!*
> *God, look triumphantly upon our foes!*
> *Scatter them by Your power and bring them*
> *down, O LORD, our shield.*
> *As for _____ and me, we shall sing of Your strength.*
> *Yes, help us joyfully sing of Your lovingkindness in the morning,*
> *for You have been our stronghold and a refuge in the day of distress.*
> *O our strength, we will sing praises to You, for You are*
> *our stronghold, the God who shows us lovingkindness.*
> *In Your strong name, Jesus~"*

Please read Psalm 60.

Meditate on verses 11-12.

> *O give us help against the adversary, for deliverance*
> *by man is in vain. Through God we shall do valiantly,*
> *and it is He who will tread down our adversaries.*

David acknowledged that he and the people had gone through difficult times, but for the glory of His name, God was even in control of hardships. Read 2 Samuel 8 to learn the rest of this story. God delivered David from his enemies and established his kingdom.

Do you and those you love feel rejected and broken by God? Psalm 60 contains good verses to pray over your situation.

Pray Psalm 60:1 and 3-5 over yourself and those for whom you stand guard as a faithful, prayerful watchman (Isaiah 62:6-7).

> *"O God, You have rejected _____ and me.*
> *You have broken us; You have been angry; O, restore us!*
> *You have made us experience hardship;*
> *You have given us wine to drink that makes us stagger.*
> *LORD, we fear You; please give us a banner that*
> *we can display because of Your truth.*
> *Please deliver Your beloved _____ ;*
> *save with Your right hand and answer us!*
> *Because of Your name, Jesus~"*

JULY 31

Please read Psalm 61.

Meditate on verses 1-2.

> *Hear my cry, O God; give heed to my prayer. From*
> *the end of the earth, I call to You when my heart is*
> *faint; lead me to the rock that is higher than I.*

David cried to the LORD to hear his prayer because God had been a refuge and tower of strength to him in the past (vs. 1, 3). David knew the LORD was a rock higher than he was; he appealed to the exalted One who was proven trustworthy.

What do you know about the LORD because you have experienced His faithfulness in the past? What do you know about the LORD because the Bible has told you His actions and attributes? Based on those facts, pray Psalm 61 over yourself and those for whom you stand guard as a faithful, prayerful watchman (Isaiah 62:6-7).

> *"Hear my cry, O God; give heed to my prayer.*
> *From the end of the earth, I call to You.*
> *_____ and my hearts are faint;*
> *lead us to the rock that is higher than we are.*
> *For You have been a refuge for us,*
> *a tower of strength against the enemy.*
> *Let us dwell in Your tent forever;*
> *let us take refuge in the shelter of Your wings.*
> *Hear our vows, O God;*
> *give us the inheritance of those who fear Your name.*
> *Prolong our lives; let our years be as many generations.*
> *Let us abide before You forever; appoint Your*
> *lovingkindness and truth that they may preserve us.*
> *Help us sing praise to Your name forever,*
> *that we may pay our vows day by day.*
> *For the sake of Your name, Jesus~"*

AUGUST

On your walls, O Jerusalem,
I have appointed watchmen;
All day and all night they
will never keep silent.
You who remind the LORD,
take no rest for yourselves;
And give Him no rest until He establishes
And makes Jerusalem a
praise in the earth.
ISAIAH 62:6-7, NASB

AUGUST 1

Please read Psalm 62.

Meditate on verses 1-2.

My soul waits in silence for God only; from Him is
my salvation. He only is my rock and my salvation,
my stronghold; I shall not be greatly shaken.

David's relationship with the LORD was intimately personal. The personal possessive pronoun "my" was used 14 times in Psalm 62. Observe what David called God:

- ◈ my salvation (vs. 1, 2, 6, 7)
- ◈ my rock (vs. 2, 6)
- ◈ my stronghold (vs. 2, 6)
- ◈ my hope (v. 5)
- ◈ my glory (v. 7)
- ◈ my strength (v. 7)
- ◈ my refuge (v. 7)

Because the LORD was his God, David gave a powerful, commanding invitation for others to trust God.

Trust in Him at all times, O people; Pour out your
heart before Him; God is a refuge for us.
—Psalm 62:8

What is your relationship with the LORD? Is He your stronghold and salvation? Are others drawn to a relationship with Christ because you know Him intimately?

Pray Psalm 62:2 and 8 over those for whom you stand guard as a faithful, prayerful watchman (Isaiah 62:6-7).

"LORD, You are my rock, my salvation, and my stronghold.
Please be _____ 's rock, salvation, and stronghold.
Do not let them be greatly shaken.
Help them trust in You at all times.
Let them pour out their heart before You.
God, be their refuge. In Your strong name, Jesus~"

AUGUST 2

Please read Psalm 63.

Meditate on verse 3.

> *Because Your lovingkindness is better than*
> *life, my lips will praise You.*

David also wrote this psalm while hiding from King Saul in the Judean wilderness (1 Samuel 22). We have been in this wilderness, and it is indeed a "dry and weary land" (v. 1).

David's lips may have been chapped and his throat parched because of his desert experience, yet he chose to praise the LORD in spite of circumstances. The lovingkindness of God was better than life (v. 3). Life was difficult, but God was faithful. The praise on David's lips brought refreshment to his soul.

You or someone you love may be in an emotionally dry and weary place. Pray with praise to the LORD of lovingkindness. Encourage the one you love to do the same.

Praising God helps you access the fountain of living water, which is the LORD (Jeremiah 17:13).

Pray Psalm 63:1, 3-4, and 6-8 over yourself and those for whom you stand guard as a faithful, prayerful watchman (Isaiah 62:6-7).

> *"O God, You are _____ and my God.*
> *We shall seek You earnestly. Our souls thirst for You;*
> *our flesh yearns for You in a dry and weary*
> *land where there is no water.*
> *Because Your lovingkindness is better than*
> *life, our lips will praise You.*
> *Help us bless You as long as we live; help us*
> *to lift up our hands in Your name.*
> *Please cause _____ to remember You on their bed,*
> *to meditate on You in the night watches.*
> *Be their help, and in the shadow of Your wings,*
> *let them sing for joy. Let their soul cling to You.*
> *Uphold them with Your right hand. In Your name, Jesus~"*

AUGUST 3

Please read Psalm 64.

Meditate on verses 1 and 10.

> *Hear my voice, O God, in my complaint; preserve my life from dread of the enemy. The righteous man will be glad in the LORD and will take refuge in Him, and all the upright in heart will glory.*

David asked God to preserve his life from dread of the enemy devising evil against him (vs. 1, 6). He trusted the LORD to take care of all his enemies; even the ones who were talking about doing him harm, but had not yet carried out their wicked plans. David wanted God to protect him from dreading what *might* happen.

Do you suffer from dread—dread of the unknown, dread of what others might be saying or thinking, dread of what you think people are scheming to do …? God wants to replace your dread with trust in Him.

Pray Psalm 64:1-2 and 10 over yourself and those for whom you stand guard as a faithful, prayerful watchman (Isaiah 62:6-7).

> *"Hear _____ and my voice, O God, in our complaint.*
> *Preserve our life from dread of the enemy.*
> *Hide us from the secret counsel of evildoers, from*
> *the tumult of those who do iniquity.*
> *Make us righteous, so we will be glad in You,*
> *LORD. We take refuge in You.*
> *Make us upright in heart, so we can glory—In Your name, Jesus~"*

Please read Psalm 65.

Meditate on verse 4a.

How blessed is the one whom You choose and bring near to You.

God choosing to draw people near to Him is a powerful reoccurring theme in the Bible. In this psalm, David reflected on the satisfaction of being with God. Being in awe of God, he wrote this beautiful thirteen-verse praise to the LORD.

As you pray these verses of praise to God (vs. 1-13), enjoy the fellowship of His presence.

"There will be silence before You, and praise in Zion, O God, and to You the vow will be performed. O You who hear prayer, to You all men come. Iniquities prevail against me; as for our transgressions, You forgive them. How blessed is the one whom You choose and bring near to You to dwell in Your courts. We will be satisfied with the goodness of Your house, Your holy temple. By awesome deeds You answer us in righteousness, O God of our salvation. You who are the trust of all the ends of the earth and of the farthest sea; who establishes the mountains by His strength, being girded with might; who stills the roaring of the seas, the roaring of their waves and the tumult of the peoples. They who dwell in the ends of the earth stand in awe of Your signs; You make the dawn and the sunset shout for joy. You visit the earth and cause it to overflow; You greatly enrich it. The stream of God is full of water; You prepare their grain, for thus You prepare the earth. You water its furrows abundantly; You settle its ridges; You soften it with showers; You bless its growth. You have crowned the year with Your bounty, and Your paths drip with fatness. The pastures of the wilderness drip, and the hills gird themselves with rejoicing. The meadows are clothed with flocks, and the valleys are covered with grain; they shout for joy, yes, they sing."

Please read Psalm 66.

Meditate on verse 16.

*Come and hear, all who fear God, and I will
tell of what He has done for my soul.*

The psalmist was excited about the LORD and wanted people to know what God had done. He recalled things the LORD did in the past, like turning the sea into dry land (v. 6). He acknowledged what God was doing in the present, like not allowing his feet to slip (v. 9). He admitted that God had tested him and laid an oppressive burden on him, but it was not without purpose; the LORD had refined him like silver (vs. 10-11). And after going through the fire, the LORD brought him to a place of abundance (v. 12).

Do you have a story to tell about journeying with the LORD? What has He done for your soul? Recall His faithfulness in the past; recognize His faithfulness today; rest assured of His faithfulness in the future.

Pray Psalm 66:8-9 and 18-20 over yourself and those for whom you stand guard as a faithful, prayerful watchman (Isaiah 62:6-7).

*"We bless You, God, and sound Your praise abroad.
Please keep _____ and me in life, and do not allow our feet to slip.
Do not let us regard wickedness in our hearts;
we want You to hear us.
Give heed to the voice of our prayers!
We bless You, God.
Do not turn away our prayers nor Your lovingkindness from us.
For the sake of Your name, Jesus~"*

AUGUST 6

Please read Psalm 67.

Meditate on verses 1-2.

> *God be gracious to us and bless us, and cause His face*
> *to shine upon us—that Your way may be known on*
> *the earth, Your salvation among all nations.*

The psalmist had a purpose in mind when he asked God to bless him. He wanted God's salvation to be known throughout the earth and for all people to praise God (vs. 2-3, 5, 7). With the request for God to bless was the understanding that when blessing came, it would point people to the Savior.

What is your motivation for asking God to bless you? Do you recognize EVERY good thing in your life as coming from God? Are you praising Him with your entire being—thoughts, words, and actions? As you do, you point a lost world to Jesus.

Pray Psalm 67:1-3 and 7 over yourself and those for whom you stand guard as a faithful, prayerful watchman (Isaiah 62:6-7).

> *"God, be gracious to _____ and me and bless us.*
> *Cause Your face to shine upon us—that Your way may be*
> *known on the earth, Your salvation among all nations.*
> *Let us praise You, O God. Let others praise You!*
> *God, bless us that all the ends of the earth may fear You.*
> *For Your sake, Jesus Christ, our Savior and LORD~"*

Please read Psalm 68 and observe God. (You may want to mark God and His synonyms and pronouns to make it easier to notice His actions and attributes.)

Meditate on verse 4.

> *Sing to God, sing praises to His name;*
> *lift up a song for Him who rides through the deserts,*
> *whose name is the LORD, and exult before Him.*

Noticing God in Psalm 68 will cause you to praise Him. Here are some truths about God:

- He daily bears your burden (v. 19).
- He is your salvation (v. 19).
- He is to you a God of deliverances (v. 20).
- He gives you strength and power (v. 35).

Verse 4 says God rides through the deserts, and verse 33 says He rides upon the highest heavens. You may be in a "highest heaven" season of life; praise God if you are and recognize that He is with you. You may be in a "desert" time of life. Which of the truths about God do you need to meditate on today, knowing that God is riding with you through the desert? Praise Him even in the desert.

Pray Psalm 68:28 and 35 over yourself and those for whom you stand guard as a faithful, prayerful watchman (Isaiah 62:6-7).

> *"God, command strength for _____ and me.*
> *Show Yourself strong on behalf of us, O God.*
> *O God, You are awesome.*
> *Please give strength and power to us.*
> *We bless You, LORD.*
> *Because of Your name, Jesus~"*

AUGUST 8

Please read Psalm 69.

Meditate on verses 1-3.

> *Save me, O God, for the waters have threatened my life. I have*
> *sunk in deep mire, and there is no foothold; I have come into deep*
> *waters, and a flood overflows me. I am weary with my crying;*
> *my throat is parched; my eyes fail while I wait for my God.*

David was in a low, depressed place when he wrote this psalm. He was transparent with God; he knew the LORD was listening to him (v. 33). If you, or someone you love, are in a similar state, Psalm 69 can help express difficult thoughts and feelings.

It is reassuring to know even David, the giant slayer and the man after God's own heart, had times of depression and despair. It is also important to remember he had an intimately honest relationship with his Savior.

Cry out to the LORD like David did on behalf of yourself and those for whom you stand guard as a faithful, prayerful watchman (Isaiah 62:6-7). Pray Psalm 69:13-17.

> *"My prayer for _____ and me is to You, O LORD.*
> *O God, in the greatness of Your lovingkindness,*
> *answer us with Your saving truth.*
> *Deliver us from the mire and do not let us sink.*
> *May we be delivered from our foes and from the deep*
> *waters. May the flood of water not overflow us nor the*
> *deep swallow us up, nor the pit shut its mouth on us.*
> *Answer us, O LORD, for Your lovingkindness is good.*
> *According to the greatness of Your compassion,*
> *turn to us, and do not hide Your face from your servants,*
> *for we are in distress; answer us quickly.*
> *In Your name, Jesus~"*

AUGUST 9

Please read Psalm 70.

Meditate on verse 4.

> *Let all who seek You rejoice and be glad in You, and let those who love Your salvation say continually, "Let God be magnified."*

When David wrote this psalm, he was not glad and rejoicing; he was afflicted and needy. He sought God to deliver him, giving God a list of his needs. Let David's honesty encourage you as you tell God your requests. David asked God to:

- ✺ hurry and deliver me (v. 1)
- ✺ hurry and help me (v. 1)
- ✺ let those be ashamed and humiliated who seek my life (v. 2)
- ✺ let those be turned back and dishonored who delight in my hurt (v. 2)
- ✺ let those be turned back because of their shame who say, "Aha, aha!" (v. 3)

Even though you seek and love the LORD, there will be seasons: days, months, or perhaps even years when you need the LORD to not delay in delivering you from what is threatening to devour you. Be honest with Him about what you need. He loves you and is faithful to provide.

Pray Psalm 70:5 over yourself and those for whom you stand guard as a faithful, prayerful watchman (Isaiah 62:6-7).

> *"LORD, _____ and I are afflicted and needy;*
> *hasten to us, O God! You are our help and our deliverer;*
> *O LORD, do not delay!*
> *For the sake of Your name, Jesus~"*

AUGUST 10

Please read and pray Psalm 71. The entire psalm is a prayer.

Meditate on verses 5-6.

> *For You are my hope; O LORD God, You are my confidence from my youth. By You, I have been sustained from my birth; You are He who took me from my mother's womb; my praise is continually of You.*

Psalm 71 was part of my (Marsha's) Bible reading the day our granddaughter was born; I wrote a note about it in my Bible. God preplanned a reading from Psalm 71 to be written into the devotional book I used months before He started weaving our granddaughter together inside her mama. He knew the date of her birth, and He knew I would be following that particular devotional plan. The LORD was pleased that I noticed His involvement in our lives.

The LORD is constantly involved like that in your life; He has been even before He took you from your mother's womb (v. 6). He wants you to notice and pay attention that He notices and pays attention to you. The psalmist recognized what God had done and was doing in his life. Because of that knowledge, he hoped in the LORD continually and praised Him more and more (v. 14).

Reread Psalm 71 and pray it specifically over yourself and those for whom you stand guard as a faithful, prayerful watchman (Isaiah 62:6-7). Here are verses 1 and 2 to get you started:

> *"In You, O LORD, _____ and I have taken refuge;*
> *let us never be ashamed.*
> *In Your righteousness deliver us and rescue us.*
> *Incline Your ear to us and save us ...*
> *In Your name, Jesus-"*

AUGUST 11

Please read Psalm 72.

Meditate on verse 17.

> *May his name endure forever; may his name increase*
> *as long as the sun shines, and let men bless themselves*
> *by him; let all nations call him blessed.*

Psalm 72 is a prayer King David prayed for his son, King Solomon. It is also a Messianic Psalm. Reread it and capitalize the *H* of *he*. The words make you think of Jesus.

> *May He judge Your people with righteousness and Your afflicted with justice. May He vindicate the afflicted of the people, save the children of the needy, and crush the oppressor. Let them fear You while the sun endures, and as long as the moon, throughout all generations. May He come down like rain upon the mown grass, like showers that water the earth. In His days, may the righteous flourish and abundance of peace till the moon is no more. May He also rule from sea to sea and from the River to the ends of the earth. Let the nomads of the desert bow before Him, and His enemies lick the dust. And let all kings bow down before Him, all nations serve Him. May His name endure forever; may His name increase as long as the sun shines,* and let men bless themselves by Him. Let all nations call Him blessed.
> —Psalm 72:2, 4-9, 11, 17

When Messiah came, He brought righteousness and peace to all who received Him. When He comes again, righteousness and peace will reign to the ends of the earth.

Pray the words of Psalm 72 for Christ to return to earth soon. Pray Psalm 72:18-20 and ask God to work wonders in your life and in the lives of those for whom you stand guard as a faithful, prayerful watchman (Isaiah 62:6-7).

> *"Blessed be You, the LORD God, the God of Israel,*
> *Who alone works wonders. LORD, work*
> *wonders for _____ and me.*
> *And blessed be Your glorious name forever; and may the*
> *whole earth be filled with Your glory. Amen and Amen."*

Please read Psalm 73.

Meditate on verses 16-17.

> *When I pondered to understand this, it was troublesome in my sight,*
> *until I came into the sanctuary of God, then I perceived their end.*

The psalmist, Asaph, described a troubling situation in Psalm 73. He envied the prosperity of the wicked and arrogant who always seemed to be at ease (vs. 3, 12). Nothing made sense until Asaph came into the sanctuary of the LORD, then he understood the truth about the wicked (vs. 17-20):

- God set them in slippery places and cast them to destruction.
- They are destroyed in a moment and utterly swept away by sudden terrors.
- The LORD will despise their form.

Being in God's presence gave Asaph insight into the world around him.

Does the news and what goes on around you make you crazy? Are there people and things in your life that make no sense? You need time-out with Jesus. Reading the Bible and talking to God will give you His perspective on the situation and bring you peace.

Pray Psalm 73:23-26 over yourself and those for whom you stand guard as a faithful, prayerful watchman (Isaiah 62:6-7).

> *"LORD, thank You that _____ and I are continually with You!*
> *Take hold of our right hands. Guide us with Your counsel,*
> *and afterward receive us to glory. Whom have we in heaven*
> *but You? And besides You, we desire nothing on earth.*
> *Our flesh and our hearts may fail, but God,*
> *be the strength of our hearts and our portion forever.*
> *In Your name, Jesus~"*

Please read Psalm 74.

Meditate on verses 1 and 12.

> *O God, why have You rejected us forever? Why does Your anger smoke against the sheep of Your pasture? Yet God is my king from of old, Who works deeds of deliverance in the midst of the earth.*

Asaph and the Israelites felt rejected by God. The enemy had damaged everything within God's sanctuary (v. 3). Asaph used words like *smashed, burned,* and *defiled* to describe what the adversary had done (vs. 6-7).

Asaph did two things in the midst of his depressing situation. He remembered God's faithfulness in the past, and He asked God to remember what the enemy did to His people (vs. 12-18).

You or someone you love may feel smashed by the enemy. Recall God's blessings and faithfulness; then cry to Him for deliverance.

Pray Psalm 74:18-23 over yourself and those for whom you stand guard as a faithful, prayerful watchman (Isaiah 62:6-7).

> *"Remember this, O LORD, that the enemy has reviled,*
> *and a foolish people has spurned Your name.*
> *Do not deliver the soul of Your turtledove, _____, and me*
> *to the wild beast; do not forget the life of Your afflicted forever.*
> *Consider the covenant, for the dark places of the land are full*
> *of the habitations of violence. Let not the oppressed return*
> *dishonored; let the afflicted and needy praise Your name.*
> *Arise, O God, and plead Your own cause; remember*
> *how the foolish man reproaches You all day long.*
> *Do not forget the voice of Your adversaries, the uproar of*
> *those who rise against You which ascends continually.*
> *For the sake of Your name, Jesus~"*

AUGUST 14

Please read Psalm 75.

Meditate on verse 1.

> *We give thanks to You, O God; we give thanks, for Your*
> *name is near; men declare Your wondrous works.*

Not only is the name of the LORD near to you; the LORD Himself is actually with you if you are in Christ Jesus. Hear what He says to you in Psalm 75; the LORD is speaking in verses 2-5:

> *"When I select an appointed time, it is I who judge with*
> *equity. The earth and all who dwell in it melt; it is I who*
> *have firmly set its pillars. I said to the boastful, 'Do not boast,'*
> *and to the wicked, 'Do not lift up the horn; do not lift up*
> *your horn on high; do not speak with insolent pride.'"*

Jesus, the Savior, is the coming Judge before whom all the world will be held accountable. Those who do not know Him as Savior and LORD will be made to drink from the cup of God's anger which is in His hand (v. 8; Revelation 14:10). The psalmist contrasted himself with the wicked who will drink that wine of wrath. Can you say the words of the psalmist? If so, pray Psalm 75:9-10 as a faithful, prayerful watchman (Isaiah 62:6-7). If you cannot, ask Jesus to be your Savior.

> *"LORD, as for me, I will declare it forever;*
> *I will sing praises to You, God of Jacob.*
> *Cut off all the horns of the wicked, but lift*
> *up the horns of the righteous.*
> *Make _____ and me righteous.*
> *Because of Your name, Jesus~"*

AUGUST 15

Please read Psalm 76.

Meditate on verses 8-9.

> *You caused judgment to be heard from heaven;*
> *the earth feared and was still when God arose to*
> *judgment to save all the humble of the earth.*

Carefully observe God in Psalm 76.

- He is known and His name is great in Israel (v.1).
- He is resplendent and majestic (v.4).
- He is to be feared (v.7).
- He judges to save all the humble of the earth (v.9).

These are important truths to remember and apply to your life.

Whom do you fear? Many people are afraid of any and everything except Almighty God. As you read God's Word, you will discover that you are to fear nothing and no one except the LORD; Satan wants you to do the opposite. Choose to fear only God.

Another truth to remember is God judges with the purpose of saving the humble. Will you be saved, or does your pride keep you from Jesus and make you the object of God's judgment and wrath? Come to the LORD in humility, and let Him change your life for eternity.

Pray Psalm 76:11 over yourself and those for whom you stand guard as a faithful, prayerful watchman (Isaiah 62:6-7).

> *"LORD my God, _____ and I make these vows to you.*
> *(Tell God the specific vows you are making.)*
> *Help us fulfill them. We bring You these gifts.*
> *(Tell God the specific gifts you are bringing.)*
> *You are to be feared. In Your name, Jesus~"*

AUGUST 16

Please read Psalm 77.

Meditate on verses 9 and 11.

> *Has God forgotten to be gracious, or has He in anger*
> *withdrawn His compassion? I shall remember the deeds of*
> *the LORD; surely I will remember Your wonders of old.*

Asaph was distressed when he wrote this psalm. He was so troubled he could not sleep, and his soul refused to be comforted (vs. 2, 4). Asaph wondered if the LORD's lovingkindness had ceased and if His promises had come to an end (v. 8).

As Asaph's grieving eyelids refused to close, he remembered the deeds of the LORD:

1. Your way, O God, is holy (v. 13).
2. You are God who works wonders (v. 14).
3. You have made known Your strength among the peoples (v. 14).
4. You have redeemed Your people by Your power (v. 15).

Sometimes it seems that God has withdrawn His compassion. If you are experiencing one of those times, remember God's faithfulness towards you and those you love. Recall that His paths are in the mighty waters; you may not be able to see His footprints, but know that they are there (v. 19).

Pray Psalm 77:1 and 19-20 over yourself and those for whom you stand guard as a faithful, prayerful watchman (Isaiah 62:6-7).

> "_____ *and my voices rise to You, God, and we will cry aloud!*
> *Our voices rise to You, God; please hear us!*
> *Keep us on Your path in these mighty waters;*
> *let us see and know Your footprints.*
> *Lead us like Your flock.*
> *By Your hand, Jesus~"*

AUGUST 17

Please read Psalm 78.

Meditate on verse 4.

We will not conceal them from their children, but tell to the generation to come the praises of the LORD, and His strength and His wondrous works that He has done.

Thankfully Asaph did not conceal God's wondrous works. He gave additional insight into the miracles God did for Israel. For example, Moses recorded that God brought water from the rock (Exodus 17:6). Asaph described that God "gave them abundant drink like the ocean depths and caused waters to run down like rivers" (vs. 15-16).

As the waters gushed and overflowed, the people questioned God's ability to give them bread and meat (v. 20). Their behavior was ungratefully rude toward God.

Do you ever whine and complain in the midst of the LORD's gushing blessings in your life? The LORD was full of wrath against Israel for their unbelief (vs. 21-22). Take heed not to repeat their sinful behavior.

Pray Psalm 78:4-8 over yourself and those for whom you stand guard as a faithful, prayerful watchman (Isaiah 62:6-7).

*"LORD, do not let _____ and me conceal
these truths from our children.
Let us tell the generation to come Your praises,
Your strength, and the wondrous works You have done.
Let us teach Your commandments to our children, so the
generation to come might know, even the children yet to be
born, that they may arise and tell them to their children.
Let us put our confidence in You, God, and not forget Your works,
but keep Your commandments. Do not let us be a stubborn
and rebellious generation. Make us a generation that prepares
its heart and whose spirit is faithful to You, God.
Because of Your name, Jesus~"*

AUGUST 18

Please read Psalm 79.

Meditate on verse 9.

> *Help us, O God of our salvation, for the glory of Your name;*
> *and deliver us and forgive our sins for Your name's sake.*

Jerusalem was in ruins and the temple defiled (v. 1). The dead were not buried properly and were eaten by the birds (v. 2). Asaph called on God to pour out His wrath on the godless nations that did those atrocities (vs. 6-7). It is good to know you can be so honest with the LORD.

But notice the sudden change in Asaph's prayer request. In the middle of his prayer, Asaph did a sin check. Was the LORD allowing such devastation to punish the people for their sins? Asaph's prayer changed from "Get them, God!" to "O LORD, forgive us."

Ask God to check you for unconfessed sins then pray the prayer of confession in Psalm 79:8-9 and 13 over yourself and those for whom you stand guard as a faithful, prayerful watchman (Isaiah 62:6-7).

> *"LORD, do not remember the iniquities*
> *of _____ and me against us.*
> *Let Your compassion come quickly to meet us,*
> *for we are brought very low.*
> *Help us, O God of our salvation, for the glory of Your name.*
> *Deliver us and forgive our sins for Your name's sake.*
> *We are Your people and the sheep of Your pasture.*
> *We will give thanks to You forever;*
> *to all generations we will tell of Your praise.*
> *For the glory of Your name, Jesus~"*

Please read Psalm 80.

Meditate on verses 3, 7, and 19.

> *O God, restore us and cause Your face to shine upon us, and we will be saved. O God of hosts, restore us and cause Your face to shine upon us, and we will be saved. O LORD God of hosts, restore us; cause Your face to shine upon us, and we will be saved.*

Asaph's prayer request sounds the same in three of the verses, but each time he adds to the name of God; "O God, O God of hosts, O LORD God of hosts ..." (vs. 3, 7, 19). You can hear the urgency as he calls on the LORD to save Israel.

Instead of Israel being fed with manna and water from the rock, God was feeding the people with the bread of tears in large measure (v. 5). Asaph asked God how long He would be angry with the prayer of His people (v. 4).

Are you or someone you love in a season of God's discipline and reproof? Remember that God disciplines those He loves (Hebrews 12:6). Call on the name of the LORD in repentance and trust.

Pray Psalm 80:17-19 over yourself and those for whom you stand guard as a faithful, prayerful watchman (Isaiah 62:6-7).

> *"LORD, let Your hand be upon _____ and me.*
> *Make us people of Your right hand,*
> *people whom You have made strong for Yourself.*
> *Do not let us turn back from You;*
> *revive us, and we will call upon Your name.*
> *O LORD God of hosts, restore us;*
> *cause Your face to shine upon us, and we will be saved.*
> *For the sake of Your name, Jesus~"*

AUGUST 20

Please read Psalm 81.

Meditate on verse 1.

> *Sing for joy to God our strength; shout joyfully to the God of Jacob.*

The LORD recalled what He did for Israel:

- ⤔ "I relieved his shoulder of the burden" (v. 6).
- ⤔ "I rescued you" (v.7).
- ⤔ "I answered you in the hiding place of thunder" (v. 7).

The LORD goes on to admonish Israel for not listening and obeying Him. If they would walk in His ways, He "would quickly subdue their enemies" (v. 14).

What does the LORD say He has done for you? Does He have a word of admonishment for you to stop having a stubborn heart?

Recall God's faithfulness. Commit to obey Him with your whole heart.

Pray Psalm 81:11-16 over yourself and those for whom you stand guard as a faithful, prayerful watchman (Isaiah 62:6-7).

> *"LORD, _____ and I are Your people.*
> *Help us listen to and obey You.*
> *Do not let us have a stubborn heart and walk in our own devices.*
> *Help us listen to You and walk in Your ways!*
> *Please quickly subdue our enemies,*
> *and turn Your hand against our adversaries.*
> *LORD, we love You; do not let us pretend to obey You.*
> *We do not want our time of punishment to be forever.*
> *Please feed us with the finest of the wheat,*
> *and satisfy us with honey from the rock.*
> *In Your name, Jesus~"*

Please read Psalm 82.

Meditate on verses 1 and 8.

> *God takes His stand in His own congregation;*
> *He judges in the midst of the rulers. Arise, O God,*
> *judge the earth! For it is You who possesses all the nations.*

This psalm begins and ends with God judging. The verses in between address human judges, exhorting them to judge righteously and fairly. The psalmist, Asaph, reminds these judges of their sacred trust to make Godly decisions like "sons of the Most High" (v. 6). Asaph tells them not to let their godlike position to make such important decisions go to their heads because they are mere men and will die like men (v. 7).

These are important verses for those in the judiciary system. Pray for those who sit in such authoritative positions to make Godly decisions and to literally be sons of the Most High through faith in Jesus Christ (John 1:12; Galatians 3:26).

As a faithful, prayerful watchman (Isaiah 62:6-7), pray Psalm 82 over judges and rulers in your land.

> *"LORD, judge in the midst of our rulers. Do not let our*
> *rulers judge unjustly and show partiality to the wicked.*
> *Let them vindicate the weak and fatherless and do justice to the*
> *afflicted and destitute. Help them rescue the weak and needy.*
> *May they deliver them out of the hand of the wicked.*
> *Make our rulers know and understand. Let them not walk about*
> *in darkness, so that the foundations of the earth are shaken.*
> *LORD, let them truly be sons of the Most*
> *High, through faith in You, Jesus.*
> *Make them realize they will die like men*
> *and fall like any one of the princes.*
> *Arise, O God, judge the earth!*
> *For it is You who possesses all the nations.*
> *Because You are the Righteous Judge, Jesus~"*

AUGUST 22

Please read Psalm 83.

Meditate on verses 1-3.

> *O God, do not remain quiet; do not be silent and, O God, do not*
> *be still. For behold, Your enemies make an uproar, and those who*
> *hate You have exalted themselves. They make shrewd plans against*
> *Your people and conspire together against Your treasured ones.*

Approximately 3,000 years ago, Asaph listed all the enemies who were hoping to annihilate the nation of Israel so that her name was no longer remembered (v. 4). Asaph asked God to pursue and terrify Israel's adversaries, shaming and humiliating them (vs. 15, 17). He hoped such dishonor would cause these wicked people to seek the name of the LORD (v. 16).

God protected Israel; she is still a nation today. And interestingly, the descendants of those enemies are Israel's current, modern day foes. They still seek the extermination of this nation loved by God, and they desire to kill Christians, who are also God's beloved. Know with certainty, God will continue to protect Israel, and He also promises to protect you.

> *But the LORD is faithful, and He will strengthen*
> *and protect you from the evil one.*
> —2 Thessalonians 3:3

Obey your LORD's command to pray for your enemies (Luke 6:27-28) by appealing to Him with Psalm 83:1-3, 16, and 18 as a faithful, prayerful watchman (Isaiah 62:6-7).

> *"O God, do not remain quiet; do not be silent and, O God,*
> *do not be still! For behold, Your enemies make an uproar, and*
> *those who hate You have exalted themselves. They make shrewd*
> *plans against Your people, and conspire together against Your*
> *treasured ones. Do what You need to do, even filling their faces*
> *with dishonor, that they may seek Your name, O LORD. May*
> *they know that You alone, whose name is the LORD, are the*
> *Most High over all the earth. In Your Most High name, Jesus-"*

Please read Psalm 84.

Meditate on verse 1.

How lovely are Your dwelling places, O LORD of hosts!

Where are God's dwelling places?

- He dwells in Jerusalem forever (1 Chronicles 23:25).
- He dwells in Zion (Psalm 9:11).
- He dwells on high (Isaiah 33:5).
- He dwells within the temple (Matthew 23:21).
- He dwells in unapproachable light (1 Timothy 6:16).
- The Spirit of God dwells in you! (Romans 8:9, 11; 1 Corinthians 3:16; 2 Timothy 1:14).

The psalmist longed to be where God was. Meditate on the fact that if you are a Christian, you are always with God because He dwells inside of you. And you are lovely because you are His dwelling place. Live so others will want to be His dwelling place, too.

Pray Psalm 84:2b and 11-12 over yourself and those for whom you stand guard as a faithful, prayerful watchman (Isaiah 62:6-7).

"My heart and my flesh sing for joy to You, the living God!
LORD God, be a sun and shield to _____ and me.
Give us grace and glory;
do not withhold any good thing from us as we walk uprightly.
O LORD of hosts, bless us as we trust in You!
In Your name, Jesus~"

Please read Psalm 85.

Meditate on verse 8.

> *I will hear what God the LORD will say; for He will speak peace to*
> *His people, to His Godly ones; but let them not turn back to folly.*

What a wonderful psalm for faithful, prayerful watchmen! It is filled with treasure verses to pray over those you love.

- ✺ LORD, forgive the iniquity of _____ and cover all their sin (v. 2).
- ✺ LORD, please withdraw Your fury from _____ and turn away from Your burning anger (v. 3).
- ✺ Restore _____, O God of our salvation, and cause Your indignation toward them to cease (v. 4).
- ✺ LORD, do not be angry forever with _____ (v. 5).
- ✺ Revive _____ again, LORD (v. 6).
- ✺ Show _____ Your lovingkindness, O LORD, and grant them Your salvation (v. 7).
- ✺ Speak peace to _____. Make them Your Godly ones (v. 8).
- ✺ LORD, do not let _____ turn back to folly (stupidity) (v. 8).

Armed with God's Word, pray at least one of the above over and over someone you are guarding as their faithful, prayerful watchman (Isaiah 62:6-7).

> *"LORD, do not let _____ turn back to stupidity.*
> *LORD, do not let _____ turn back to stupidity.*
> *LORD, do not let _____ turn back to stupidity ...*
> *For the sake of Your name, Jesus~"*

AUGUST 25

Please read Psalm 86.

Meditate on verse 1.

> *Incline Your ear, O LORD, and answer me;*
> *for I am afflicted and needy.*

Psalm 86 is a prayer of David. Perhaps you want to write your name next to David's in your Bible and make it your prayer, too.

David was afflicted and needy, and he wanted God to help him. Observe David's prayer requests, and make them your own:

- Preserve my soul (v. 2).
- Be gracious to me (v. 3).
- Make my soul glad (v. 4).
- Give ear to my prayer (v. 6).
- Give heed to my supplications (v. 6).
- Teach me Your way (v. 11).
- Let me walk in Your truth (v. 11).
- Unite my heart to fear Your name (v. 11).
- Turn to me (v. 16).
- Grant me Your strength (v. 16).
- Save me (v. 16).
- Show me a sign for good (v. 17).
- Help me and comfort me (v. 17).

Reread Psalm 86, saying it as a personal prayer to your LORD.

> *"Incline Your ear, O LORD, and answer me; for I am afflicted*
> *and needy. Preserve my soul, for I am a Godly person;*
> *O You my God, save Your servant who trusts in You.*
> *Be gracious to me, O LORD, for to You I cry all day long.*
> *Show me a sign for good, that those who hate me may*
> *see it and be ashamed, because You, O LORD,*
> *have helped me and comforted me.*
> *In Your name, Jesus-"*

Please read Psalm 87.

Meditate on verses 2 and 6.

> *The LORD loves the gates of Zion more than all the other*
> *dwelling places of Jacob. The LORD will count when*
> *He registers the peoples, "This one was born there."*

Zion was the southwestern hill of Jerusalem where David built his palace; it became the "city of David[1]." The LORD loves Zion and calls it the "city of God" (vs. 2-3). Everyone born in Zion is counted and registered by the LORD Himself (vs. 5-6).

As a Christian, "you have come to Mount Zion and to the city of the living God, the heavenly Jerusalem" (Hebrews 12:22). And this is what Jesus says about you:

> *"He who overcomes, I will make him a pillar in the temple*
> *of My God, and he will not go out from it anymore; and I*
> *will write on him the name of My God, and the name of*
> *the city of My God, the new Jerusalem, which comes down*
> *out of heaven from My God, and My new name."*
> —Revelation 3:12

Through Jesus Christ, you are born into the city of God. The LORD counts and registers you as a citizen of His household (Ephesians 2:19). Amazing!

Pray Psalm 87:6 over those who need to be born into the city of God. Pray Psalm 87:7 in thanksgiving for your permanent residence there.

> *"LORD, cause _____ to be born into You,*
> *so when You count and register the peoples,*
> *You will say of them, 'This one was born there.'*
> *LORD, all my springs of joy are in You.*
> *Because of Your name, Jesus~"*

---

1. *Easton's Bible Dictionary*

AUGUST 27

Please read Psalm 88.

Meditate on verse 10a.

Will You perform wonders for the dead?

The psalmist was in very low and depressed state. From the pit, he asked God six questions (vs. 10-12):

- Will You perform wonders for the dead?
- Will the departed spirits rise and praise You?
- Will Your lovingkindness be declared in the grave?
- Will Your faithfulness be declared in Abaddon (place of destruction)?
- Will Your wonders be made known in the darkness?
- Will Your righteousness be made known in the land of forgetfulness?

The answer to all of these questions is: "In Jesus Christ, YES!"

> *For the LORD Himself will descend from heaven with a shout,*
> *with the voice of the archangel and with the trumpet of God,*
> *and the dead in Christ will rise first. Then we who are alive and*
> *remain will be caught up together with them in the clouds to meet*
> *the LORD in the air, and so we shall always be with the LORD.*
> —1 Thessalonians 4:16-17

Perhaps you or those you love are in a dark place. Use the words from Psalm 88 to cry out to your LORD then look up "because your redemption is drawing near" (Luke 21:28).

Pray Psalm 88:1-2 over yourself and those for whom you stand guard as a faithful, prayerful watchman (Isaiah 62:6-7).

> *"O LORD, the God of my salvation,*
> *I have cried out by day and in the night before You.*
> *Let my prayer come before You; incline Your ear to my cry!*
> *(Pour out your heart to the LORD.)*
> *In Your name, Jesus~"*

AUGUST 28

Please read Psalm 89.

Meditate on verse 1.

> *I will sing of the lovingkindness of the LORD forever; to all generations I will make known Your faithfulness with my mouth.*

Lovingkindness and *faithfulness* are important repeated words in this psalm; both are used seven times. God's promises surrounding these words were originally made to David, God's anointed servant (v. 20). In Christ Jesus, you, too, are an anointed servant of God (2 Corinthians 1:21; Revelation 19:5), so His promises apply to you. Ponder these truths about God's lovingkindness and faithfulness:

- Lovingkindness will be built up forever, and God will establish His faithfulness (v. 2).
- God's faithfulness surrounds Him (v. 8).
- Lovingkindness goes before Him (v. 14).
- God's faithfulness and lovingkindness are with His anointed (v. 24).
- God keeps His lovingkindness for His anointed (v. 28).
- God will not break off His lovingkindness nor deal falsely in His faithfulness (v. 33).

Tell others these truths from God's Word and pray them over yourself and those for whom you stand guard as a faithful, prayerful watchman (Isaiah 62:6-7). Pray Psalm 89:20-22, 24a, 26, and 28-29.

> *"LORD, _____ and I are Your servants.*
> *Anoint us with Your holy oil. Let Your hand be*
> *established with us, and let Your arm strengthen us.*
> *Do not let the enemy deceive us nor the son of wickedness afflict us.*
> *Let Your faithfulness and lovingkindness be with us.*
> *You are our Father, our God, and the Rock of our salvation!*
> *Keep Your lovingkindness for us forever and*
> *confirm Your covenant with us.*
> *Establish our descendants forever.*
> *In Your name, Jesus~"*

AUGUST 29

Please read Psalm 90.

Meditate on verse 1.

LORD, You have been our dwelling place in all generations.

Since the beginning of time, God made the opportunity to dwell with Him available to all people. You were created to praise Him! You were created to be His family, and He lavishly pours out His love on you. The LORD simply wants to be with you.

Ponder these truths about God (vs. 2, 8):

- The One who gave birth to the earth and the world wants to be with you.
- The One who is from everlasting to everlasting God wants to be with you.
- The One who knows your secret sins wants to be with you.
- The One who placed your sins before Him wants to be with you, so much so that He became your sins and died for them, so He can be with you (2 Corinthians 5:21).

If you are a Christian, then the LORD is your dwelling place; He is forever with you.

Pray Psalm 90:1, 14, and 16-17 over yourself and those for whom you stand guard as a faithful, prayerful watchman (Isaiah 62:6-7).

"LORD, thank You for being _____ and my dwelling place. Satisfy us in the morning with Your lovingkindness that we may sing for joy and be glad all our days. Let Your work appear to us, Your servants, and Your majesty to our children and grandchildren. O LORD our God, let Your favor be upon us. Establish the work of our hands; yes, establish the work of our hands. In Your name, Jesus-"

AUGUST 30

Please read Psalm 91. It is often called "The Warrior's Psalm." Many modern day warriors cling to it, even carrying a copy in their uniform pockets as they go into battle.

Meditate on verses 1 and 5a.

> *He who dwells in the shelter of the Most High*
> *will abide in the shadow of the Almighty.*
> *You will not be afraid of the terror by night …*

The psalmist wrote at least 3,000 years ago, yet his words speak about things happening today: terror, destruction, evil … And just like the psalmist's only sure shelter from wickedness was Almighty God, the Most High is your shield and bulwark, protecting you from plague and pestilence. As you totally depend on the LORD, hear Him talking to you:

> *"Because he has loved Me, therefore I will deliver him;*
> *I will set him securely on high because he has known My name.*
> *He will call upon Me, and I will answer him; I will be with*
> *him in trouble; I will rescue him and honor him. With a*
> *long life I will satisfy him and let him see My salvation."*
> —Psalm 91:14-16

If you love and know the LORD, claim His promises and pray Psalm 91:2-4 over yourself and those for whom you stand guard as a faithful, prayerful watchman (Isaiah 62:6-7).

> *"LORD, You are my refuge and my fortress,*
> *My God in whom I trust!*
> *Deliver _____ and me from the snare of the*
> *trapper and from the deadly pestilence.*
> *Cover us with Your pinions,*
> *and under Your wings let us seek refuge.*
> *Your faithfulness is our shield and bulwark.*
> *Because of Your name, Jesus~"*

AUGUST 31

Please read Psalm 92.

Meditate on verses 1-2.

> *It is good to give thanks to the LORD and to sing praises to Your name, O Most High; to declare Your lovingkindness in the morning and Your faithfulness by night.*

Why is it good to give God thanks?

- ✺ The works of His hands are great, and they make you glad (v. 4-5).
- ✺ His thoughts are very deep (v. 5).
- ✺ He is on high forever (v. 8).
- ✺ His enemies will perish, and all who do iniquity will be scattered (v. 9).
- ✺ He makes you righteous, so you flourish like the palm tree (v. 12).
- ✺ He plants in His house where you flourish in His courts (v. 13).
- ✺ He lets you yield fruit, even in old age (v. 14).

The LORD does all of the above, so you can declare that He is upright, that He is your rock, and that there is no unrighteousness in Him (v. 15).

So much to be thankful for! Spend this day thanking Him. And pray Psalm 92:1-2 and 12-15 as a faithful prayerful watchman (Isaiah 62:6-7).

> *"LORD, it is good to give You thanks and sing praises to Your name, O Most High.*
> *I will declare Your lovingkindness in the morning and Your faithfulness by night.*
> *Make _____ and me righteous.*
> *Let us flourish like the palm tree and grow like a cedar in Lebanon.*
> *Plant us in Your house, LORD, and let us flourish in Your courts.*
> *Let us still yield fruit in old age; let us be full of sap and very green, to declare that You are upright;*
> *You are our Rock, and there is no unrighteousness in You.*
> *Because You are the LORD Jesus~"*

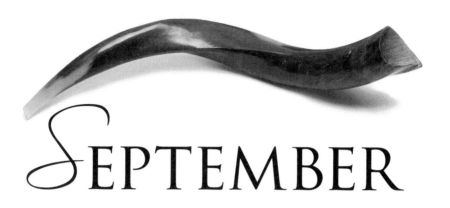

SEPTEMBER

On your walls, O Jerusalem,
I have appointed watchmen;
All day and all night they
will never keep silent.
You who remind the LORD,
take no rest for yourselves;
And give Him no rest until He establishes
And makes Jerusalem a
praise in the earth.
ISAIAH 62:6-7, NASB

September 1

Please read Psalm 93.

Meditate on verse 5.

> *Your testimonies are fully confirmed; holiness*
> *befits Your house, O LORD, forevermore.*

As a child of God, you are the house of God.

> *Christ was faithful as a Son over His house—whose house we are ...*
> —Hebrews 3:6

As a child of God, you are holy because He is holy.

> *Like the Holy One who called you, be holy yourselves also in all your*
> *behavior because it is written, "You shall be holy, for I am holy."*
> —1 Peter 1:15-16

As a child of God, you are fully confirmed in the LORD Jesus Christ.

> *Our LORD Jesus Christ will also confirm you to the end,*
> *blameless in the day of our LORD Jesus Christ.*
> —1 Corinthians 1:7b-8

Ponder these truths about who you are in Christ, and pray Psalm 93 in confident praise to your LORD.

> *"LORD, You reign! You are clothed with majesty.*
> *LORD, You have clothed and girded Yourself with strength.*
> *Indeed, the world is firmly established, it will not be moved.*
> *Your throne is established from of old; You are from everlasting. O*
> *LORD, the floods have lifted up their voice and their pounding waves.*
> *But more than the sounds of many waters and the mighty*
> *breakers of the sea, You, the LORD on high, are mighty!*
> *Your testimonies are fully confirmed.*
> *Thank You for confirming them in _____ and me.*
> *Holiness befits Your house. Make us holy, O LORD, forevermore.*
> *Because of You, LORD Jesus~"*

SEPTEMBER 2

Please read Psalm 94.

Meditate on verse 19.

*When my anxious thoughts multiply within
me, Your consolations delight my soul.*

The psalmist asked God questions which you may also have asked:

- ❧ O LORD, how long will the wicked exult (v. 3)?
- ❧ He who planted the ear, does He not hear; He who formed the eye, does He not see (v. 9)?
- ❧ He who chastens the nations and teaches man knowledge, will He not rebuke (v. 10)?
- ❧ Who will stand up for me against evildoers and those who do wickedness (v. 16)?
- ❧ Can a throne of destruction and mischief be allied with the LORD (v. 20)?

When you ask God questions, listen for His answers:

- ❧ A pit is dug for the wicked (v. 13).
- ❧ The LORD will not abandon His people (v. 14).
- ❧ Judgment will again be righteous for the upright in heart to follow (v. 15).
- ❧ The LORD is your help, and His lovingkindness will hold you up (vs. 17-18).
- ❧ The LORD is your stronghold and rock of refuge (v. 22).
- ❧ The LORD your God will bring wickedness back on the wicked and destroy them in their evil (v. 23).

Be consoled by the LORD and His Word and pray Psalm 94:17-19 and 22 over yourself and those for whom you stand guard as a faithful, prayerful watchman (Isaiah 62:6-7).

*"LORD, You are _____ and my help! Our souls will not
dwell in the abode of silence. When our feet slip, Your lovingkindness,
O LORD, will hold us up. When our anxious thoughts multiply
within us, Your consolations delight our souls. LORD, You are
our stronghold, and God, You are the Rock of our refuge, Jesus~"*

Please read Psalm 95.

Meditate on verses 7b-8a.

Today, if you would hear His voice, do not harden your hearts …

In a world full of wickedness and evil, it is tempting to be cynical and calloused; however, God exhorts you not to harden your heart. Heed His Words from Psalm 95:8-11:

> *"I loathed that hard-hearted generation who had seen My work, yet they tested and tried Me. They erred in their heart and did not know My ways. Therefore I swore in My anger, truly they shall not enter into My rest."*

Hear the LORD speaking to you, and accept His invitation to come into His presence with thanksgiving, joyfully singing and shouting to the Rock of your salvation (vs. 1-2). It is the cure for callousness and the antidote to hard-heartedness.

Come, worship, bow down, kneel before the LORD your Maker (v. 6) and praise Him with Psalm 95:3-5 and 7-8 as a faithful, prayerful watchman (Isaiah 62:6-7).

> *"LORD, You are a great God and a great King above all gods, in whose hand are the depths of the earth. The peaks of the mountains are Yours also. The sea is Yours, for You made it, and Your hands formed the dry land. You are _____ and my God! We are the people of Your pasture and the sheep of Your hand. Today, let us hear Your voice, and do not let us harden our hearts. For the sake of Your name, Jesus~"*

Please read Psalm 96.

Meditate on verse 2.

> *Sing to the LORD; bless His name; proclaim good
> tidings of His salvation from day to day.*

Psalm 96 answers many questions about worship.

- ⌘ Who is to worship?
  - All the earth (v. 1, 9)
  - Families of the peoples (v. 7)
- ⌘ What is worship?
  - Singing a new song to the LORD (v. 1)
  - Blessing His name and proclaiming good tidings of His salvation (v. 2)
  - Telling of His glory and wonderful deeds (v. 3)
  - Ascribing to God glory and strength, the glory of His name (vs. 7-8)
  - Bringing an offering and coming to His courts (v. 8)
- ⌘ Where does worship take place?
  - Among the nations and all the peoples (v. 3)
  - In His courts (v. 8)
- ⌘ When is worship?
  - From day to day (v. 2)
- ⌘ Why worship the LORD?
  - He is great, greatly to be praised, and to be feared above all gods (v. 4).
  - He made the heavens (v. 5).
  - Splendor, majesty, strength, and beauty are before Him and in His sanctuary (v. 6).
  - He is coming to judge the earth, the world, and the peoples in righteousness and faithfulness (v. 13).

◈ How do you worship?

- Trembling before Him in holy attire (v. 9) "Put on the LORD Jesus Christ ..." (Romans 13:14).
- By saying, "The LORD reigns; indeed the world is firmly established; it will not be moved. He will judge the peoples with equity" (v. 10).

The heavens, earth, sea and all it contains, field and all that is in it, and all the trees of the forest are worshipping the LORD (vs. 11-12). Join them by starting your worship with Psalm 96:4a.

"LORD, You are great and greatly to be praised ..."

Continue to worship all day, everyday.

SEPTEMBER 5

Please read Psalm 97.

Meditate on verses 9-10a.

> *For You are the LORD Most High over all the earth; You are exalted far above all gods. Hate evil, you who love the LORD...*

Some of the truths about the LORD from Psalm 97 are:

- ❧ He reigns (v. 1).
- ❧ Righteousness and justice are the foundation of His throne (v. 2).
- ❧ Fire goes before Him and burns up His adversaries (v. 3).
- ❧ He is LORD of the whole earth (v. 5).
- ❧ The heavens declare His righteousness, and all people have seen His glory (v. 6).
- ❧ He is Most High over all the earth and exalted far above all supernatural powers (v. 9).
- ❧ He preserves the souls of His Godly ones and delivers them from the wicked (v. 10).

Based on these truths about the LORD:

- ❧ Hate evil (v. 10)
- ❧ Be glad in Him (v. 12)
- ❧ Give thanks to His holy name (v. 12)

Pray Psalm 97:9-12 to the LORD as a faithful, prayerful watchman (Isaiah 62:6-7).

> *"LORD, You are Most High over all the earth.*
> *You are exalted (praised) far above all gods.*
> *_____ and I love You, LORD, and we hate evil.*
> *We are Your Godly ones; preserve our souls and*
> *deliver us from the hand of the wicked.*
> *Keep us righteous and upright in heart; sow light and gladness for us.*
> *We are Your righteous ones; we will be glad in You, LORD.*
> *We give thanks to Your holy name, Jesus~"*

Please read Psalm 98.

Meditate on verse 4.

> *Shout joyfully to the LORD, all the earth; break*
> *forth and sing for joy and sing praises.*

Psalm 98 tells you why the LORD is worthy of worship:

- ✤ He has done wonderful things (v. 1).
- ✤ His right hand and His holy arm have gained the victory for Him (v. 1).
- ✤ He has made known His salvation (v. 2).
- ✤ He has revealed His righteousness in the sight of the nations (v. 2).
- ✤ He has remembered His lovingkindness and His faithfulness to Israel (v. 3).
- ✤ All the ends of the earth have seen His salvation (v. 3).
- ✤ He is coming to judge the world with righteousness and equity (v. 9).

Join the sea, rivers, and mountains in roaring, clapping, and singing for joy to your LORD the King (vs. 6-7).

Praise Him with Psalm 98 as a faithful, prayerful watchman (Isaiah 62:6-7).

> *"LORD, You have done wonderful things! Your right hand and holy*
> *arm have gained the victory. You have made known Your salvation.*
> *You have revealed Your righteousness in the sight of the nations.*
> *You have remembered Your lovingkindness and faithfulness*
> *to the house of Israel. Thank You for remembering Your*
> *lovingkindness and faithfulness to my house, too.*
> *All the ends of the earth have seen Your salvation.*
> *Cause _____ to see Your salvation before You*
> *come to judge the world with righteousness and equity.*
> *You are worthy of all the shouting, singing, praising,*
> *roaring, and clapping, Our LORD, our King, Jesus~"*

Please read Psalm 99.

Meditate on verse 9.

> *Exalt the LORD our God and worship at His*
> *holy hill, for holy is the LORD our God.*

God expects you to exalt and worship Him because He is holy, great, and awesome (v. 3). There is no one and nothing in the entire universe that compares with Him.

You live in a world where people are easily awe-struck. The presence of actors, athletes, authors, authorities, etc. can create excitement and uproar. But before swooning over a human, keep in mind:

> *The LORD reigns; let the peoples tremble.*
> *He is enthroned above the cherubim; let the earth shake!*
> —Psalm 99:1

The only One worthy of people trembling and shaking is the LORD. As you ponder Him, realize only He deserves your awe.

Pray Psalm 99:1-5 and 9 in awesome wonder to your LORD.

> *"LORD, You reign; let the peoples tremble!*
> *You are enthroned above the cherubim; let the earth shake!*
> *LORD, You are great in Zion, and You*
> *are exalted above all the peoples.*
> *Let us praise Your great and awesome name; You are holy.*
> *Your strength, O King, loves justice; You have established*
> *equity; You have executed justice and righteousness in Jacob.*
> *Please execute justice and righteousness in our land.*
> *I exalt You, LORD our God, and worship at Your footstool.*
> *You are holy!I exalt You, LORD our God,*
> *and worship at Your holy hill,*
> *For You are holy, LORD our God, Jesus~"*

Please read Psalm 100.

Meditate on verses 1 and 5.

> *Shout joyfully to the LORD, all the earth. For the LORD is good; His lovingkindness is everlasting and His faithfulness to all generations.*

In the midst of daily life: family, jobs, activities, illness, national and global crises ... it is easy to lose focus on the LORD. Thankfully, God gave you His *Psalms*, the book of 150 prayers, praises, and songs that declare truth about Him. *Psalms* helps you regain the focus God expects from His creation. It gives you ways to articulate moments in life too glorious and/ or difficult for words. *Psalms* helps you intimately and genuinely worship your Creator and Savior.

Hopefully the past 100 days, your summer of psalms, have given you the holy habit of meditating on and praising God. Thank Him for what He has taught you and pray Psalm 100 as a faithful, prayerful watchman (Isaiah 62:6-7).

> *"I shout joyfully to You, LORD! I will serve You with gladness and come before You with joyful singing. LORD, I know You are God. You made _____ and me, and not we ourselves. We are Your people and the sheep of Your pasture. Let us enter Your gates with thanksgiving and Your courts with praise. We give thanks to You and bless Your name, for You are good. Your lovingkindness is everlasting and Your faithfulness to all generations. Thank You, LORD Jesus, in Your Holy name~"*

SEPTEMBER 9

Please read Jeremiah 1.

Meditate on verse 9.

> *Then the LORD stretched out His hand and touched my mouth, and the LORD said to me, "Behold, I have put My Words in your mouth."*

For the next 52 days, you will read the book of *Jeremiah*. Jeremiah was a preacher in Jerusalem for 53 years. His ministry started in 627 BC, 22 years before Judah was first conquered by the Babylonians.

God called Jeremiah to preach to people who needed to hear and heed His Word. God put His words in Jeremiah's mouth and told him to speak everything He commanded him to say (vs. 9, 17). The people would fight against Jeremiah, but he was not to be dismayed; God would deliver him.

If you are a follower of Jesus Christ, you have a calling from God. He expects you to obey His plan for your life. Do not be dismayed! The LORD promises to always be with you (Matthew 28:19-20).

Pray Jeremiah 1:7-9 over yourself and those for whom you stand guard as a faithful, prayerful watchman (Isaiah 62:6-7).

> *"LORD, help _____ and me stop making excuses. Everywhere You send us, help us go.*
> *All You command us, let us speak.*
> *Help us not be afraid of people.*
> *Thank You for being with us to deliver us.*
> *Touch our mouths, LORD,*
> *and put Your Words into our mouths.*
> *For Your name's sake, Jesus~"*

Please read Jeremiah 2.

Meditate on these phrases from verses 4 and 31.

> *Hear the Word of the LORD ... O generation,*
> *heed the Word of the LORD...*

The book of *Jeremiah* contains the Words of the LORD which God put into Jeremiah's mouth (Jeremiah 1:9). Jeremiah spoke the Words, and his scribe, Baruch, recorded them (Jeremiah 36:4). 2,600 years later, you have the privilege of holding God's Words in your hand and reading them. Amazing!

God issued a timeless command, "O generation, heed the Word of the LORD" (v. 31). Your current generation is commanded by God to heed, observe carefully, and give attention to His Word.

Do you hear and heed God's Word, or do you give your attention to things that offend God? The Israelites were so deluded by sin they thought they were innocent (v. 35). God judged them severely for their wickedness, but He first had Jeremiah proclaim, "Thus says the LORD ..." (v. 2).

God is talking to you. Hear and heed what He says as you read His Words in *Jeremiah*.

Pray Jeremiah 2:5, 9, 13, and 31 over yourself and those for whom you stand guard as a faithful, prayerful watchman (Isaiah 62:6-7).

> *"LORD, help _____ and me not go far from You.*
> *Let us not walk after emptiness and become empty.*
> *LORD, we do not want You to have to contend with us*
> *or with our children's children. Help us to never forsake*
> *You, the fountain of living waters. Do not let us hew for*
> *ourselves broken cisterns that can hold no water.*
> *Make us the generation that heeds Your Word,*
> *LORD. In Your name, Jesus~"*

Please read Jeremiah 3.

Meditate on verse 22a.

> *"Return, O faithless sons; I will heal your faithlessness."*

God allegorized the history of Israel in Jeremiah 3. God compared Himself to a husband; Israel was His wife. Because of idol worship, Israel was an unfaithful wife with many lovers. God called her idolatry, "harlotry," and reasoned with her that He should divorce her for her wickedness. Yet God in His undying love, made one of the saddest statements in the Bible, "I thought, 'After she has done all these things, she will return to Me,' but she did not return" (v. 7).

The Assyrians destroyed Israel in 722 BC. Her "sister" Judah watched the destruction, yet she, too, refused God's undeserved invitation to return to Him with all her heart, which resulted in her destruction by the Babylonians beginning in 605 BC.

God recorded this story because He wants you to be wiser than Israel and Judah, and He desires you to accept His invitation to come to Him.

Pray Jeremiah 3:12-13, 15, 17, and 22 over yourself and those for whom you stand guard as a faithful, prayerful watchman (Isaiah 62:6-7).

> *"LORD, may _____ and I heed*
> *Your invitation to return to You.*
> *Thank You for being gracious and not looking upon us*
> *in anger. Thank You for not being angry forever. We*
> *acknowledge our iniquity. We have transgressed against*
> *You, LORD our God, and not obeyed Your voice.*
> *Make us shepherds after Your own heart. Let us feed on*
> *Your knowledge and understanding. Do not let us walk*
> *anymore after the stubbornness of our evil heart!*
> *LORD our God, we return to You; heal our faithlessness.*
> *Because of Your name, Jesus~"*

SEPTEMBER 12

Please read Jeremiah 4.

Meditate on verse 14.

> *Wash your heart from evil, O Jerusalem, that you may be saved.*
> *How long will your wicked thoughts lodge within you?*

The people of Judah had heart issues. Bitter evil touched their hearts; the wicked thoughts lodged within them made their hearts evil (vs. 14, 18). God told them to "remove the foreskins" of their sin hardened hearts (v. 4). His approaching judgment would make the heart of the king and the princes fail (v. 9).

When God told Jeremiah of the coming devastation because of the people's rebellious ways, his soul was in anguish. Jeremiah cried out, "Oh, my heart! My heart is pounding in me" (v. 19).

The Word of the LORD caused Jeremiah's heart to pound. His heart was tender towards God. His Word so affected Jeremiah he spent 53 years of his life not keeping silent but proclaiming the Word of God.

How does God's Word impact you? Is your heart hardened by the deceitfulness of sin, or is it circumcised by Jesus Christ (Hebrews 3:13; Colossians 2:11)?

Pray Jeremiah 4:19 and 22 over yourself and those for whom you stand guard as a faithful, prayerful watchman (Isaiah 62:6-7).

> *"LORD, may _____ and my heart*
> *pound when we hear Your Word.*
> *Let us not keep silent about what we hear.*
> *Do not let us be foolish people. Let us know You, LORD.*
> *Stop us from being stupid children who have no understanding.*
> *Do not let us be shrewd to do evil.*
> *Teach us to do good.*
> *In Your name, Jesus~"*

SEPTEMBER 13

Please read Jeremiah 5.

Meditate on verse 24a.

They do not say in their heart, "Let us now fear the LORD our God."

Refusing to fear the LORD, the people used God's name in vain and lied about Him. Their homes were filled with deceit. They were wealthy, so they thought their relationship with God was just fine. Instead of speaking God's Word, their preachers preached falsely, and their priests ruled by their own authority, and the people loved it (vs. 2-4, 12, 24, 27, 31).

God warned Judah of His coming judgment because of such arrogant rebellion. Even the waves of the sea obey God and stay within the boundaries He sets for them, yet the people defied God's ways and refused to tremble in His presence (v. 22).

Hear and heed the Word of the LORD! Who do you fear people or God? Do your preachers and teachers speak the truth of God's Word, or do they teach lies?

At the end of Jeremiah 5, God asks a question, "What will you do at the end of it?" How will you answer Him?

Pray Jeremiah 5:22-23 over yourself and those for whom you stand guard as a faithful, prayerful watchman (Isaiah 62:6-7).

"LORD, You have established boundaries
for _____ and me; do not let us cross them.
You have issued eternal decrees; do not
allow us to prevail against them.
May we fear You and tremble in Your presence, LORD.
Remove our stubborn and rebellious heart.
Do not let us turn aside and depart from You.
In Your name, Jesus~"

Please read Jeremiah 6.

Meditate on this sentence from verse 15.

> *They were not even ashamed at all; they*
> *did not even know how to blush.*

God prepared war and great destruction against Jerusalem for refusing to walk in His ways. The LORD condemned the people for their abominations. Some of His indictments included:

- They kept their wickedness fresh (v. 7).
- Everyone dealt falsely (v. 13).
- They had no shame (v. 15).
- They did not even know how to blush (v. 15).
- They refused to walk in the good path (v. 16).
- They refused to listen to God's Words (v. 19).
- They were stubbornly rebellious (v. 28).

There were preachers among the people who healed their brokenness superficially instead of teaching how to walk with God deeply, in holiness (13-14). God appointed Jeremiah as His messenger of truth. His sermons were not superficial; they were God's Words that truly heal brokenness.

God's Words spoken 2,600 years ago are still fresh today. Examine your life by His Word. Does "stubbornly rebellious" describe you? Is there fresh wickedness in your family? Hear and heed God's Word, and pray it over yourself and those for whom you stand guard as a faithful, prayerful watchman (Isaiah 62:6-7).

Pray Jeremiah 6:16.

> *"LORD, _____ and I are standing by the ways,*
> *looking and asking for the ancient paths where Your good way is.*
> *We want to walk in it. As we do, let us find rest for our souls.*
> *In Your name, Jesus~"*

SEPTEMBER 15

Please read Jeremiah 7.

Meditate on what God said in verse 23.

> *"Obey My voice, and I will be your God, and you will be My people; and you will walk in all the way which I command you, that it may be well with you."*

God prepared Jeremiah to be a preacher from the time he was in his mother's womb. His first recorded sermon was at the gate of the LORD's house (Jeremiah 1:5-9; 7:2).

The people worshipped in the beautiful temple built by King Solomon, and they were proud of it. They thought going to the temple freed them to spend the rest of their week stealing, murdering, committing adultery, swearing falsely, walking after other gods, and even sacrificing their own children (vs. 8-10, 31-32).

Jeremiah's sermon was one of warning with an opportunity to repent before it was too late. God would destroy the temple and pour out His wrath on the people and the land unless they changed their behavior.

Examine your life. Do you justify behaviors that are detestable to the LORD? Who and what are you sacrificing to get ahead? Are you proud of the church you attend, but ignore Jesus who is the Head of your church?

Pray Jeremiah 7:23-24 over yourself and those for whom you stand guard as a faithful, prayerful watchman (Isaiah 62:6-7).

> *"LORD, help _____ and me obey Your voice.*
> *We want You to be our God; we want to be Your people.*
> *May we walk in the way You command*
> *us, that it may be well with us.*
> *Help us to obey and incline our ear to You.*
> *Do not let us walk in our own counsels and*
> *in the stubbornness of an evil heart.*
> *May we stop going backward! Let us go forward*
> *with You, LORD! In Your name, Jesus~"*

Please read Jeremiah 8.

Meditate on what God said in verse 7.

"My people do not know the ordinance of the LORD."

Jeremiah preached to people who chose to live in sin and wickedness instead of the LORD's righteousness. Choosing sin was choosing death, and the time would come when the people would be left with only dead bones to spread out to the sun, moon, and stars they worshipped (vs. 1-2).

The people were in a pathetic place. They surrounded themselves with others who condoned their sinful behavior. The scribes wrote lies and rejected God's Word. The people were not ashamed of their disgusting behavior (vs. 8-9, 12).

Jeremiah preached God's Word; he told about the coming judgment for refusing to repent. The horrible sin, lack of repentance, and impending destruction caused Jeremiah to be sorrowful beyond healing. He was broken for the brokenness of his people (vs. 18, 21).

What is your attitude toward sin? Does it break your heart to see lives destroyed by it? Your world is grievously similar to Jeremiah's. Do not be tempted to condone behavior that is an abomination to God. Hear and heed the Word of the LORD and share it with others.

Pray Jeremiah 8:7 and 13a over yourself and those for whom you stand guard as a faithful, prayerful watchman (Isaiah 62:6-7).

"LORD, even the stork, the turtledove, the swift,
and the thrush know the seasons and the
migrations You have appointed for them.
LORD, make _____ and me know Your ordinances,
so You will not have to snatch us away.
In Your name, Jesus~"

Please read Jeremiah 9.

Meditate on verse 24.

> *Let him who boasts boast of this, that he understands*
> *and knows Me, that I am the LORD who exercises*
> *lovingkindness, justice, and righteousness on earth, for*
> *I delight in these things, declares the LORD.*

Jeremiah is described as the "weeping prophet." His eyes were a fountain of tears as he grieved for his people steeped in sin (vs. 1, 10).

Instead of annihilation, God offered the people something truly remarkable, something they could even boast about. Their Creator desired these sinful, idolatrous people to understand and intimately know Him.

Ponder that truth because God's invitation is for you and those you love. The LORD wants you to understand and know Him. He even gives you permission to boast that you do. Why would anyone choose to know sin when the Creator of your soul draws you into a personal relationship of knowing Him?

Pray Jeremiah 9:13-14, 23-24, and 26 over yourself and those for whom you stand guard as a faithful, prayerful watchman (Isaiah 62:6-7).

> *"LORD, _____ and I have forsaken*
> *Your law which You set before us.*
> *Forgive us for not obeying Your voice nor*
> *walking according to Your Word.*
> *Help us stop walking after the stubbornness of our heart.*
> *LORD, we are done boasting about our wisdom*
> *and our might and our riches.*
> *Let us boast of this, that we understand and know You,*
> *that You are the LORD who exercises lovingkindness,*
> *justice, and righteousness on earth.*
> *You delight in those things.*
> *LORD, circumcise our hearts!*
> *In Your name, Jesus~"*

Please read Jeremiah 10.

Meditate on verse 8.

> *But they are altogether stupid and foolish. In their*
> *discipline of delusion—their idol is wood!*

God expressed clearly what He thinks about idols and the people who put their trust in them. Idols are like scarecrows in a cucumber field that have to be carried because they cannot walk; those who trust in such things instead of trusting the LORD "are altogether stupid and foolish" (vs. 5, 8).

God used the word stupid three times in this chapter. People are stupid and devoid of knowledge when they trust in the works of their hands and do not seek the LORD (vs. 14, 21).

God contrasted Himself to idols in verses 10 and 12.

    ∞ The LORD is:
- the true God
- the living God
- the everlasting King
- the One who made the earth by His power
- the One who established the world by His wisdom

What are you hoping will make your life better, but it is actually adding to your burden? Do not be stupid; let the true and living God, who made the earth by His power, establish and care for you and those you love.

Pray Jeremiah's prayer of confession in Jeremiah 10:23 and 24 over yourself and those for whom you stand guard as a faithful, prayerful watchman (Isaiah 62:6-7).

> *"O LORD, the way You want _____ and*
> *me to go is not in ourselves. It is not in us to be*
> *able to direct our own steps; we need You.*
> *O LORD, correct us with your justice;*
> *not with Your anger.*
> *For Your name's sake, Jesus~"*

Please read Jeremiah 11.

Meditate on what God says in verse 4.

"Listen to My voice, and do according to all which I command you..."

Jeremiah's next sermon was in the cities of Judah and the streets of Jerusalem (v. 6). The message from God was simple: "Hear the words of this covenant and do them" (v. 6). The people responded to the sermon as their ancestors had done before them; each person walked in the stubbornness of his evil heart (v. 8). God promised to respond with disaster.

When Jeremiah delivered the message to his hometown of Anathoth, the people wanted to kill him (Jeremiah 1:1; 11:21). It is not always easy to tell people the truth of God's Word. Thankfully, the LORD protected Jeremiah from those who did not want to hear about His covenant.

When God told Jeremiah the message, he responded with: "Amen, O LORD" (v. 5). When the people heard the message, they responded with: "Let us cut him off from the land of the living that his name be remembered no more" (v. 19).

What is your response to the Word of God? Jeremiah's "amen" meant, "so be it." Do you respond to the LORD by saying, "So be it God; I am ready to do whatever you tell me"?

Pray Jeremiah 11:4-5 and 8 over yourself and those for whom you stand guard as a faithful, prayerful watchman (Isaiah 62:6-7).

"LORD, help _____ and me listen to Your voice
and do according to all which You command us.
We want to be Your people, and we want You to be our God.
Do not let us walk after the stubbornness of our evil hearts.
Amen, O LORD Jesus~"

Please read Jeremiah 12.

Meditate on verse 3a.

> *But You know me, O LORD; You see me, and You*
> *examine my heart's attitude toward You.*

Jeremiah preached to people who said the name "God," yet He was the farthest thing from their mind (v. 2). They did not think about the LORD and His Word as they made decisions and walked through their days. They pleased themselves, their idols, and the wicked people around them (vs. 14-17). They refused to listen and take God and His Word to heart (vs. 11,17).

Jeremiah was the opposite. He had an intimate relationship with the LORD. Jeremiah discussed matters with God, and he knew the LORD saw him and was listening to him (vs. 1, 3).

Think about your walk with the LORD. Do you attend church, sing a few songs about God, then go through the rest of your week without giving Him another thought? Or do you live life with the LORD, wanting to please Him, discussing everything with Him, aware that He knows everything about you?

Pray Jeremiah 12:2-3 over yourself and those for whom you stand guard as a faithful, prayerful watchman (Isaiah 62:6-7).

> *"LORD, You have planted _____ and me.*
> *We have taken root; we grow and produce fruit.*
> *Make it good fruit for You!*
> *LORD, be near to our lips and on our minds.*
> *You know us, O LORD; You see us,*
> *and You examine our heart's attitude toward You.*
> *Make us pleasing to You.*
> *In Your name, Jesus-"*

Please read Jeremiah 13.

Meditate on verse 15.

Listen and give heed, do not be haughty, for the LORD has spoken.

God told Jeremiah to create an interesting sermon illustration. Jeremiah took a waistband, put it around his waist, went to the Euphrates River, and hid it in a rock crevice. After many days, he returned to the Euphrates and dug out the waistband, which was totally ruined (vs. 1-7).

The waistband was a picture of Judah's pride. Like a waistband clings to the waist, the people clung to their foolish pride instead of clinging to God. In their wickedness, God declared them totally worthless just like the worthless waistband (v. 10).

Jeremiah begged the people to listen to the LORD, but they refused. They were eventually taken captive by the Babylonians and marched from Jerusalem to Babylon. Their route took them by the Euphrates River where Jeremiah had once buried a waistband. The sermon illustration was no longer ridiculous to them. "Oh, if we had only heeded the Word of the LORD before it was too late!"

God's Word is timeless truth, carefully preserved, so you do not repeat mistakes from the past. Hear and heed His Word! Let go of pride and cling to God.

Pray Jeremiah 13:11 and 15-16 over yourself and those for whom you stand guard as a faithful, prayerful watchman (Isaiah 62:6-7).

"LORD, as the waistband clings to the waist of a man, _____ and I want to cling to You. We want to be Your people for Your renown, praise, and glory. Help us listen to You! We want to listen, give heed, and not be haughty. We give glory to You, God! Do not let our feet stumble. In Your name, Jesus~"

SEPTEMBER 22

Please read Jeremiah 14.

Meditate on verse 9b.

> *You are in our midst, O LORD, and we are*
> *called by Your name; do not forsake us!*

Sin took its toll, not only on the people of Judah, but on the land and the animals. The water was gone; the ground was cracked, and the animals abandoned their newborn babies because there was no grass (vs. 1-6).

Amazingly, in the midst of the drought, the false prophets said there would not be a famine. In the name of the LORD, they said everything was going to be fine. God said they were preaching the deception of their own minds (vs. 13-14).

As you read Jeremiah, does the attitude of the people and the false preachers remind you of today? False teachers preach that God just wants you to be happy, prosperous, and blessed. People do whatever feels good with no regard for what God thinks about their behavior.

Do not be deceived! Just because current laws or religious teachings legalize and condone sin, God still hates sin and punishes those participating in and approving it. Surround yourself with God's Word and with people who are not afraid to teach what the LORD says.

Pray Jeremiah 14:20-22 over yourself and those for whom you stand guard as a faithful, prayerful watchman (Isaiah 62:6-7).

> *"We know our wickedness, O LORD.*
> *_____ and I have sinned against You.*
> *Do not despise us for Your name's sake;*
> *do not disgrace the throne of Your glory.*
> *Remember and do not annul Your covenant with us.*
> *We hope in You, O LORD our God, Jesus Christ~"*

Please read Jeremiah 15.

Meditate on verse 16.

> *Your Words were found and I ate them, and Your Words*
> *became for me a joy and the delight of my heart, for I have*
> *been called by Your name, O LORD God of hosts.*

As the people of Judah forsook God, they kept going backward. God grew tired of relenting on behalf of those living in unrelenting sin, so He declared their destiny: death, famine, captivity, anguish, and dismay (vs. 1-8).

Jeremiah did not forsake the LORD. God and His Word became the delight of Jeremiah's heart (v. 16). God was pleased with Jeremiah and promised to save and deliver him from the hand of the wicked (vs. 20-21).

How would you describe your life; are you going backward or forward? Cling to God and devour His Word. When you do, you will experience His joy.

Pray Jeremiah 15:19-21 over yourself and those for whom you stand guard as a faithful, prayerful watchman (Isaiah 62:6-7).

> *"LORD, _____ and I want to return*
> *to You and be restored to You.*
> *Let us stand before You. Help us to extract*
> *the precious from the worthless.*
> *Make us Your spokesmen.*
> *Make us a fortified wall of bronze,*
> *and though others may fight against us,*
> *do not let them prevail over us.*
> *Be with us to save us and deliver us.*
> *Deliver us from the hand of the wicked and*
> *redeem us from the grasp of the violent.*
> *For Your name's sake, Jesus-"*

Please read Jeremiah 16.

Meditate on verse 21.

> *Therefore behold, I am going to make them **know**—this
> time I will make them **know** My power and My might;
> and they shall **know** that My name is the LORD.*

Up to this point in Israel's history, the nation was famous for the LORD bringing them out of slavery in Egypt. God was about to banish them to Babylon because of their stubbornness and refusal to listen to Him. From that point on, they would be remembered for the LORD sending them to Babylon and other nations as punishment for forsaking Him (vs. 10-15). The Babylonian exile became a cornerstone in Israel's history.

God was and still is unrelenting in His pursuit of Israel. He brings calamity on them, rather than allowing them to continue in their iniquity, because He wants them to **know** that they **know** that they **know** He is the LORD (vs. 10, 17, 21).

God pursues you and those you love with the same diligence. He wants you to **know** that you **know** that you **know** He is the LORD. He wants you to be like Jeremiah who intimately knew God as his strength, his stronghold, and his refuge (v. 19).

Pray Jeremiah 16:19 and 21 over yourself and those for whom you stand guard as a faithful, prayerful watchman (Isaiah 62:6-7).

> *"LORD, You are _____ and my strength and stronghold.*
> *You are our refuge in the day of distress. _____ has*
> *inherited nothing but falsehood, futility, and things of no profit.*
> *Make them know—this time, make them*
> *know Your power and might.*
> *Make them know Your name is the LORD.*
> *In Your name, LORD Jesus~"*

Please read Jeremiah 17.

Meditate on verse 7.

> *Blessed is the man who trusts in the LORD*
> *and whose trust is the LORD.*

God gave a sharp contrast between trusting in mankind and trusting in Him. Those who make flesh their strength and whose heart turns away from the LORD are cursed. Those who trust in the LORD are blessed; they are like a tree planted by water that is not anxious even in a year of drought (vs. 5-8).

Why would anyone choose a life of curses instead of God's blessings? People make sinful decisions because the heart is deceitful and desperately sick (v. 9).

Jeremiah knew the One who cures sin sickness. He cried out, "Heal me, O LORD, and I will be healed; save me and I will be saved, for You are my praise!" (v. 14).

Let the LORD heal you. Choose to listen to Him and obey His Word.

Pray Jeremiah 17:7-8 and 14 over yourself and those for whom you stand guard as a faithful, prayerful watchman (Isaiah 62:6-7).

> *"LORD, may _____ and I be people who trust in You.*
> *LORD, be our trust! Make us like a tree planted by*
> *the water that extends its roots by a stream.*
> *Do not let us fear when the heat comes, but let our leaves be green.*
> *Do not let us be anxious in a year of drought nor cease to yield fruit.*
> *Heal us, O LORD, and we will be healed;*
> *save us and we will be saved,*
> *for You are our praise, LORD Jesus~"*

Please read Jeremiah 18.

Meditate on verse 6.

> *"Can I not, O house of Israel, deal with you as this potter*
> *does?" declares the LORD. "Behold, like the clay in the*
> *potter's hand, so are you in My hand, O house of Israel."*

God sent Jeremiah to the potter's house for another sermon illustration. Jeremiah watched the potter remake a spoiled vessel into a vessel that pleased him. God told Jeremiah He would use calamity to reshape Judah into a nation pleasing to Him (v. 11).

The people responded to God's invitation to repent with willful disobedience.

> *"We are going to follow our own plans, and each of us will*
> *act according to the stubbornness of his evil heart."*
> —Jeremiah 18:12b

God called them appalling (v. 13). He promised calamity, and when it came, they would only see God's back and not His face (v. 17).

Hear and heed the Word of the LORD! If you are a child of God, He will mold you into a vessel pleasing to Him. And you have a choice to make. You can be a malleable vessel, easily molded by the Potter. Or you can be a stubborn vessel fighting His every touch. It is a pathetic place to be when God fashions calamity because a person refuses to be fashioned by their Creator.

Pray Jeremiah 18:4 and 6 over yourself and those for whom you stand guard as a faithful, prayerful watchman (Isaiah 62:6-7).

> *"LORD, forgive _____ and me for being spoiled.*
> *Make us into vessels that please You.*
> *We want to be clay in Your hands that You mold,*
> *not clay that You have to deal with.*
> *In Your name, Jesus~"*

Please read Jeremiah 19.

Meditate on verse 15.

> *Thus says the LORD of hosts, the God of Israel, "Behold, I*
> *am about to bring on this city and all its towns the entire*
> *calamity that I have declared against it, because they have*
> *stiffened their necks so as not to heed My Words."*

While Jeremiah was at the potter's house, God told him to buy an earthenware jar. He took the jar along with some of the elders and senior priests to the valley of Ben-Hinnom, the valley where the people sacrificed their children by fire as part of their Baal worship. The elders and senior priests should have taught and upheld truth to the people; rather they allowed heinous atrocities to take place. God promised calamity. Jeremiah spoke the Word of the LORD to the men then broke the jar in front of them to represent the irreparable breaking God would do to the people.

Jeremiah then walked to the court of the LORD's house, not far from the valley of Slaughter, and spoke to all the people. His sermon was simple; God promised to bring on Jerusalem and all its towns the entire calamity because the people had stiffened their necks so as not to heed His Words (v. 15).

If you are a teacher/preacher of God's Word, fearlessly speak the Word of Truth. People are perishing for lack of knowledge of what the Bible says (Hosea 4:6). If you are a hearer of the Word, heed and obey what God tells you to do.

Pray Jeremiah 19:11 and 15 over yourself and those for whom you stand guard as a faithful, prayerful watchman (Isaiah 62:6-7).

> *"LORD, let _____ and me live to please You,*
> *so You do not have to break us like one breaking a potter's vessel,*
> *which cannot again be repaired.*
> *Do not let us stiffen our necks.*
> *May we heed Your Words.*
> *In Your name, Jesus-"*

SEPTEMBER 28

Please read Jeremiah 20.

Meditate on verse 11a.

But the LORD is with me like a dread champion.

Jeremiah needed a dread champion (one to be greatly feared) as he preached God's Word and was persecuted for it. Jeremiah had thoughts about no longer speaking the Word of the LORD, but those thoughts created a burning in his heart and bones. He had to speak God's truth (vs. 7-9).

The sermon he delivered in the court of the temple (Jeremiah 19:14-15) resulted in beatings and being put in the stocks by Pashhur, the chief priest. Upon his release, Jeremiah delivered another message; this one was personally for Pashhur. The LORD promised to make the false prophet Pashhur a terror to himself and all his friends. His friends would be killed, and Pashhur would die as an exile in Babylon (vs. 3-6).

Do you proclaim the truth of God's Word despite what others say and do? Or are you a Pashhur, telling people what they want to hear?

In the face of opposition and persecution, Jeremiah prayed. Pray his prayer from Jeremiah 20:11-13 over yourself and those for whom you stand guard as a faithful, prayerful watchman (Isaiah 62:6-7).

"LORD, be with _____ and me like a dread champion;
let our persecutors stumble and not prevail.
Let them be utterly ashamed because they have failed with
an everlasting disgrace that will not be forgotten.
O LORD of hosts, You test the righteous;
You see the mind and the heart;
let us see Your vengeance on them, for to You,
we set forth our cause.
We sing to You, LORD; we praise You!
Deliver our needy souls from the hand of evildoers.
For Your name's sake, Jesus~"

Please read Jeremiah 21. Pashhur in this chapter is not the same Pashhur in Jeremiah 20; they have different fathers (Jeremiah 20:1; 21:1).

Meditate on verse 8b.

> *Thus says the LORD, "Behold, I set before you*
> *the way of life and the way of death."*

Observe carefully what God said in this chapter.

> *"I Myself will war against you with an outstretched hand*
> *and a mighty arm, even in anger and wrath and great*
> *indignation. I will also strike down the inhabitants of this city,*
> *both man and beast; they will die of a great pestilence. For I*
> *have set My face against this city for harm and not for good.*
> *I will punish you according to the results of your deeds."*
> —Jeremiah 21:5-6, 10a, 14a

Did you know God has anger, wrath, and great indignation? Does it surprise you that God sets His face against people to punish them for their sinful deeds? Does knowing these truths about God impact your choices and behaviors? How will you apply these truths to your life?

God gave the people of Judah a choice; they could choose the way of life or the way of death. God gives you the same choice; which do you pick?

Pray Jeremiah 21:12 over yourself and those for whom you stand guard as a faithful, prayerful watchman (Isaiah 62:6-7).

> *"LORD, help _____ and me to administer*
> *justice every morning and deliver the person who has*
> *been robbed from the power of his oppressor.*
> *We do not want Your wrath to go forth like fire*
> *and burn with none to extinguish it.*
> *LORD, keep us from evil deeds.*
> *For the sake of Your name, Jesus~"*

Please read Jeremiah 22.

Meditate on this phrase from verses 2 and 29.

Hear the Word of the LORD.
Hear the Word of the LORD!

Jeremiah's next pulpit was at the palace of the king of Judah. He delivered a six-point sermon. The LORD told the king, his servants, and all the people to do the following (v. 3):

- Do justice.
- Do righteousness.
- Deliver the one who has been robbed from the power of his oppressor.
- Do not mistreat the stranger, orphan, or widow.
- Do not do violence to the stranger, orphan, or widow.
- Do not shed innocent blood.

If the king and his people obeyed God, they would continue to have a king on the throne; if they disobeyed, God would make the palace a desolation (vs. 4-5). King Jehoiakim refused to hear and heed God's Word. God promised him a donkey's burial beyond the gates of Jerusalem (v. 19).

Hear the Word of the LORD! God does not want your life to be desolate. Sin desolates; obedience averts desolation. Ask God to show you areas of disobedience. Repent and commit to walk obediently with Him.

Pray the opposite of Jeremiah 22:21 to be true in your life and the lives of those for whom you stand guard as a faithful, prayerful watchman (Isaiah 62:6-7).

"LORD, when You speak to _____ and me, we will listen!
Forgive the practices from our youth not to obey Your voice.
Help us practice obedience now! Let it be the practice of
our children from their youth to obey Your voice.
In Your name, Jesus~"

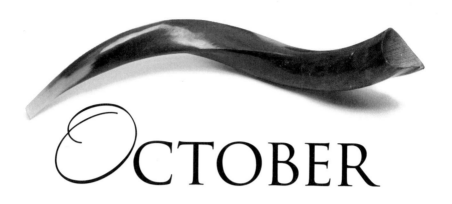

OCTOBER

On your walls, O Jerusalem,
I have appointed watchmen;
All day and all night they
will never keep silent.
You who remind the LORD,
take no rest for yourselves;
And give Him no rest until He establishes
And makes Jerusalem a
praise in the earth.
ISAIAH 62:6-7, NASB

OCTOBER 1

Please read Jeremiah 23. It describes your world.

Meditate on verse 28b. God is talking.

> *"Let him who has My Word speak My Word in truth."*

God addressed preachers, prophets, teachers, and anyone who declared, "I have a word from the LORD." God is against those who prophesy false dreams and declare lies in His name (vs. 31-32). He warned people not to claim revelation from the LORD that is actually born from "the deception of their own heart" (v. 26).

Do not be deceived! Everything you read and hear must be filtered through the truth of the Bible. If someone declares they have a word from the LORD, it must not contradict the LORD's Word; if it does, that person has "perverted the Words of the living God" (v. 36).

As you continue to read and study the Bible, you will be able to discern truth from lies. Ask God to give you His Biblical worldview.

Pray Jeremiah 23:22 and 28 over yourself and those for whom you stand guard as a faithful, prayerful watchman (Isaiah 62:6-7).

> *"LORD, let _____ and me announce Your Words to Your people.*
> *Use Your Words to turn us back from our evil*
> *way and from the evil of our deeds.*
> *We have Your Word;*
> *let us speak Your Word in truth.*
> *In Your name, Jesus~"*

Please read Jeremiah 24.

Meditate on verse 7.

> *I will give them a heart to know Me, for I am the LORD;*
> *and they will be My people, and I will be their God,*
> *for they will return to Me with their whole heart.*

God took Jeremiah back to His temple to preach the fig sermon. The LORD showed Jeremiah two baskets of figs; one contained very rotten figs, and the other contained very good figs (v 2). The good figs represented the people exiled to Babylon. At the time of this sermon, ten thousand Jews had recently been taken captive to Babylon (2 Kings 24:10-17). God promised to keep His eyes on them for good, to build them up, plant them, give them a heart to know Him, and bring them back to the land of Israel (vs. 5-7). Those left behind in Jerusalem were like the bad figs that were too rotten to eat. God promised to destroy them (vs. 8-10).

Which fig are you? Is God taking you through trials of exilic proportions for the purpose of building and planting you? He wants you firmly established in Him, so you will not be overthrown and plucked up. God has His eyes on you for good.

Pray Jeremiah 24:2 and 7 over yourself and those for whom you stand guard as a faithful, prayerful watchman (Isaiah 62:6-7).

> *"LORD, make _____ and me first-ripe, very good figs.*
> *Do not let us be very bad, rotten figs.*
> *Give us a heart to know You, for You are the LORD.*
> *Make us Your people and be our God.*
> *We return to You with our whole heart.*
> *In Your name, Jesus~"*

Please read Jeremiah 25.

Meditate on verse 30b.

> *The LORD will roar from on high and utter His voice from His holy*
> *habitation; He will roar mightily against His fold. He will shout like*
> *those who tread the grapes, against all the inhabitants of the earth.*

At this point in Jeremiah's ministry, he had preached the Word of the
LORD for 23 years. The people refused to listen and obey God. It was
605 BC, and the first wave of exiles was taken captive to Babylon. God's
judgment had arrived.

The LORD also had Jeremiah preach to all the nations. God used calamity
to punish Jerusalem; the other inhabitants of the earth would not be free
from God's punishment for disobedience. Jeremiah's sermon illustration
was a cup of the wine of the wrath of God, which all the inhabitants on
earth will be forced to drink if they do not hear and heed the Word of the
LORD (vs. 15-29; Revelation 19:15).

When God says He will roar "against all the inhabitants of the earth," He
is not jesting (v. 30). In light of current world events, pray Jeremiah 25:5-6
over yourself and those for whom you stand guard as a faithful, prayerful
watchman (Isaiah 62:6-7).

> *"LORD, may _____ and I turn from our*
> *evil way and from the evil of our deeds.*
> *We want to dwell with You in Your land forever and ever.*
> *We will stop going after other gods to serve and worship them.*
> *We do not want to provoke You to anger with the*
> *work of our hands. LORD, do not do us harm.*
> *Because of Your salvation, Jesus~"*

Please read Jeremiah 26.

Meditate on verse 2.

> *Thus says the LORD, "Stand in the court of the LORD's house, and speak to all the cities of Judah who have come to worship in the LORD's house all the words that I have commanded you to speak to them. Do not omit a word!"*

Jeremiah was preaching in the court of the temple to everyone who came to worship. God commanded him not to omit a word of his sermon! The LORD hoped the people would listen and turn from their evil way, so He could repent of the calamity He had planned "because of their evil deeds" (vs. 2-3).

The people responded to Jeremiah's sermon by wanting to kill him. The priests and the prophets demanded a death sentence. But when the city officials heard Jeremiah's sermon, they recognized it as the Word of the LORD, and they spared his life (vs. 8-16).

How do you share God's Word? Do you omit the words that are not politically correct or might make someone upset? How do you respond to God's Word? Are you willing to change your lifestyle, so you can experience God's blessings instead of His wrath?

Pray Jeremiah 26:2-3 over yourself and those for whom you stand guard as a faithful, prayerful watchman (Isaiah 62:6-7).

> *"LORD, help _____ and me speak the*
> *Words You command us to speak.*
> *Do not let us omit a Word! Help us and*
> *others listen to Your every Word.*
> *May we desire to turn from our wicked way,*
> *so You will repent of the calamity which You are*
> *planning to do because of the evil of our deeds.*
> *For Your name's sake, Jesus~"*

Please read Jeremiah 27.

Meditate on verse 5. God is speaking.

> *I have made the earth, the men, and the beasts which are on the face of the earth by My great power and by My outstretched arm, and I will give it to the one who is pleasing in My sight.*

God gave Jeremiah a sermon to preach with bonds and yokes on his neck (vs. 1-2). The main point of the sermon was God would give the land to one pleasing in His sight, and the people were to serve whom God chose. God chose Nebuchadnezzar, king of Babylon. He was a terrorist ruler who tortured and murdered his enemies (2 Kings 25). God was pleased to use this man to punish His people for refusing to hear and heed His Word.

As Jeremiah preached God's Word, false prophets told the people they would not serve the king of Babylon (v. 9). However, God's Word prevailed, and He used Nebuchadnezzar to subdue and bring His people back in line with His will.

Are you or someone you love in a yoke and bond situation? What is the LORD teaching you? Is He drawing you out of sin and into a right relationship with Him? Jesus Himself said, "Take My yoke upon you and learn from Me" (Matthew 11:29a).

Pray Jeremiah 27:5 and 12 over yourself and those for whom you stand guard as a faithful, prayerful watchman (Isaiah 62:6-7).

> *"LORD, You have made the earth, the men,*
> *and the beasts which are on the face of the earth by*
> *Your great power and outstretched arm.*
> *Make _____ and me pleasing in Your sight.*
> *Let us bring our necks under Your yoke, King Jesus,*
> *and serve You and Your people, so we will live!*
> *Because of Your name, Jesus~"*

Please read Jeremiah 28.

Meditate on verse 15.

> *Then Jeremiah the prophet said to Hananiah the prophet,*
> *"Listen now, Hananiah, the LORD has not sent you,*
> *and you have made this people trust in a lie."*

Jeremiah was preaching the yoke sermon when another prophet, Hananiah, started preaching a false yoke sermon. Hananiah preached what the people wanted to hear instead of the truth of God's Word. He told the people their exile to Babylon would last a brief two years then everything would be back to normal. Hananiah even took the yoke off of Jeremiah's neck and broke it. God told Jeremiah to tell Hananiah his false prophecy would put the people into yokes of iron, and he would be dead within that year because he had counseled rebellion against the LORD (vs. 1-17).

Hear and heed the Word of the LORD (Jeremiah 13:15)! Appraise what you hear and read by the Word of God. Are you trusting in the truth of the Bible, or are you trusting in a lie? Ironclad bondage occurs when you do not hear the true Word from God.

Use Jeremiah 28:15-16 to pray for God's protection from the "Hananiahs," for yourself and those whom you stand guard as a faithful, prayerful watchman (Isaiah 62:6-7).

> *"LORD, protect _____ and me from*
> *false prophets like Hananiah,*
> *prophets that You have not sent.*
> *Do not let us trust in a lie.*
> *Let us not listen to anyone who would counsel*
> *rebellion against You, LORD.*
> *For Your name's sake, Jesus~"*

Please read Jeremiah 29 and Daniel 9.

Meditate on verse 13.

> *You will seek Me and find me when you*
> *search for Me with all your heart.*

The word *seek* in Jeremiah 29:13 means to search out by prayer and worship. The same word is used in Daniel 9:

> *... I, Daniel, observed ... the Word of the LORD to*
> *Jeremiah the prophet ... So I gave my attention to the LORD*
> *God to seek Him by prayer and supplications ...*
> —Daniel 9:2-3

Jeremiah sent a letter to those exiled to Babylon; Daniel was one of them. Daniel 9 records him reading that letter, the same letter you read in Jeremiah 29. Daniel took God's Words to heart to seek Him through prayer. While praying, Gabriel appeared and said, "O Daniel, I have now come forth to give you insight with understanding" (Daniel 9:22b).

Notice the sequence of events. As Daniel observed God's Word, he talked to the LORD. During that intense prayer time, God sent Gabriel to give Daniel insight with understanding into incredible revelations from Him. The LORD let Daniel find Him when Daniel searched for Him.

As you read God's Word, let it draw you into an intimate prayer time. The LORD will give you great depth of understanding about Himself.

Pray Jeremiah 29:11-13 over yourself and those for whom you stand guard as a faithful, prayerful watchman (Isaiah 62:6-7).

> *"LORD, _____ and I trust You for the plans You have for us, plans*
> *for welfare and not for calamity, to give us a future and a hope.*
> *We call upon You and come and pray to You.*
> *Please listen to us, LORD. We seek You;*
> *let us find You as we search for You with all our hearts.*
> *In Your name, Jesus~"*

Please read Jeremiah 30.

Meditate on verse 22.

You shall be My people, and I will be your God.

God described a hopeless situation for Israel. Her wound was incurable, and her injury was serious because her iniquity was great and her sins numerous (vs. 12, 15). Israel was desperately sick, and a cure was impossible, yet God said in verse 17, "I will restore you to health, and I will heal you of your wounds."

Imagine a doctor telling you that you are going to die and then saying, "I will restore you to health." That is what the LORD told Israel.

And that is what the LORD tells you. Without Christ, you are terminal, deadly sick in sin. But God, in His love and compassion, died for you, so you don't have to die from sin sickness. Jesus is the cure for the hopeless situation caused by sin. Have you let Him heal you?

Pray Jeremiah 30:12-13, 15, 17, and 22 over those for whom you stand guard as a faithful, prayerful watchman (Isaiah 62:6-7), who need to be spiritually healed by the LORD.

> *"LORD, _____ have an incurable wound;*
> *their injury is serious. Plead their cause, LORD!*
> *They need healing and recovery because their iniquity*
> *is great, and their sins are numerous.*
> *LORD, restore them to health; heal their wounds.*
> *Let them be Your people and You their God.*
> *For the sake of Your name, Jesus~"*

OCTOBER 9

Please read Jeremiah 31.

Meditate on verse 4a.

Again I will build you, and you will be rebuilt, O virgin Israel!

God told Jeremiah to preach sermons about impossible situations. In Jeremiah 30, the topic was: "Your Wound Is Incurable; God Will Heal Your Wounds" (vs. 12, 17). Today's sermon could be titled: "Virgin Again."

Before Jeremiah 31, God often referred to Israel as a harlot, an adulteress who left God for man-made idols (Jeremiah 3:6-8). You would think God would be done with Israel, but then He called her a "virgin"—after He called her a harlot! Impossible! How can someone become a virgin again?

> *And looking at them Jesus said to them, "With people this*
> *is impossible, but with God all things are possible."*
> —Matthew 19:26

Be encouraged that despite past sins, confessing those sins and accepting God's forgiveness covers you and cleans you of sin, guilt, and shame. God's forgiveness is so complete that in His eyes, you can be a virgin again; you can be made holy because God is holy. Let God turn your impossible situation into an opportunity to glorify Him.

Pray Jeremiah 31:3-4a and 34 over yourself and those for whom you stand guard as a faithful, prayerful watchman (Isaiah 62:6-7).

> *"LORD, You have loved _____ and me with an*
> *everlasting love and drawn us with lovingkindness.*
> *Build us, and we will be rebuilt; make us virgins again!*
> *LORD, we want to know You.*
> *Forgive our iniquity and remember our sin no more.*
> *For the sake of Your name, Jesus~"*

OCTOBER 10

Please read Jeremiah 32.

Meditate on verse 17.

> *"Ah LORD God! Behold, You have made the heavens*
> *and the earth by Your great power and by Your*
> *outstretched arm! Nothing is too difficult for You.*

Impossible! Jeremiah was imprisoned; Jerusalem was under the control of the Chaldeans (Babylonians), and Jeremiah's cousin, Hanamel, asked him to buy some local land conquered by Babylon. Who, in their right mind, would buy land controlled by another nation? But when Jeremiah heard the offer, he knew it "was the word of the LORD" (v. 8). He bought the land and made the transaction public, so everyone knew what crazy Preacher Jeremiah had done.

The rest of the story is Babylon ceased to exist, being conquered by the Medes and Persians (Daniel 5:30-31). Cyrus, king of Persia, allowed the Jews to return to their land of Israel (2 Chronicles 36:22-23). And if you research the price of land in Israel today, Jeremiah was wise to obey God!

What has God told you to do that does not make sense in the eyes of the world and requires total dependence on Him? Trust and obey the LORD; rich blessings await your obedience.

Pray Jeremiah 32:17-19 over yourself and others who are in impossible situations as a faithful, prayerful watchman (Isaiah 62:6-7).

> *"Ah LORD God! Behold You have made the heavens and the*
> *earth by Your great power and by Your outstretched arm!*
> *Nothing is too difficult for You!*
> *Show lovingkindness to _____ and me.*
> *Forgive us of our iniquity, so it is not repaid into the*
> *bosom of our children, O great and mighty God!*
> *LORD of hosts, counsel us with Your great*
> *counsel; show us your mighty deeds.*
> *Keep Your eyes on our ways.*
> *Let the fruit of our deeds please You.*
> *For the sake of Your name, Jesus~"*

Please read Jeremiah 33.

Meditate verse 3.

> *"Call to Me and I will answer you, and I will tell you*
> *great and mighty things, which you do not know."*

Jeremiah 33 tells about another impossible situation that only God could remedy. Jerusalem was filled with the corpses of people slain by the Chaldeans (Babylonians) because God, in His anger and wrath, punished them for their wickedness (v. 5). Then God said the impossible would happen; He would bring healing, peace, truth, restoration, and cleansing to His people (vs. 6-8).

God wants to do the same in your life and in the lives of those you love. Only God can cleanse and pardon you. Only God can restore and rebuild you. Only God can bring health and healing and give you an abundance of peace and truth.

Bring to the LORD the "corpse-filled situations" you are praying over as a faithful, prayerful watchman (Isaiah 62:6-7). Pray Jeremiah 33:6-11.

> *"LORD, bring health and healing to _____ and me.*
> *Reveal to us an abundance of peace and truth. Restore and rebuild us.*
> *Cleanse us from all iniquity by which we have sinned against You.*
> *Pardon all our iniquities by which we have sinned and transgressed*
> *against You. Let us be to You a name of joy, praise, and glory.*
> *Let everyone hear of the good You have done for us, so they will*
> *fear and tremble before You, God. In our lives that have become*
> *a desolate waste, let the voice of joy, the voice of gladness, the*
> *voice of the bridegroom, and the voice of the bride be heard.*
> *We give You thanks, LORD of hosts, for You are good;*
> *Your lovingkindess is everlasting.*
> *Thank You for restoring our fortunes as they were at first.*
> *For Your name's sake, Jesus~"*

Please read Jeremiah 34.

Meditate on verses 15b-16a.

> *You had made a covenant before Me in the house which is called*
> *by My name. Yet you turned and profaned My name...*

King Zedekiah, his officials, and some of the people made a covenant to free their Hebrew servants. They cut a calf in half and passed between the pieces. Vows were made saying if they did not keep the promises, may what happened to the animal or worse happen to them. They freed the servants as promised but then took them back. They wanted their servants more than they wanted to keep their covenant vows.

God was mad! Because of their broken covenant promises, worse would happen to them—their dead bodies would become bird and animal food (vs. 17-20).

Do not think for a moment that God takes cutting covenant lightly. When a married couple says, "I promise to love, honor, and cherish you until death," what is ringing in the ears of Almighty God is, "If I do not love, honor, and cherish you, may what happened to this sacrificed animal or worse happen to me." Covenants are made to NEVER be broken (*The Covenant Maker* by Marsha Harvell).

As a faithful, prayerful watchman (Isaiah 62:6-7), use Jeremiah 34:14-16 to pray for yourself and those you love to keep your covenant promises.

> *"LORD, let _____ and me obey You and incline our ear to You.*
> *Help us turn and do what is right in Your sight.*
> *Let us keep the covenants we have made before You;*
> *do not let us turn from those covenants and profane Your name.*
> *For Your name's sake, Jesus~"*

OCTOBER 13

Please read Jeremiah 35.

Meditate on verse 13b.

*"Will you not receive instruction by listening
to My words?" declares the LORD.*

God told Jeremiah to take the Rechabite boys to the temple and offer them wine to drink. They immediately refused because their father had commanded them not to ever drink wine (vs. 5-6).

These men were Jeremiah's sermon illustration as he spoke this Word from the LORD:

The words of Jonadab, the son of Rechab, which he commanded his sons not to drink wine, are observed. So they do not drink wine to this day, for they have obeyed their father's command. But I have spoken to you again and again, yet you have not listened to Me.
—Jeremiah 35:14

The Rechabite boys obeyed their father completely. Why did the people treat God the Father with less respect? The LORD rewarded the Rechabites for their obedience; they would not lack a man to stand before Him always (vs. 19).

There are valuable lessons from this sermon. God rewards those who honor and obey their parents. God rewards those who honor and obey Him.

Pray Jeremiah 35:16 over yourself and those for whom you stand guard as a faithful, prayerful watchman (Isaiah 62:6-7).

*"LORD, help _____ and me observe the commands
of our father. Help us listen and obey You, Father.
For the sake of Your name, Jesus-"*

Please read Jeremiah 36.

Meditate on verse 7.

> *Perhaps their supplication will come before the LORD, and everyone will turn from his evil way, for great is the anger and the wrath that the LORD has pronounced against this people.*

After preaching 23 years, God told Jeremiah to write His Words on a scroll. Jeremiah spent a year dictating God's messages to his scribe, Baruch. Afterward Baruch read all the Words to the people at the LORD's house (vs. 1-9).

Notice the various responses to God's Word. When the people heard the Words, one of the men, Micaiah, went to the palace and declared to the king's officials all that he had heard. When the officials heard God's Words, they were afraid and told the king all of the Words. When the king heard the Words, he took a knife, cut off sections of the scroll, and threw them into the fire.

What is your response to the Word of God? Do you tell others what God's Word says? Do His Words cause you to fear and honor Him? Or, do you treat the Bible with contempt, cutting out the parts you do not like or think apply to you?

As a faithful, prayerful watchman (Isaiah 62:6-7), pray to have a Jeremiah 36:7 response to God's Word and not a Jeremiah 36:24 reaction.

> *"LORD, may the supplication of _____ and me come before You.*
> *We want to turn from our evil way, so You do not have*
> *to pronounce Your anger and wrath against us.*
> *In fear of Your Word, we rend our garments*
> *in mourning for our sins against You.*
> *Because of Your name, Jesus~"*

OCTOBER 15

———◆◇◆———

Please read Jeremiah 37.

Meditate on verse 3b.

Please pray to the LORD our God on our behalf.

It is important to notice the context of the meditation verse. No one in the land of Judah was listening to the Words of the LORD, yet King Zedekiah called for Jeremiah to pray on their behalf. Zedekiah wanted Jeremiah to ask God to make everything okay and for the Chaldeans not to destroy Jerusalem. He wanted God's blessings even though he and the people refused to listen and obey God's Word.

Examine your life. Do you hear and heed the Word of God, or do you ignore God's commands and precepts yet continue to ask for and expect Him to bless you?

Use the words from Jeremiah 37:2-3 to pray over yourself and those for whom you stand guard as a faithful, prayerful watchman (Isaiah 62:6-7).

"LORD, I pray on behalf of _____ and me.
Help us listen to Your Words.
In Your name, Jesus~"

Please read Jeremiah 38.

Meditate on verse 20b.

> *Please obey the LORD in what I am saying to you,*
> *that it may go well with you, and you may live.*

Jeremiah again became a living sermon illustration for the Word he preached. He was thrown into a cistern for declaring God's truth. After Jeremiah was pulled out of the miry mud, King Zedekiah summoned him to proclaim a Word from the LORD. Jeremiah told the king he was being misled and overpowered by his close friends, and his feet were sinking in the mire (v. 22).

Like Jeremiah's feet sank into the muddy cistern, Zedekiah and the people of Judah were sinking into the mire of their sin-filled lives. They were stuck. Like Jeremiah, they needed help getting out. God wanted to help them; they simply had to obey Him.

This sermon is for you. Are you stuck in the mire of sin? A slave named Ebed-melech rescued Jeremiah from the muddy cistern. Jesus Christ took the form of a bond-servant and died on a cross to save you from life mired in sin (Philippians 2:5-11). Jeremiah had to put the ropes offered by Ebed under his armpits to be pulled out of the mud. You must choose to accept the salvation offered by Jesus Christ to be pulled out of your sin.

Pray Jeremiah 38:20 and 22 over those for whom you stand guard as a faithful, prayerful watchman (Isaiah 62:6-7). You may need to insert your own name into the blank.

> *"LORD, _____'s close friends have misled and overpowered them.*
> *Their feet have sunk into the mire.*
> *Please cause them to obey You in what You say,*
> *that it may go well with them, and they may live.*
> *In Your name, Jesus~"*

OCTOBER 17

Please read Jeremiah 39.

Meditate on verses 17-18.

> *"But I will deliver you on that day," declares the LORD,*
> *"and you will not be given into the hand of the men whom*
> *you dread. For I will certainly rescue you, and you will not*
> *fall by the sword; but you will have your own life as booty*
> *because you have trusted in Me," declares the LORD.*

Jeremiah 39 records important events which occurred in 588 BC, during the third and final siege of Jerusalem by the Babylonians. King Zedekiah and his family were captured. His young children were slaughtered before his eyes, and his eyes were blinded by the Babylonians. The last thing he saw was his children killed. God punished Zedekiah for breaking covenant promises and rebelling against Him (Jeremiah 34).

Jeremiah was released from prison and moved freely throughout Judah. God left His faithful preacher in Judah to shepherd the ones who appeared rejected by God but were still loved by Him.

Ebed-melech, the Ethiopian slave who rescued Jeremiah from the cistern (Jeremiah 38), was delivered from the disaster that occurred in Jerusalem. Life was his reward because he trusted and obeyed God (vs. 16-18).

With whom do you most relate in this chapter? Is God disciplining you because of disobedience? Do you feel rejected by God and need assurance of His love? Is God asking you to care for the rejected? Do you trust God to deliver you?

Pray Jeremiah 39:17-18 over yourself and those for whom you stand guard as a faithful, prayerful watchman (Isaiah 62:6-7).

> *"LORD, please deliver _____ and me from*
> *the hand of the men we dread.*
> *Rescue us and do not let us fall; give us life.*
> *We trust in You! For the sake of Your name, Jesus~"*

OCTOBER 18

Please read Jeremiah 40.

Meditate on verse 10.

> *Now as for me, behold, I am going to stay at Mizpah to stand*
> *for you before the Chaldeans who come to us; but as for you,*
> *gather in wine and summer fruit and oil, and put them in your*
> *storage vessels, and live in your cities that you have taken over.*

Gedaliah was appointed by King Nebuchadnezzar to be in charge of the remnant left in Judah (v. 7). God gave the people favor and compassion in the sight of Gedaliah, and he allowed them to gather "wine and summer fruit in great abundance" (v. 12).

Gedaliah was speaking in the meditation verse. He went to Mizpah to represent the people before the Babylonians (Chaldeans). *Mizpah* means "watchtower." Gedaliah was at a place where he could watch over the people put in his care.

Who has God placed in your care? Have you stationed yourself at *Mizpah*, a place where you can discern the physical and spiritual needs of those you love? Do you bring those needs to the LORD and ask Him to provide from His abundance?

God has appointed you to be a *Gedaliah* for at least one person, and He wants you be faithful in the watchtower.

Use the words from Jeremiah 40:10 and 12 to pray over yourself and those for whom you stand guard as a faithful, prayerful watchman (Isaiah 62:6-7).

> *"LORD, I will stay at Mizpah to stand in prayer for _____.*
> *Let them gather in wine, summer fruit,*
> *and oil to put in their storage vessels.*
> *Let them live in You, Jesus!*
> *Let them gather in the fruit of Your Spirit in great abundance.*
> *For Your name's sake, Jesus~"*

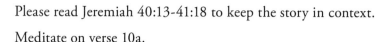

Please read Jeremiah 40:13-41:18 to keep the story in context.

Meditate on verse 10a.

> *Then Ishmael took captive all the remnant of*
> *the people who were in Mizpah ...*

Gedaliah was appointed by the king of Babylon to care for the remnant in Judah. Johanan warned him about an enemy named Ishmael. Johanan wanted to kill Ishmael for Gedaliah, but Gedaliah forbade him and accused him of lying about Ishmael (Jeremiah 40:13-16). Gedaliah's refusal to heed Johanan's warning resulted in his death and the deaths of many other people, enough to fill a cistern with their corpses. Ishmael took the survivors captive to Ammon (Jeremiah 41:1-10).

Heed the warning of this story. Satan wants sin to capture and destroy you and your family. God's Word tells you what sin is and that it brings death. Do not ignore God's warnings and make excuses to do things contrary to God's will. Sin is not to be toyed with; sin must be destroyed before it destroys you and those you love.

Use the words from Jeremiah 40:14-15; 41:10 and 12 to pray over yourself and those for whom you stand guard as a faithful, prayerful watchman (Isaiah 62:6-7).

> *"LORD, please kill the sin that wants to*
> *take the life of _____ and me.*
> *Do not let it take us captive,*
> *so we have to fight against it.*
> *In Your name, Jesus–"*

Please read Jeremiah 42.

Meditate on the people's request from verses 2-3.

> *"Please let our petitions come before you, and pray for us to the LORD your God, that the LORD your God may tell us the way in which we should walk and the thing that we should do.*

The remnant in Judah said they wanted to know God's will for their lives. They asked Jeremiah to pray for them, so they could hear the Word of the LORD. They promised to do everything God said (vs. 5-6).

Jeremiah prayed. God faithfully answered with instructions to remain in Judah and NOT go to Egypt. The people chose to …

You will find out the rest of their story tomorrow in Jeremiah 43.

Do you desire to hear God's will for your life? When He reveals it to you through the Bible and the Holy Spirit inside of you, do you obey what He says? What will be the rest of your story?

Pray Jeremiah 42:5-6 over yourself and those for whom you stand guard as a faithful, prayerful watchman (Isaiah 62:6-7).

> *"LORD, be a true and faithful witness against us*
> *if _____ and I do not act in accordance with Your whole message.*
> *Whether it is pleasant or unpleasant, we will listen*
> *to Your voice so that it may go well with us when*
> *we listen to Your voice, LORD our God.*
> *In Your name, Jesus~"*

Please read Jeremiah 43.

Meditate on this phrase from verse 4.

The people did not obey the voice of the LORD …

The people promised to obey the whole message from God (Jeremiah 42:5). Jeremiah told "**all** the people **all** the words of the LORD their God—that is, **all** these words—" (v. 1). **All** the arrogant men accused Jeremiah of lying, so "**all** the people did not obey the voice of the LORD" (vs. 2, 4).

God told the people to remain in Judah. Instead, they fled to Egypt. Jeremiah went with them; he had another sermon to deliver. He preached the Word of the LORD at the entrance of one of Pharaoh's palaces. The Jews thought the Egyptians would save them from King Nebuchadnezzar; however, he was about to destroy Egypt; there would be no salvation for the Jews in that country. The LORD God was their only hope for salvation (vs. 8-13).

Ask God to search your life. What do you hope will save you from a difficult situation? Is your hope in God? Do you ignore the lies that would cause you to doubt God? Trust the LORD and obey His Word.

Use Jeremiah 43:1-2 and 4 to pray over yourself and those for whom you stand guard as a faithful, prayerful watchman (Isaiah 62:6-7). Pray not to be like those who disobeyed the LORD.

"LORD our God, tell _____ and me all Your Words.
Do not let us be arrogant and call Your Words a lie.
Help us to obey Your voice.
In Your name, Jesus~"

Please read Jeremiah 44.

Meditate on verse 23.

> *Because you have burned sacrifices and have sinned against*
> *the LORD and not obeyed the voice of the LORD or walked*
> *in His law, His statutes, or His testimonies; therefore,*
> *this calamity has befallen you, as it has this day.*

In disobedience, the Jews fled to Egypt hoping for safe haven. Their wickedness provoked God to anger, yet they refused to fear God and walk in His ways (vs. 7-10). The preacher God had given them for the past 41 years was still with them proclaiming the Word of the LORD. Yet in total defiance, the people said to Jeremiah, "As for the message that you have spoken to us in the name of the LORD, we are not going to listen to you! But rather we will certainly carry out every word that has proceeded from our mouths ..." (vs. 16-17).

As you read the words in Jeremiah 44, does it remind of people today? The Word of the LORD is proclaimed, yet often ignored. Many choose to heed their own words instead of God's. God still proclaims that His Words will surely stand (vs. 28-29).

Hear the Word of the LORD and use the words from Jeremiah 44:5 and 9-11 to pray over yourself and those for whom you stand guard as a faithful, prayerful watchman (Isaiah 62:6-7).

> *"LORD, let _____ and me listen and incline*
> *our ears to turn from our wickedness.*
> *Do not let us forget our wickedness, but let us be contrite and fear*
> *and walk in Your law and statutes which You have set before us.*
> *We do not want You to set Your face against us.*
> *In Your name, Jesus~"*

Please read Jeremiah 45.

Meditate on verse 5a.

> *"But you, are you seeking great things for yourself?*
> *Do not seek them ..." declares the LORD.*

"Ah, woe is me!" Have you ever thought that? Baruch, Jeremiah's faithful scribe said those words; he felt sorry for himself. He had carefully written all the Words of the LORD as dictated by Jeremiah only to have them burned in the fire by King Jehoiakim. Jeremiah gave Baruch another scroll, and for a year, he rewrote those Words plus many others as directed by God through Jeremiah (Jeremiah 36).

The LORD put a stop to Baruch's pity party. God was going to bring disaster on the people, but He would spare Baruch. Instead of feeling sorry for himself, Baruch needed to be thankful for the life God gave him.

The LORD says something similar to you in Luke 17:10.

> *"So you too, when you do all the things which are*
> *commanded you, say, 'We are unworthy slaves; we have*
> *done only that which we ought to have done.'"*

What has the LORD called you to do? What kind of attitude do you have for serving Him? Do you serve with thankfulness for the life Christ has given you?

Pray Jeremiah 45:5 over yourself and those for whom you stand guard as a faithful, prayerful watchman (Isaiah 62:6-7).

> *"LORD, let _____ and me stop seeking great things for ourselves.*
> *Let us be thankful for the life You give us in all the places we go.*
> *In Your name, Jesus~"*

Please read Jeremiah 46.

Meditate on verse 13.

> *This is the message which the LORD spoke to Jeremiah*
> *the prophet about the coming of Nebuchadnezzar*
> *king of Babylon to smite the land of Egypt.*

Jeremiah 46 begins a sermon series the LORD gave Jeremiah concerning the nations surrounding Israel. The first message was addressed to Egypt. The LORD was going to thrust down the mighty Egyptians and make them prostrate. They could not stand against the King. God makes even powerful oppressors stumble and fall (vs. 15-18).

Be encouraged by the Word of the LORD. God avenged Himself in the past, and He continues to avenge Himself on His foes; the day of vengeance belongs to the LORD God of hosts (v. 10). But, if you belong to Jesus Christ, you need not fear that day. The LORD promises to save you (Romans 5:8-10).

As a servant of the LORD, pray Jeremiah 46:27 over yourself and those for whom you stand guard as a faithful, prayerful watchman (Isaiah 62:6-7).

> *"LORD, let _____ and me not fear or be dismayed.*
> *Save us! Save those we love from the land of their captivity to sin.*
> *Let us return to You and be undisturbed and*
> *secure, with no one making us tremble.*
> *For the sake of Your name, Jesus–"*

Please read Jeremiah 47.

Meditate on verse 3b.

> *The fathers have not turned back for their children*
> *because of the limpness of their hands.*

When Jeremiah received his calling from God, he was appointed to be a prophet, not only to Judah, but also to the nations (Jeremiah 1:5). Jeremiah 47 contains the prophecy the LORD gave him concerning the Philistines (v. 1).

The Philistines were one of the nations used by God to test Israel to find out if they would obey His commandments (Judges 3:1-4). Has God allowed some "Philistines" to be part of your life to test your faith and ability to handle situations with Christ-control and obedience to Him?

Observe that God controlled the Philistine situation in Jeremiah 47. He knew what would happen in the future (v.2). He caused the future (v.4). The LORD gave the orders and the assignments (v. 7). When you know these truths about God, your hands can stop being limp; you can be "strong in the LORD and in the strength of His might" (Ephesians 6:10).

Pray Jeremiah 47:3 over yourself and fathers for whom you stand guard as a faithful, prayerful watchman (Isaiah 62:6-7).

> *"LORD, do not let _____ and me be afraid of the*
> *noise, tumult, and rumbling going on around us.*
> *Cause _____ to turn back to his children.*
> *Let his hands no longer be limp.*
> *Because of Your strength, Jesus~"*

OCTOBER 26

Please read Jeremiah 48.

Meditate on verse 42.

> *Moab will be destroyed from being a people because*
> *he has become arrogant toward the LORD.*

Moab was part of present-day Jordan. The Moabites originated as the result of the incestuous relationship between Lot and his oldest daughter (Genesis 19:30-37).

The LORD's message to Moab was one of calamity and destruction, not because of their shameful beginnings, but because of their pride.

> *For because of your trust in your own achievements and*
> *treasures, even you yourself will be captured …*
> —Jeremiah 48:7a

> *Make him drunk, for he has become arrogant toward*
> *the LORD; so Moab will wallow in his vomit,*
> *and he also will become a laughingstock.*
> —Jeremiah 48:26

> *"I know his fury," declares the LORD, "but it is futile;*
> *his idle boasts have accomplished nothing."*
> —Jeremiah 48:30

Does the LORD's message apply to you, your family, your nation? Hear and heed the Word of the LORD! God will not leave the arrogant unpunished.

Pray Jeremiah 48:29 in confession to the LORD for yourself and those for whom you stand guard as a faithful, prayerful watchman (Isaiah 62:6-7).

> *"LORD, please forgive the pride of*
> *_____ and me—we are very proud.*
> *Let our haughtiness, pride, arrogance,*
> *and self-exaltation cease.*
> *In Your name, Jesus~"*

OCTOBER 27

Please read Jeremiah 49.

Meditate on this phrase from verse 16.

The arrogance of your heart has deceived you.

Jeremiah 49 contains more messages from the LORD for the nations surrounding Israel. Ammon and Edom are present-day Jordan (vs. 1-22). Damascus is still Damascus today (vs. 23-27). Kedar and Hazor are present-day Saudi Arabia (vs. 28-33). And Elam is in present-day Iraq and Iran where their borders touch on the northern end of the Persian/Arabian Gulf.

It is fascinating to understand God's Word in light of current events. Notice what the LORD says in this chapter:

*"Behold, **I** am going to bring terror upon you."*
—Jeremiah 49:5

*"**I** will bring the disaster of Esau upon him at the time **I** punish him."*
—Jeremiah 49:8

*"**I** will set fire to the wall of Damascus."*
—Jeremiah 49:27

*"So **I** will shatter Elam before their enemies and before those who seek their lives; and **I** will bring calamity upon them, even My fierce anger, and **I** will send out the sword after them until **I** have consumed them."*
—Jeremiah 49:37

Appraise and filter what you read and hear in the news through the Word of God. Remember that He is in charge, and **ALL** of His plans have and will come to pass.

Trust in the LORD, and pray Jeremiah 49:16 over yourself and those for whom you stand guard as a faithful, prayerful watchman (Isaiah 62:6-7).

"LORD, do not let the arrogance of _____ and my hearts deceive us. Bring us down from our high places. In Your name, Jesus~"

Please read Jeremiah 50.

Meditate on verse 24. God is talking.

> *"I set a snare for you and you were also caught, O Babylon,*
> *while you yourself were not aware; you have been found and also*
> *seized because you have engaged in conflict with the LORD."*

Jeremiah 50 and 51 contain the sermon God gave Jeremiah concerning Babylon. Babylon has existed since the beginning of nations (Genesis 10:6-10). Their first ignoble act was trying to make a name for themselves (Genesis 11:1-9). The geographic location of Babylon is present-day Iraq. Babylon is also an ideological place, the dwelling of demons and every unclean spirit (Revelation 18:2). "For all the nations have drunk of the wine of the passion of her (Babylon's) immorality, and the kings of the earth have committed acts of immorality with her, and the merchants of the earth have become rich by the wealth of her sensuality" (Revelation 18:3).

The LORD describes Babylon as arrogant against Him; therefore, He is against her (vs. 29-31). God declares, "the arrogant one will stumble and fall with no one to raise him up" (v. 32a).

Hear and heed the Word of the LORD and examine your life. Is the LORD of hosts your strong Redeemer (v. 34), or are you ensnared by Babylon—pride, sensuality, wealth, immorality …?

Pray Jeremiah 50:7 over yourself and those for whom you stand guard as a faithful, prayerful watchman (Isaiah 62:6-7).

> *"LORD, _____ and I are guilty;*
> *we have sinned against You.*
> *LORD, be the habitation of righteousness for us.*
> *You are the hope of our fathers.*
> *We make You our hope.*
> *In Your name, Jesus~"*

OCTOBER 29

Please read Jeremiah 51.

Meditate on verse 17a.

All mankind is stupid, devoid of knowledge...

In *Jeremiah*, you have read a series of sermons that God gave preacher Jeremiah: temple sermons, street sermons, palace sermons, potter house sermons, cistern sermons, sermons to the nations, etc. *Jeremiah* is organized by those sermons. The last sermon series is addressed to Babylon. Some of the prophecies in the message have been fulfilled; the Medes overthrew the kingdom of Babylon in 539 BC (Daniel 5:31). The ideological kingdom of Babylon still exists and "reigns over the kings of the earth" (Revelation 17:18). The full title of this kingdom is "Babylon the Great, the Mother of Harlots and of the Abominations of the Earth" (Revelation 17:5)[1]. God's Word is fascinating! As you read and study it, you can put the events happening around you into a Biblical perspective. You can see things the way God does.

The LORD, "who made the earth by His power, who established the world by His wisdom" (v. 15) declared, "All mankind is stupid, devoid of knowledge" (v. 17). Apart from God, indeed people are devoid of His wisdom and understanding. But God does not want people to stay stupid. If you are in relationship with God through Jesus Christ, then you have the mind of Christ (1 Corinthians 2:16). You are no longer "stupid and devoid of knowledge," and you can choose not to live a "Babylonian" lifestyle.

Pray Jeremiah 51:45 over yourself and those for whom you stand guard as a faithful, prayerful watchman (Isaiah 62:6-7).

"LORD, help _____ and me come forth
from the midst of Babylon.
Save us from Your fierce anger, LORD!
In Your name, Jesus~"

1. *Read Revelation 16-19 to recognize the kingdom of Babylon that still exists today.*

Please read Jeremiah 52.

Meditate on verse 2a.

> *He did evil in the sight of the LORD ...*

Jeremiah is a book about hearing and heeding the Word of the LORD. Preacher Jeremiah faithfully spoke God's Word for 53 years. Some people listened, like Daniel. He was a young boy growing up in Jerusalem when Jeremiah was delivering messages from the LORD. Daniel heeded God's Word and made up his mind not to defile himself (Daniel 1:8). Even though he was exiled to Babylon, God protected Daniel. He lived to be at least 80 years old and spent his life pleasing the LORD.

King Zedekiah heard God's Word preached as well, but he chose to disobey the LORD (Jeremiah 34). Jeremiah 52 records the end of his life. The Babylonians took Zedekiah and his family captive when he was 32 years old. His young children were slaughtered before his eyes, and his eyes were blinded, so the last thing he saw was his children being killed. He died in a Babylonian prison.

As you read the Words of the LORD in *Jeremiah,* what did God say to you, and will you heed what you heard?

Pray not to do and experience Jeremiah 52:2-3. Pray it over yourself and those for whom you stand guard as a faithful, prayerful watchman (Isaiah 62:6-7).

> *"LORD, let _____ and me not do evil in your*
> *sight like Zedekiah and Jehoiakim did.*
> *We do not want to experience Your anger*
> *or be cast from Your presence.*
> *In Your name, Jesus~"*

Please read 1 Samuel 1.

Meditate on verse 17.

> *Then Eli answered and said, "Go in peace, and may the God*
> *of Israel grant your petition that you have asked of Him."*

There is much to learn about praying from Hannah, a woman of prayer, who desperately wanted a child.

- ❧ She prayed and wept bitterly to the LORD (v. 10).
- ❧ She promised the LORD that her son would be His all the days of his life (v. 11).
- ❧ She continued praying before the LORD (v. 12).
- ❧ She spoke to God in her heart (v. 13).
- ❧ She poured out her soul before the LORD (v. 15).
- ❧ She spoke continually to the LORD about her great concern (v. 16).
- ❧ When she had peace that God would grant her request, she was able to eat and was no longer sad (vs. 17-18).
- ❧ She worshipped before the LORD (v. 19).

Does your prayer life look like Hannah's? Do not cease to pray for your loved ones. As you see the LORD miraculously working, you will be thankful you persevered.

Pray 1 Samuel 1:11, 22-23, and 28 over yourself and those for whom you stand guard as a faithful, prayerful watchman (Isaiah 62:6-7).

> *"LORD, I give _____ and me to You all the days of our lives.*
> *Let us appear before You and stay there forever.*
> *LORD, confirm Your Word to us.*
> *Let us be dedicated to You, LORD, as long as*
> *we live. LORD, we worship You.*
> *In Your name, Jesus~"*

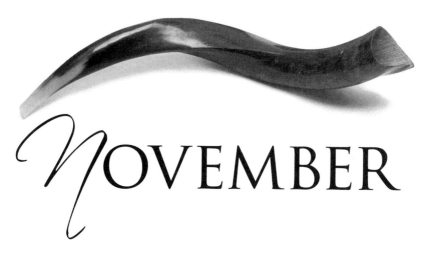

NOVEMBER

On your walls, O Jerusalem,
I have appointed watchmen;
All day and all night they
will never keep silent.
You who remind the LORD,
take no rest for yourselves;
And give Him no rest until He establishes
And makes Jerusalem a
praise in the earth.
ISAIAH 62:6-7, NASB

Please read 1 Samuel 2.

Meditate on verses 12 and 26.

> *Now the sons of Eli were worthless men; they did not know*
> *the LORD. Now the boy Samuel was growing in stature*
> *and in favor both with the LORD and with men.*

There are sharp contrasts between Samuel and the sons of Eli, Hophni and Phinehas. These young men were worthless and refused to know the LORD. They despised the things of God, even having sexual relations with women serving at the door of the tabernacle. God said these evil men would die because of their sin.

God held Eli accountable for his sons' behavior. Because Eli honored his sons above God and did not make them stop sinning, his family lost the privilege of the priesthood.

While Hophni and Phinehas behaved disgustingly, young Samuel ministered before the LORD, growing in favor with both God and men. The LORD made Samuel a faithful priest.

Learn from Eli, Hophni, Phinehas, and Samuel. Even if everyone around you is behaving contrary to the heart and soul of God, stay faithful to Christ and minister true to His Word. Lead your family, even your adult children, to obey and honor Him.

Pray 1 Samuel 2:18, 26, and 35 over yourself and those for whom you stand guard as a faithful, prayerful watchman (Isaiah 62:6-7).

> *"LORD, let _____ and me minister before You.*
> *Let us grow in stature and in favor with both You and men.*
> *Let us do according to what is in Your heart and*
> *in Your soul. Build us an enduring house.*
> *For the honor of Your name, Jesus~"*

Please read 1 Samuel 3.

Meditate on verse 3b.

> *Samuel was lying down in the temple of the*
> *LORD where the ark of God was.*

Picture what happened so far in 1 Samuel. From the time he was approximately three years old, Hannah left her precious gift from God, Samuel, with Eli at the tabernacle (1 Samuel 1:24). Eli's two sons were also at the tabernacle committing all kinds of evil, and everyone knew and talked about it (1 Samuel 2:24). Surprisingly, Hannah kept her promise to God and allowed Samuel to stay at the temple, despite the atrocities surrounding him. Samuel slept near where the ark of God was. The ark was in the Holy of Holies and represented the presence of God. Despite evil all around him, Samuel was safe because he was with the LORD.

God wants you to rest in the same place as Samuel; in the presence of the LORD, there is security despite the evil all around. God wants you to trust your loved ones to Him. He is calling you into His presence; say, "Here I am, LORD" (v. 4).

Pray 1 Samuel 3:9-10, 19, and 21 over yourself and those for whom you stand guard as a faithful, prayerful watchman (Isaiah 62:6-7).

> *"LORD, call _____ and me by name.*
> *Speak, LORD, for Your servants are listening.*
> *Speak, LORD, for Your servants are listening.*
> *LORD, be with us, and let none of our words fail.*
> *Reveal Yourself to us by Your Word.*
> *In Your name, Jesus~"*

Please read 1 Samuel 4.

Meditate on verse 3.

> *When the people came into the camp, the elders of Israel said, "Why has the LORD defeated us today before the Philistines? Let us take to ourselves from Shiloh the ark of the covenant of the LORD, that it may come among us and deliver us from the power of our enemies."*

In an attempt to turn the tide of the battle against the Philistines, the Israelites took the ark of the covenant out of the tabernacle hoping it would deliver them from their enemies. Instead of trusting the LORD to deliver them, they trusted in a religious object. God was not pleased; He let the Philistines kill 30,000 Israelite soldiers and steal the ark.

Beware not to give people or things credit for taking care of you; the credit belongs to the LORD. Ask Him to intervene in everything that is happening in your life. God loves it when you totally rely on Him to accomplish what concerns you (Psalm 138:8).

Pray the opposite of 1 Samuel 4:22 over yourself and those for whom you stand guard as a faithful, prayerful watchman (Isaiah 62:6-7).

> *"LORD, do not let Your glory depart*
> *from _____ and me.*
> *Because You are in our midst, Jesus~"*

Please read 1 Samuel 5.

Notice the repeated word "hand."

Meditate on verse 11b.

> *For there was a deadly confusion throughout the*
> *city; the hand of God was very heavy there.*

The Philistines took the ark of God to Ashdod and placed it in the temple of Dagon, their fertility god[1]. The next morning, the idol was face down on the ground before the ark. The people put Dagon back in his place, and when they returned the following morning, the head and the hands were cut off. The hand of God was heavy on those idol worshippers, bringing very great confusion to the people of Ashdod and causing tumors to break out on them.

Do not be tempted to put the LORD beside anyone or anything as the object of your trust and supreme affection. If the LORD's hand is heavy upon you, ask Him to show you idols in your life that need to be destroyed.

Pray for God not to have to do 1 Samuel 5:6-7, 9, and 11 to you and those for whom you stand guard as a faithful, prayerful watchman (Isaiah 62:6-7).

> *"LORD, may _____ and I live pleasing to You,*
> *so Your hand will not have to be heavy and severe on us.*
> *We do not want Your hand against us with great*
> *confusion. Do not let tumors break out on us.*
> *Please return to Your proper place in our lives.*
> *Remove the deadly confusion.*
> *May Your hand not be very heavy on us.*
> *In Your name, Jesus~"*

---

1. *Retrieved from https://www.blueletterbible.org/lang/lexicon/lexicon.cfm?Strongs=H1712&t=NASB.*

Please read 1 Samuel 6.

Meditate on verse 6a.

> *Why then do you harden your hearts as the Egyptians*
> *and Pharaoh hardened their hearts?*

Smitten with tumors and deadly confusion, the Philistines experienced the severe hand of God. They wanted the ark of the LORD removed to hopefully bring relief. It was placed on a cart pulled by two untrained milk cows and sent out of town. The same hand of God that heavily struck the Philistines gently guided those cows to Beth-shemesh.

What does the LORD's hand feel like on you, today? If it is heavy, "humble yourself under the mighty hand of God that He may exalt you at the proper time" (1 Peter 5:6). He wants to gently lead you in the way you should go.

Pray 1 Samuel 6:5-6 over yourself and those for whom you stand guard as a faithful, prayerful watchman (Isaiah 62:6-7).

> *"LORD God, I give You glory.*
> *Please ease Your hand from _____.*
> *Let _____ and me not harden our hearts.*
> *May You not have to deal severely with us.*
> *In Your name, Jesus~"*

Please read 1 Samuel 7.

Meditate on verse 12b.

Thus far the LORD has helped us.

It had been 20 years since the Philistines returned the ark of the LORD, and it was still not in the tabernacle. The people grieved because its absence made them feel separated from God; plus, they were still plagued by their enemies, the Philistines. Samuel addressed their real problem:

> *"If you return to the LORD with all your heart, remove*
> *the foreign gods and the Ashtaroth from among you and*
> *direct your hearts to the LORD and serve Him alone; and*
> *He will deliver you from the hand of the Philistines."*
> —1 Samuel 7:3

The people didn't need the ark in the proper place; they needed their hearts in the proper place. Only the LORD delivers those who come to Him in humble repentance.

Do you want the LORD to deliver and rescue you? Seek His help by:

- ✍ returning to the LORD with all your heart
- ✍ removing your idols (anything more important to you than God)
- ✍ directing your heart to the LORD
- ✍ serving only Him

Pray 1 Samuel 7:3, 6, 10, and 12 over yourself and those for whom you stand guard as a faithful, prayerful watchman (Isaiah 62:6-7).

> *"LORD, _____ and I have sinned against You.*
> *Help us return to You with all our heart.*
> *Remove the foreign gods from among us.*
> *Direct our hearts to You, and let us serve You alone.*
> *Deliver us from the hand of our enemies; thunder*
> *against them; confuse and rout them.*
> *Because You are our help, LORD Jesus~"*

Please read 1 Samuel 8.

Meditate on these phrases from verses 7, 11, and 14.

> *The LORD said to Samuel, "They have rejected Me from being king over them." This will be the procedure of the king who will reign over you: He will take the best...*

The LORD wanted to be King of Israel, but the people wanted to be like all the other nations around them and have a human king. Despite warnings from Samuel and the consequences of their choice being spelled out by God Himself, the Israelites insisted on getting what they wanted. God said, "Okay."

Be careful what you ask for; sometimes God will give it to you. If your request is contrary to God's will, it will come with His chastisement. Ask the LORD to show you anything or anyone you have made king of your life instead of Jesus. All those other "kings" will take God's best from you. The best comes when you truly let God reign supreme.

Pray to be the opposite of 1 Samuel 8:7-8 over yourself and those for whom you stand guard as a faithful, prayerful watchman (Isaiah 62:6-7).

> *"LORD, do not let _____ and me*
> *reject You from being King over us.*
> *Do not let us forsake You and serve other gods.*
> *In Your name, King Jesus~"*

NOVEMBER 8

Please read 1 Samuel 9.

Meditate on verse 20b.

> *And for whom is all that is desirable in Israel? Is it*
> *not for you and for all your father's household?*

Saul was taken aback when Samuel spoke to him about having everything that is desirable in Israel. Saul was from the smallest of the Israelite tribes, and his family was the least in that tribe of Benjamin; he certainly did not deserve such honor. The LORD often chooses those who are weak and despised to bring honor to Himself (1 Corinthians 1:26-31).

Even Samuel, the prophet of God, came from humble beginnings. His father was from the tribe of Ephraim, yet because of his mother's vow to dedicate him to the LORD, Samuel lived in the tabernacle with Eli, the priest (1 Samuel 1). Although he was not from the tribe of Levi, God raised Samuel up to be His faithful priest (1 Samuel 2:35).

Is the LORD calling you to do something that you feel inadequate to accomplish? Your adequacy comes from God (2 Corinthians 3:5). Let your obedience bring glory to Him.

Pray 1 Samuel 9:6 over yourself and those for whom you stand guard as a faithful, prayerful watchman (Isaiah 62:6-7).

> *"LORD, make _____ and me people of God,*
> *people held in honor who speak the truth.*
> *For the sake of Your glory, Jesus~"*

Please read 1 Samuel 10.

Meditate on verse 6.

> *Then the Spirit of the LORD will come upon you mightily, and you shall prophesy with them and be changed into another man.*

Notice God's power:

- ✺ The Spirit of the LORD came upon Saul mightily; he prophesied and was changed into another man (vs. 6, 10).
- ✺ God was with Saul and chose him (v. 7, 24).
- ✺ God touched and changed hearts (vs. 9, 26).
- ✺ God delivered Israel from the Egyptians and from the power of all the kingdoms that oppressed them (v. 18).
- ✺ God delivers you from all your calamities and distresses (v. 19).
- ✺ After the LORD did the miraculous for Saul, worthless men despised and doubted him. They questioned his ability to lead (v. 27).

When the LORD calls and anoints you for His service, trust His Spirit to come upon you mightily. He will give you the abilities you need. When others doubt what God is doing, ignore their negativity and focus on God's power and deliverance.

Pray 1 Samuel 10:6-7, 9-10, and 19 over yourself and those for whom you stand guard as a faithful, prayerful watchman (Isaiah 62:6-7).

> *"Spirit of the LORD, come upon _____ and me mightily.*
> *Change us into the people You need us to be.*
> *God, be with us and change our hearts.*
> *Spirit of God, come upon us mightily.*
> *Deliver us from all our calamities and distresses.*
> *In Your name, Jesus~"*

NOVEMBER 10

Please read 1 Samuel 11.

Meditate on verse 7b.

> *Then the dread of the LORD fell on the people,*
> *and they came out as one man.*

The Ammonites besieged Jabesh-gilead. In desperation, the Israelites living in Jabesh sought to make a covenant with their enemies. The cost of this agreement would be the gouging out of every resident's right eye. When word of the horrific situation reached Saul, he was mad. By the Spirit of God, he sent the vivid message to all the people that they would lose much more than an eye if they did not align themselves with him and Samuel. "Then the dread of the LORD fell upon the people," and God delivered them from their enemies (vs. 7, 13).

Who or what are you dreading? God's Word says to fear only Him; dreading anybody or anything else will tear you apart. The LORD will deliver you from all your fears when you fear and trust Him (Psalm 34:4; Proverbs 3:25-26).

Pray 1 Samuel 11:6-7 and 13 over yourself and those for whom you stand guard as a faithful, prayerful watchman (Isaiah 62:6-7).

> *"God, let Your Spirit come upon _____ and me mightily.*
> *Let the dread of You fall upon us and our nation,*
> *and let us come together as one.*
> *LORD, accomplish deliverance from our enemies.*
> *In Your name, Jesus~"*

Please read 1 Samuel 12.

Meditate on verse 14.

> *If you will fear the LORD and serve Him, and listen to His voice*
> *and not rebel against the command of the LORD, then both you and*
> *also the king who reigns over you will follow the LORD your God.*

The Israelites realized their sinful foolishness in asking for a king, yet they lived with the consequences of that sin. Kings ruled them for nearly 500 years. But God in His mercy, gave the way forward in the midst of the consequences (v. 14):

- Fear and serve the LORD
- Listen to His voice
- Do not rebel against His commands

Are you or someone you love living in the consequences of sin? Do not lose hope; God has not abandoned you. Obey and pray 1 Samuel 12:14 and 20-24.

> *"LORD, let _____ and me fear and serve You.*
> *Help us listen to Your voice and not rebel against Your*
> *commands, so we and our leaders will follow You.*
> *Do not let us turn aside from following You*
> *and serving You with all our heart.*
> *Let us stop going after futile things which can not*
> *profit or deliver because they are futile.*
> *Thank You for not abandoning us on account*
> *of Your great name, LORD.*
> *As for me, I will not sin against You by ceasing to pray.*
> *Help me instruct others in the good and right way.*
> *LORD, let us fear You and serve You in truth with all our heart.*
> *Let us always consider what great things You have done for us.*
> *In Your name, Jesus~"*

Please read 1 Samuel 13.

Meditate on verse 13.

> *You have acted foolishly; you have not kept the commandment*
> *of the LORD your God, which He commanded you, for now the*
> *LORD would have established your kingdom over Israel forever.*

The Israelites were hard-pressed and overcome by the Philistines. In desperation, Saul sacrificed a burnt offering hoping to obtain God's favor to defeat the Philistine enemies. Instead, Saul experienced God's wrath for foolishly disobeying His commandments. Saul's kingdom was effectively over at this point. Saul trusted in religious rituals; he did not have a heart to seek and obey the LORD.

What do you do when you are hard-pressed and overcome? The LORD uses difficult situations to establish you in holiness. Press into Him and His Word, seeking His favor. Ask the LORD to give you His heart for what is happening. Let the LORD accomplish what concerns you (Psalm 138:8).

Pray not to be like Saul in 1 Samuel 13:12-14 over yourself and those for whom you stand guard as a faithful, prayerful watchman (Isaiah 62:6-7).

> *"LORD, I am asking for Your favor.*
> *Do not let _____ and me act foolishly.*
> *Let us keep Your commandments.*
> *Establish us forever in You.*
> *Make us people after Your own heart.*
> *In Your name, Jesus~"*

Please read 1 Samuel 14.

Meditate on verse 24.

> *Now the men of Israel were hard-pressed on that day, for Saul had put the people under oath, saying, "Cursed be the man who eats food before evening, and until I have avenged myself on my enemies." So none of the people tasted food.*

Saul and his men were in the middle of battling the Philistines when Saul commanded them to stop eating until he put an end to his enemies. Instead of letting his soldiers have the nourishment needed to win a war, he crippled his own army by refusing to let them eat. If the edict had remained in effect, Saul's army would have starved to death because the Philistines warred against Saul for the rest of his life.

Have you ever issued a foolish decree? What were the consequences? Are you and those you love in a hard-pressed situation because of words rashly spoken?

Ask for forgiveness from the LORD and those you love, and pray 1 Samuel 14:29.

> *"LORD, I have troubled the land.*
> *Help me to brighten the eyes of those I love.*
> *Give us a taste of Your honey.*
> *In Your name, Jesus~"*

Please read 1 Samuel 15.

Meditate on these phrases from verses 22-23.

*To obey is better than sacrifice… Rebellion
is as the sin of divination…*

The LORD commanded Saul to utterly destroy the Amalekites. In disobedience, Saul spared their king, Agag, along with the best of their animals. God was mad. Samuel confronted Saul in his sin, and with the surviving animals providing background music, Saul bold-faced lied to Samuel, telling him that he obeyed God. As the truth came out, Saul admitted to fearing the people and doing what they wanted instead of what God wanted.

This chapter from God's Word demands immediate application. What does God want you to utterly destroy: thoughts, words, activities … that are displeasing to Him? Are you partially obeying the LORD? Have you justified your actions and convinced yourself and others you are fully obeying God? Do you fear people and listen to their voice, or do you fear and please the LORD?

Pray 1 Samuel 15:22-23 over yourself and those for whom you stand guard as a faithful, prayerful watchman (Isaiah 62:6-7).

*"LORD, let _____ and me delight
You by obeying Your voice.
Help us to obey and heed You.
Keep us from rebellion and insubordination,
for they are as divination, iniquity, and idolatry.
Do not let us reject Your Word, LORD.
In Your name, Jesus-"*

Please read 1 Samuel 16.

Meditate on verse 7b.

> *God sees not as man sees, for man looks at the outward*
> *appearance, but the LORD looks at the heart.*

King Saul had a heart issue. He did not wholeheartedly follow God; he did ungodly things and tried to justify them as Godly. "The LORD regretted that He had made Saul king over Israel" (1 Samuel 15:35). He chose another to be king: David, a young man who pursued the heart of God, desiring to do all of God's will (Acts 13:22).

The world tells you to follow your heart. God says to follow His heart; to hate what is evil and cling to what is good; to pursue faith and righteousness; and to know God and walk with Him with your whole heart (Romans 12:9; 2 Timothy 2:22; Jeremiah 7:23; 24:7). Ask the LORD to search your heart for areas not pleasing to Him. Give yourself wholeheartedly to the LORD, living without regrets.

Pray 1 Samuel 16:13 and 18 over yourself and those for whom you stand guard as a faithful, prayerful watchman (Isaiah 62:6-7).

> *"LORD, anoint _____ and me.*
> *Let Your Spirit come upon us mightily.*
> *Make us skillful, mighty people of valor, warriors,*
> *prudent in speech, and handsome.*
> *LORD, be with us.*
> *Because of Your heart's desires, Jesus~"*

NOVEMBER 16

Please read 1 Samuel 17.

Meditate on verse 51b.

When the Philistines saw that their champion was dead, they fled.

The Philistine warrior, Goliath, was called "champion" three times in this chapter (vs. 4, 23, 51). For 40 days, the Israelite armies shook in their boots because of him, until a young musician/shepherd arrived. Appalled by Goliath's words, David quickly volunteered to fight. David had a proven Champion that would battle for him, delivering him and his nation from this Philistine bully.

Do you need a champion? There are two other verses in the Bible that talk about a champion; as you read them, be encouraged and emboldened like David.

They will cry to the LORD because of oppressors, and He will send them a Savior and a Champion, and He will deliver them.
—Isaiah 19:20b

But the LORD is with me like a dread champion; therefore my persecutors will stumble and not prevail.
—Jeremiah 20:11a

Appeal to the LORD as your Champion and pray 1 Samuel 17:37 over yourself and those for whom you stand guard as a faithful, prayerful watchman (Isaiah 62:6-7).

*"LORD, deliver _____ and me
from the hand of _____.
Thank You that wherever we go, You are with us.
Because You are our Savior and Champion, Jesus~"*

Please read 1 Samuel 18.

Meditate on verse 30b.

> *David behaved himself more wisely than all the servants*
> *of Saul. So his name was highly esteemed.*

After the death of Goliath, David soon faced a new enemy, jealous King Saul. Saul's gratitude for his young musician's victory over the enemy turned to deadly envy. Saul conceived plot after plot to kill him, yet David's LORD Champion was always with him, keeping him safe, even in impossible circumstances. Just as he trusted God to save him from lions, bears, and giants (1 Samuel 17:34-37), David trusted the LORD to save him from a crazy king, keeping his behavior above reproach despite how Saul behaved.

You often encounter ungodly people. They may be family members, friends, coworkers, or a stranger in the car next to you. How do you respond? Do you reflect their words, actions, and attitudes, or do you behave more wisely than those around you because Christ controls you? Trust your Savior and Champion to fight your battles (Isaiah 19:20).

Pray 1 Samuel 18:14 and 30 over yourself and those for whom you stand guard as a faithful, prayerful watchman (Isaiah 62:6-7).

> *"LORD, let _____ and me prosper*
> *in all our ways for You are with us.*
> *Let us behave ourselves more wisely than others.*
> *May our name be highly esteemed.*
> *Because of Your name, Jesus~"*

Please read 1 Samuel 19.

Meditate on verse 9.

> *Now there was an evil spirit from the LORD on Saul*
> *as he was sitting in his house with his spear in his hand,*
> *and David was playing the harp with his hand.*

Perhaps you noticed a repeated phrase in the last four chapters of 1 Samuel: "an evil spirit from the LORD" (1 Samuel 16:14-16, 23; 18:10; 19:9). Sovereign and all-powerful God controls evil spirits. Ask the LORD to help you accept and understand this truth as stated in His Word.

Another repeated phrase in 1 Samuel is: "the Spirit of God came upon" (1 Samuel 10:10; 11:6; 19:20, 23). Throughout the Old Testament, the Spirit of God came upon individuals to meet the needs of the situation. (See also: Numbers 11, 24; Judges 3, 6, 11, 13).

As a New Testament follower of Jesus Christ, you have the Spirit of God living inside you, and He will never leave you. Bask in Jesus' Words:

> *"I will ask the Father, and He will give you another Helper, that*
> *He may be with you forever; that is the Spirit of truth, whom the*
> *world cannot receive, because it does not see Him or know Him, but*
> *you know Him because He abides with you and will be in you."*
> —John 14:16-17

Use the words from 1 Samuel 19:9 and 23 to pray over yourself and those for whom you stand guard as a faithful, prayerful watchman (Isaiah 62:6-7).

> *"LORD, do not allow an evil spirit to come upon*
> *_____ and me.*
> *Thank You that Your Spirit has come upon us and lives in us.*
> *May we speak continually of You.*
> *Let Your Spirit come upon _____,*
> *who needs to follow You.*
> *In Your name, Jesus~"*

NOVEMBER 19

Please read 1 Samuel 20.

Meditate on verse 8a.

> *Therefore deal kindly with your servant, for you have brought*
> *your servant into a covenant of the LORD with you.*

After David killed Goliath, he and Jonathan (Saul's son) entered into a covenant relationship with each other (1 Samuel 18:3-4). Jonathan gave David his princely robe and his armor. The exchange was poignant, foreshadowing that David would be king instead of Jonathan and promising that Jonathan would protect David at all costs. 1 Samuel 20 confirms that covenant relationship between Jonathan and David.

When you are in a covenant relationship with Jesus, similar exchanges are made. Jesus takes your sin and robes you with Himself.

> *But put on the LORD Jesus Christ, and make no*
> *provision for the flesh in regard to its lusts.*
> —Romans 13:14

Jesus also promises to protect you in this covenant relationship.

> *But the LORD is faithful, and He will strengthen*
> *and protect you from the evil one.*
> —2 Thessalonians 3:3

Pray 1 Samuel 20:8 and 15 over yourself and those for whom you stand guard as a faithful, prayerful watchman (Isaiah 62:6-7).

> *"LORD, deal kindly with Your servants, _____ and me,*
> *for You have brought Your servants into a covenant with You.*
> *Thank You that You put Yourself to death for our iniquity.*
> *Thank You that You will not cut off Your lovingkindness*
> *from our house forever, not even when You cut off every*
> *one of Your enemies from the face of the earth.*
> *Because of Your sacrifice, Jesus~"*

Please read 1 Samuel 21.

Meditate on verse 6a.

> *So the priest gave him consecrated bread; for there was*
> *no bread there but the bread of the Presence...*

David went from being the famous warrior, renowned for killing ten thousands, to a man running for his life. When he arrived at Gath, Goliath's hometown (1 Samuel 17:4), he entered as a lunatic instead of a victorious conqueror. Fear can drive a person to pathetic places.

As David began his flight from King Saul, he obtained some of the consecrated tabernacle bread, the bread of the Presence. Oh, how David needed that tangible reminder of God's presence at one of the scariest times of his life!

Are you in need of the tangible? Hold your Bible and read Psalm 56 aloud. It is one of David's psalms written during his scary time. Take communion/ the LORD's Supper. As you eat the bread, remember that His Presence, the Holy Spirit, lives inside of you giving you life, help, and strength (John 6:53; 14:16; Ephesians 3:16).

Be encouraged that even a great warrior like David needed the LORD to deliver him from all his fears (Psalm 34:4).

Pray 1 Samuel 21:4 and 6 over yourself and those for whom you stand guard as a faithful, prayerful watchman (Isaiah 62:6-7).

> *"LORD, _____ and I are in need of no ordinary bread;*
> *we need consecrated bread, the bread of Your Presence.*
> *LORD, we need You!*
> *In Your name, Jesus~"*

Please read 1 Samuel 22 and Psalm 52.

David wrote Psalm 52 because of the events in 1 Samuel 22.

Meditate on 1 Samuel 22:22 and Psalm 52:1.

> *Then David said to Abiathar, "I knew on that day, when Doeg the Edomite was there, that he would surely tell Saul. I have brought about the death of every person in your father's household."*
>
> *Why do you boast in evil, O mighty man? The lovingkindness of God endures all day long.*

David's decision to get bread from Ahimelech (1 Samuel 21) resulted in the deaths of 85 priests and their families. Can you imagine being in David's situation, and how would you handle it if you were?

David took responsibility for the deaths and offered shelter to Abiathar, the lone survivor. Then, according to Psalm 52, David put the situation into God's perspective. He knew the LORD would deal with Doeg and punish him for his wickedness. David kept His focus on God, trusting in His lovingkindness and giving Him thanks (Psalm 52:8-9).

Reread Psalm 52 aloud. Then pray 1 Samuel 22:14 and Psalm 52:8 over yourself and those for whom you stand guard as a faithful, prayerful watchman.

> *"LORD, make _____ and me faithful.*
> *Give us honor in our homes.*
> *Make us like a green olive tree in Your house, God.*
> *We trust in Your lovingkindness forever and forever.*
> *Thank You, LORD Jesus~"*

Please read 1 Samuel 23.

Meditate on verse 4.

> *Then David inquired of the LORD once more. And the*
> *LORD answered him and said, "Arise, go down to Keilah,*
> *for I will give the Philistines into your hand."*

It was approximately 15 years after his kingly anointing before David actually wore the crown. God used those years to prepare David for His high calling. Instead of going to finishing school, the young shepherd boy was plucked from his familiar pastures outside of Bethlehem and chased by King Saul throughout Israel. God used the school of difficulties to teach David about the land and the people he would eventually govern. God used the school of impossible circumstances to discipline David to rely on Him and seek His guidance before making decisions.

How is the LORD preparing you for His future plans? Is He using a difficult situation to draw you into richer faith and wholehearted reliance on Him? Sometimes the LORD's training grounds are unorthodox; trust His sovereignty and learn from the individualized lessons He daily prepares for you.

Use the words from 1 Samuel 23:2, 4, and 16 to pray over yourself and those for whom you stand guard as a faithful, prayerful watchman (Isaiah 62:6-7).

> *"LORD, help _____ and me always inquire*
> *of You where we should go and what we should do.*
> *Answer us and help us to hear and obey.*
> *As we go, let us encourage others in You.*
> *In Your name, Jesus~"*

Please read 1 Samuel 24.

Meditate on verse 5.

> *It came about afterward that David's conscience bothered*
> *him because he had cut off the edge of Saul's robe.*

The LORD continued to teach David how to be a king, and in a cave, God gave him a test. When presented with a great opportunity to advance his kingdom, would David heed the advice of friends or obey the counsel of God?

What were the chances of David and Saul being in the same cave together in a wilderness full of caves? "Surely the LORD gave Saul into David's hand to finally put an end to this unrelenting enemy," David's men reasoned. But David chose to listen to God instead of his friends; he passed the test, refusing to kill Saul.

Be mindful of similar tests in your life. You are presented daily with choices and opportunities. As you encounter each one, seek God's wisdom before heeding the counsel of advisors and friends. Ask the LORD to help you discern advice contrary to His will and to give you the courage to make Godly choices.

Pray 1 Samuel 24:11b over yourself and those for whom you stand guard as a faithful, prayerful watchman (Isaiah 62:6-7).

> *"LORD, let there be no evil or rebellion*
> *in _____ and my hands.*
> *Do not let us sin against You or others.*
> *For the sake of Your name, Jesus~"*

Please read 1 Samuel 25.

Meditate on verses 32-33.

> *Then David said to Abigail, "Blessed be the LORD God of Israel, who sent you this day to meet me, and blessed be your discernment, and blessed be you, who have kept me this day from bloodshed and from avenging myself by my own hand."*

When David was in a murderous rage, God sent Abigail to keep him from sinning. David wisely listened to the counsel of this God-given advisor. Abigail's interruption paused David long enough to think before he did something regrettable.

There is much to learn from this story and virtuous Abigail. Abigail was submissive, bold, intelligent, diplomatic, and brilliant. Be mindful when God sends people like her into your life; learn from them and emulate their Godly characteristics. Thank the LORD when He interrupts your life with "Abigails" sent to keep you from the regrettable.

Pray 1 Samuel 25:32-33 over yourself and those for whom you stand guard as a faithful, prayerful watchman (Isaiah 62:6-7).

> *"I bless You, LORD God of Israel,*
> *for sending _____ to meet me.*
> *Blessed be their discernment, and bless them for keeping me*
> *from bloodshed and from avenging myself by my own hand.*
> *LORD, make _____ and me that kind of people,*
> *people of discernment who keep others from sinning.*
> *In Your name, Jesus~"*

Please read 1 Samuel 26.

Meditate on verse 12.

> *So David took the spear and the jug of water from beside*
> *Saul's head, and they went away, but no one saw or knew*
> *it, nor did any awake, for they were all asleep, because*
> *a sound sleep from the LORD had fallen on them.*

Can you imagine 3,000 people and a king, all sound asleep at the same time in a camp? Not one single person stirred because God made them sleep. David moved among 3,001 of his enemies, taking the spear Saul used to try to kill both him and Jonathan (1 Samuel 18:10-11; 19:9-10; 20:33). With spear in hand, David could have killed King Saul, but David acknowledged Saul as the LORD's anointed because God had not yet taken Saul's life. David trusted God and maintained his integrity.

Are you ever tempted to compromise your integrity? Someone maligned you; now you have information to hurt them. Do you stab them like they did you, or will you trust the LORD to take care of the situation? You ought to receive a certain position. Do you work angles to promote yourself, or will you wait for God to promote you when His time is right? Let God work on your behalf, so you can have a life filled with "because God ..." moments.

Pray 1 Samuel 26:24-25 over yourself and those for whom you stand guard as a faithful, prayerful watchman (Isaiah 62:6-7).

> *"LORD, let _____ and my life*
> *be highly valued in Your sight.*
> *Deliver us from all distress.*
> *Bless us, LORD.*
> *May we accomplish much and surely prevail.*
> *Because of You, Jesus~"*

November 26

Please read 1 Samuel 27.

Meditate on verse 1a.

> *Then David said to himself, "Now I will perish one*
> *day by the hand of Saul. There is nothing better for me*
> *than to escape into the land of the Philistines."*

At this point in David's life, he felt safer with his enemies, the Philistines, than with his own countrymen. He lived among foes for a year and four months. During that time, the LORD used David to take care of unfinished business. The Geshurites, Girzites, and Amalekites were inhabitants of Canaan that God commanded the armies of Joshua and Saul to utterly destroy (Joshua 13:13; 1 Samuel 15). During this waiting time, David and his men did what God commanded, attacking and killing these enemies of Israel.

David could have spent those 16 months whining and complaining to God about the last 15 years of his life. Instead, he productively used the time doing God's will, removing enemies from the kingdom that would one day be his.

Are you in one of God's waiting times? Look around; what unfinished business does the LORD want you to complete? Ask Him to give you the energy and the courage to remove surrounding "enemies." (These could be "enemies" that rob you of time, energy, health, spiritual growth, etc.)

Use the words from 1 Samuel 27:4-5 to pray over yourself and those for whom you stand guard as a faithful, prayerful watchman (Isaiah 62:6-7).

> *"LORD, let _____ and my enemies*
> *no longer search for us.*
> *Give us favor in Your sight and in the sight*
> *of _____. Give us what we need …*
> *For the sake of doing Your will, Jesus~"*

364 | *The* WATCHMAN *on the* WALL ————————

Please read 1 Samuel 28.

Meditate on verse 6.

> *When Saul inquired of the LORD, the LORD did not*
> *answer him, either by dream or by Urim or by prophets.*

Saul was in a pathetic place. He had no one to advise him; God wouldn't talk to him; Samuel the prophet was dead, and he had alienated his son, Jonathan. In desperation, he looked to a medium for answers. This spiritist was even surprised when her phony and demonic powers appeared to conjure up dead Samuel. The point of the entire encounter was to tell Saul, one last time, why his life was so miserable: he refused to obey the LORD. When Saul did not destroy the Amalekites and justified his disobedience as sacrificing for God, God became his adversary (1 Samuel 15; 28:16, 18). Saul's rebellion resulted in a tormented life.

Examine your life. Do you delight in the LORD and His Word? Is it your heart's desire to obey and please God? Ask Him to show you every area of your life where you are justifying disobedience, even rationalizing your behavior as sacrificing for God. Repent and walk wholeheartedly with Jesus Christ.

Pray for the opposite of 1 Samuel 28:6, 16, and 18 over yourself and those for whom you stand guard as a faithful, prayerful watchman (Isaiah 62:6-7).

> *"LORD, I am inquiring of You; please answer me.*
> *LORD, never depart from _____ and me.*
> *Never become our adversary.*
> *Help us to listen to Your voice, obey You,*
> *and execute everything You tell us to do.*
> *By Your power, LORD Jesus~"*

Please read 1 Samuel 29.

Meditate on verse 2.

> *And the lords of the Philistines were proceeding on by*
> *hundreds and by thousands, and David and his men*
> *were proceeding on in the rear with Achish.*

Picture this impossible situation. After taking refuge among the Philistines for at least two years, David and his 600 men were tagging along with them to fight the Israelites. Achish presumed David to be loyal to the Philistine cause; the Philistine commanders discerned differently and refused to take David and his men into battle with them. The LORD used pagans to keep David from being expected to kill his fellow countrymen.

Take encouragement from God's Word. People who do not acknowledge the LORD and His Word have surrounded His people throughout human history. God has and will continue to use the ungodly for His purposes. He cares for you and prepares a table for you in the presence of your enemies (Psalm 23:5). Jesus prayed for the Father to protect you in His name and to keep you from the evil one (John 17:11, 15). Trust Him with the impossible situations you face in the midst of the enemy.

Pray 1 Samuel 29:6 over yourself and those for whom you stand guard as a faithful, prayerful watchman (Isaiah 62:6-7).

> *"LORD, let even our enemies say this of _____ and me:*
> *'As the LORD lives, you have been upright,*
> *and your going out and your coming in*
> *with me are pleasing in my sight;*
> *for I have not found evil in you from the day*
> *of your coming to me to this day.'*
> *For the glory of Your name, Jesus~"*

Please read 1 Samuel 30.

Meditate on verse 6b.

But David strengthened himself in the LORD his God.

David's trials just kept coming! When he and his men returned to Ziklag, they found the city overthrown and burned, and their women and children captured. The people left behind wanted to stone David, and his mighty men wept uncontrollably.

What would you do in such a horrific situation? Observe how David:

- wept with the people (v. 4)
- strengthened himself in the LORD (v. 6)
- asked the LORD what to do (v. 8)
- did not force the 200 exhausted men to go with him (v. 10)
- fed a sick Egyptian (v. 11-13)
- shared the spoil with all 600 men and Judah's elders (v. 21-26)

Despite devastating trials, David cared about others. The LORD gave him strength and wisdom to stop an angry mob, track down a band of invading kidnappers, and share with hundreds who would soon be his loyal subjects. God had indeed raised up a shepherd boy to be a king. Only God would choose such an incredible 15-year journey to groom a monarch.

The LORD has you on a journey. As you travel with Him, rely on His wisdom and strength; care for others and share with them what God shares with you along the way.

Pray 1 Samuel 30:6 and 8 over yourself and those for whom you stand guard as a faithful, prayerful watchman (Isaiah 62:6-7).

> *"LORD, please strengthen _____ and me in You.*
> *We inquire of You concerning _____.*
> *Tell us what to do.*
> *In Your name, Jesus~"*

Please read 1 Samuel 31.

Meditate on verse 3a.

> *The battle went heavily against Saul ...*

What a sad chapter in God's Word! How did a man go from being chosen and anointed by God to lead a nation to dying with his sons, armor bearer, and all his men, then having his headless body paraded among his enemies? 1 Chronicles 10:13-14 gives additional insight into this tragedy:

> *So Saul died for his trespass which he committed against the LORD, because of the word of the LORD which he did not keep; and also because he asked counsel of a medium, making inquiry of it, and did not inquire of the LORD. Therefore He killed him and turned the kingdom to David the son of Jesse.*

God killed Saul because he had disobeyed Him.

Learn well from the stories in God's Word. He carefully recorded them, not merely for a history lesson, but to disciple you into Godliness.

- Keep God's Word.
- Seek God's counsel.
- Do not be tempted to seek guidance from a fortune-teller, horoscope, etc.
- Live as a person with a heart for God.

Pray for the opposite of 1 Samuel 31:1-3 over yourself and those for whom you stand guard as a faithful, prayerful watchman (Isaiah 62:6-7).

> *"LORD, as _____ and I obey You,*
> *do not let our enemies fight against us and overtake us.*
> *Do not let the battle go heavily against us.*
> *Do not let us be hit by our enemies and badly wounded.*
> *For the sake of Your name, Jesus~"*

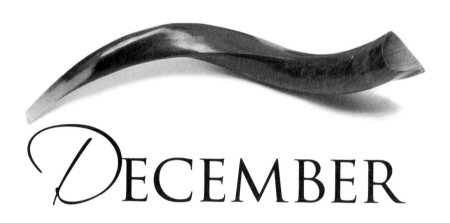

DECEMBER

On your walls, O Jerusalem,
I have appointed watchmen;
All day and all night they
will never keep silent.
You who remind the LORD,
take no rest for yourselves;
And give Him no rest until He establishes
And makes Jerusalem a
praise in the earth.
ISAIAH 62:6-7, NASB

DECEMBER 1

Please read 2 Samuel 1.

Meditate on verse 16.

> *David said to him, "Your blood is on your head, for your mouth has testified against you, saying, 'I have killed the LORD's anointed.'"*

The true account of Saul's death is recorded in 1 Samuel 31. The Amalekite in this chapter gave a very different version of Saul's death. This young man wanted be a hero by telling David he killed Saul. His deceitful, prideful words resulted in his death.

Remember this story when you are tempted to tell an embellished tale of your accomplishments. Ask yourself these questions: Is it the truth? Even if it is, does it need to be told? If so, who is glorified in the telling, you or God?

Use the words from 2 Samuel 1:16 to pray over yourself and those for whom you stand guard as a faithful, prayerful watchman (Isaiah 62:6-7).

> *"LORD, do not let _____ and my mouth testify against us. In Your name, Jesus~"*

As you prepare for celebrating Jesus' birth, you will continue to read the story of King David, the great, great, great ... grandfather of Jesus. David's story foreshadows Messiah's coming. In today's reading, the Amalekite symbolizes Satan, who thought he killed the LORD's Anointed on the cross. On the third day (v. 2), the Amalekite came to David, and his lie was exposed. On the third day, Jesus rose from the dead; Satan's lie was exposed, and he was defeated.

Pray 2 Samuel 1:16 in thanksgiving for Jesus' triumph over Satan.

> *"LORD, thank You that Satan did not kill Your Anointed.*
> *Thank You that Satan's blood is on his head*
> *for the lies his mouth testifies.*
> *Because of Your blood, Jesus~"*

DECEMBER 2

Please read 2 Samuel 2.

Meditate on verses 1 and 4a.

> *Then it came about afterwards that David inquired of the LORD, saying, "Shall I go up to one of the cities of Judah?" And the LORD said to him, "Go up." So David said, "Where shall I go up?" And He said, "To Hebron." Then the men of Judah came and there anointed David king over the house of Judah.*

David was anointed king at Hebron. Hebron is first mentioned in Genesis 13:18 where Abraham built an altar to the LORD because of faith in God's promises for land, descendants, and blessings (Genesis 12:1-2; 13:14-18). David was one of those descendants and blessings. And through Abraham and David, came the ultimate descendant and blessing, Jesus. "The record of the genealogy of Jesus the Messiah, the son of David, the son of Abraham …" (Matthew 1:1).

Jesus descended from the royal line of David because He is King of kings (1 Timothy 6:14-15). Is He your King? Do you have a Hebron, a place where you believed the promises of God and made Jesus King of your life? If not, let today become your Hebron.

Pray 2 Samuel 2:4 and 6 over yourself and those for whom you stand guard as a faithful, prayerful watchman (Isaiah 62:6-7).

> *"LORD Jesus, I anoint You King over me and my house.*
> *Show Your lovingkindness, truth, and goodness to us.*
> *Because You are King Jesus~"*

DECEMBER 3

Please read 2 Samuel 3.

Meditate on verse 14a.

> *So David sent messengers to Ish-bosheth, Saul's*
> *son, saying, "Give me my wife Michal ..."*

David wanted his bride. Michal, Saul's daughter, was betrothed to David, but Saul later gave her to Paltiel to marry instead (1 Samuel 18:20-27; 25:44). Michal loved David; he had fought and killed 200 Philistines to win her hand in marriage. Now, as David's kingdom was being established, he wanted his bride, Michal, with him.

The parallels in this story to Christ and His bride, the church, are poignant. Christians are the bride of Christ. When Jesus came 2,000 years ago, it was for the purpose of dying and resurrecting to win His bride. Satan and the world would love to steal that precious bride, but Jesus knows who she is, and He will make her His own when He returns to establish His Kingdom (Revelation 19:7-9).

To whom are you betrothed, Christ or the world? Be aware that when you choose to become the bride of Christ, the world will come chasing after you, even weeping, like Paltiel did for Michal (v. 16). Do not be swayed in your decision to follow Jesus; His love for you is eternal, and His is the only everlasting Kingdom (Revelation 11:15).

Use the words from 2 Samuel 3:18 and 21 to pray over yourself and those for whom you stand guard as a faithful, prayerful watchman (Isaiah 62:6-7).

> *"LORD, by Your hand save _____ and me.*
> *Save us from all our enemies.*
> *Gather Your people to make a covenant with You.*
> *Be King over all that Your soul desires.*
> *In Your name, King Jesus~"*

DECEMBER 4

Please read 2 Samuel 4.

Meditate on verse 9b.

> *David said to them, "As the LORD lives, who*
> *has redeemed my life from all distress..."*

As the regime change from Saul's kingdom to David's kingdom became obvious, people started to panic, thinking David would want to kill Saul's family to secure his place on the throne. A fleeing nurse carrying Jonathan's son, Mephibosheth, dropped and crippled him. Rechab and Baanah, two of Saul's commanders, thought they could find favor with David by killing Saul's son, Ish-bosheth, but their bad decision resulted in their own deaths.

The people in these stories did not know the heart of King David. He would never kill a descendant of Jonathan, and he trusted God's intervention to take care of his enemies. He did not want humans preempting the LORD's provision.

What sends you into a panic and causes you to make crippling choices? Know and trust the heart of Jesus; He promises to take care of you.

Pray 2 Samuel 4:9b over yourself and those for whom you stand guard as a faithful, prayerful watchman (Isaiah 62:6-7).

> *"LORD, as You live,*
> *redeem _____ and my life*
> *from all distress.*
> *Thank You, Jesus~"*

DECEMBER 5

Please read 2 Samuel 5.

Meditate on verse 2b.

> *And the LORD said to you, 'You will shepherd My*
> *people Israel, and you will be a ruler over Israel.'"*

These words spoken to King David are strikingly similar to words from the Christmas story:

> *And you Bethlehem, land of Judah, are by no means least*
> *among the leaders of Judah; for out of you shall come*
> *forth a Ruler who will shepherd My people Israel.*
> —Matthew 2:6

After reigning over Judah seven-and-a-half years, David shepherded the combined kingdom of Israel and Judah for 33 years. David ruled a total of 40 years, but a Ruler was coming who would reign and shepherd eternally.

Jesus is the everlasting Ruler and Shepherd. Have you made Him Ruler and Shepherd of your life?

Although David was king, he acknowledged God established the kingdom for His purposes (v. 12). Do you live with the same intentionality?

Pray 2 Samuel 5:12 over yourself and those for whom you stand guard as a faithful, prayerful watchman (Isaiah 62:6-7).

> *"LORD, let _____ and me realize*
> *why You have established us.*
> *Use us to exalt Your Kingdom for the sake of Your people.*
> *In Your name, King Jesus~"*

DECEMBER 6

Please read 2 Samuel 6.

Meditate on verse 2.

> *And David arose and went with all the people who were*
> *with him to Baale-judah to bring up from there the ark*
> *of God which is called by the Name, the very name of the*
> *LORD of hosts who is enthroned above the cherubim.*

The ark of God was kept at Abinadab's house for 20 years (1 Samuel 7:1-2). It was the visual reminder of God's presence, and King David wanted it back inside the tabernacle in the City of David. His first attempt at returning the ark went terribly wrong because David did it the wrong way. The ark was not to be put on a cart; it was to be carried with poles on the shoulders of Levites and not touched by human hands. David was significantly rattled when God killed Uzzah just for touching the ark, trying to steady it when the cart became unstable. In fear of God, David left the ark at the home of Obed-edom until he made proper preparations for moving it (1 Chronicles 15:13-15).

God still has specific requirements for being in His presence. Those who do not know God and obey the Gospel of the LORD Jesus will "pay the penalty of eternal destruction, away from the presence of the LORD" (2 Thessalonians 1:8-9). But those who come into the presence of God through Jesus Christ receive eternal life and eternal blessings.

Pray 2 Samuel 6:12 over your house/family as a faithful, prayerful watchman (Isaiah 62:6-7).

> *"LORD, bless my house and all that belongs*
> *to my family on account of Your presence.*
> *Because You are Immanuel, God with us, Jesus~"*

DECEMBER 7

Please read 2 Samuel 7.

Meditate on verse 16. God is speaking to David.

> *"Your house and your kingdom shall endure before Me*
> *forever; your throne shall be established forever."*

2 Samuel 7 contains the Davidic covenant, God's forever promises to King David. Some of those covenant promises are:

- ✎ God will establish the kingdom of David's descendant forever (vs. 12-13).
- ✎ God's lovingkindness will not depart from David's descendant (v. 15).
- ✎ David's house and kingdom will endure before God forever, and his throne will be established forever (v. 16).

Jesus Christ is the fulfillment of the Davidic covenant:

- ✎ Jesus was born a descendant of David (Romans 1:1-3).
- ✎ Jesus is the Messiah, the son of David (Matthew 1:1).
- ✎ God found David to be a man after His heart, and from his descendants, according to God's promise, God brought to Israel a Savior Jesus (Acts 13:22-23).

If you are in a covenant relationship with Jesus, sit before the LORD and pray David's words in 2 Samuel 7:18-29. This is a prayer formed with some of those words:

> *"Who am I, O LORD God, and what is my house, that You have*
> *brought me this far? Thank You for knowing me, O LORD God!*
> *For the sake of Your Word and according to Your own heart,*
> *You have done all this greatness. For this reason, You are great,*
> *O LORD God; for there is none like You,*
> *and there is no God besides You.*
> *May my family be established before You. May it please You to*
> *bless my family that we may continue forever before You.*
> *For You, O LORD God, have spoken, and with Your blessing may*
> *my family, Your servants, be blessed forever. In Your name, Jesus~"*

DECEMBER 8

Please read 2 Samuel 8.
Meditate on this sentence from verses 6 and 14.

And the LORD helped David wherever he went.

David was quite a warrior, killing most of his enemies and enslaving the rest. Perhaps you are thinking this is the chapter where the Christ parallels end. However, consider these words from Revelation 19:13-16 and 21.

He is clothed with a robe dipped in blood, and His name is called The Word of God. From His mouth comes a sharp sword, so that with it He may strike down the nations, and He will rule them with a rod of iron; and He treads the wine press of the fierce wrath of God, the Almighty. And on His robe and on His thigh He has a name written, "KING OF KINGS, AND LORD OF LORDS." And the rest were killed with the sword which came from the mouth of Him who sat on the horse, and all the birds were filled with their flesh.

Jesus, the baby born in a manger to die for the sins of the world, will return to earth as the conquering Warrior King and LORD, slaying His enemies who refused His sacrifice for their sins. That is the entire story of Christmas. Ask the LORD to help you tell the whole Christmas story this year; people must know how the story ends.

Pray 2 Samuel 8:6b and 14b over yourself and those for whom you stand guard as a faithful, prayerful watchman (Isaiah 62:6-7).

"LORD, help _____ and me wherever we go.
LORD, help _____ and me wherever we go.
In Your name, Jesus~"

DECEMBER 9

Please read 2 Samuel 9.

Meditate on verses 8 and 11b.

> *Again he prostrated himself and said, "What is your*
> *servant, that you should regard a dead dog like me?"*
> *So Mephibosheth ate at David's table as one of the king's sons.*

The covenant promises David made to Jonathan extended to his family (1 Samuel 20:15). So after Jonathan and his father, Saul, and brother, Ishbosheth died, David longed to show lovingkindness to a descendant of Jonathan. Mephibosheth was the blessed recipient of that kindness, and even though David's soul hated the lame and the blind (2 Samuel 5:8), this crippled man ate at the king's table regularly because of covenant promises.

The remarkable story of King David and Mephibosheth is the picture of your covenant relationship with Jesus Christ. God hates sin and cannot be in its presence. You were blind and lame in sin and could not come close to God. Jesus became your crippling sin and died because of it (2 Corinthians 5:21). Now you come to God the Father through Jesus the Son; He extends His lovingkindness to you, and you get to eat with the LORD regularly as one of the King's children (John 14:6; Revelation 3:20). Amazing!

Pray 2 Samuel 9:8, 11, and 13 in thanksgiving and commitment to your King Jesus.

> *"My LORD, I prostrate myself before You.*
> *What is Your servant, that You should regard a dead dog like me?*
> *Thank You that I get to eat at Your table as a King's child!*
> *Thank You that I live with You and get to eat at Your table regularly.*
> *Because of You, King Jesus~"*

DECEMBER 10

Please read 2 Samuel 10.

Meditate on verse 12.

> *Be strong, and let us show ourselves courageous for the*
> *sake of our people and for the cities of our God; and*
> *may the LORD do what is good in His sight.*

David's kind intentions to send condolences were misunderstood and assigned as false motives by Hanun, the Ammonite king. Messengers sent on behalf of King David were horribly humiliated by Hanun, resulting in war between David's armies and the combined forces of the Ammonites and Arameans. Under the command of Joab and Abishai, the Israelites were victorious.

Have your intentions, words, and actions ever been misunderstood? Christians are often lied about and humiliated by those who do not know God and His Word. Be encouraged by the story of David and Hanun. "The LORD is faithful, and He will strengthen and protect you from the evil one" (2 Thessalonians 3:3). King Jesus and His armies will be victorious (Revelation 19:11-21).

Pray 2 Samuel 10:12 over yourself and those for whom you stand guard as a faithful, prayerful watchman (Isaiah 62:6-7).

> *"LORD, help _____ and me be strong,*
> *and let us show ourselves courageous for the*
> *sake of Your people and for You, God.*
> *LORD, do what is good in Your sight.*
> *In Your name, Jesus~"*

Please read 2 Samuel 11.

Meditate on verses 1a, c, and 27b.

> *Then it happened in the spring, at the time when kings go*
> *out to battle, that David stayed at Jerusalem. But the thing*
> *that David had done was evil in the sight of the LORD.*

Keep in mind that David is merely a foreshadowing picture of Messiah; he is NOT Jesus. In fact, parts of his life are the reason Jesus came to the earth: to die for David's sins ... and your sins ... and my sins ...

Learn well from 2 Samuel 11, and let the LORD use His Truths to keep you from sinning. Observe the path of sin David took:

- David stayed home instead of fighting with his men (v. 1). Where does God want you? Stay in the trenches of God's will, prayerfully fighting spiritual battles.

- David was bored at home, so he went looking for something to interest him (v. 2). Are you busy doing the LORD's work? It will keep you from doing and looking at things you shouldn't.

- David asked about the bathing woman (v. 3). Do not even inquire about the forbidden. Entertaining sinful ideas opens the door to disaster.

- David sent for Bathsheba, took her, and slept with her (v. 4). Stop yourself before it is too late. Ask the LORD not to let sin be accomplished in your life.

- David's sin resulted in the murder of Uriah, one of his mighty men (v. 21; 2 Samuel 23:39). Sin always ends in death. Do not let it deceive you!

Pray 2 Samuel 11:27b to begin a prayer of confession to God.

> *"LORD, the thing that I have done is evil in Your sight.*
> *Forgive me by Your sacrifice, Jesus~"*

DECEMBER 12

Please read 2 Samuel 12.

Meditate on verse 9a.

> *Why have you despised the Word of the*
> *LORD by doing evil in His sight?*

The LORD sent Nathan, the prophet, to confront David about his sins. David was quick to confess, and the LORD was quick to forgive. God even removed some of the consequences; David was allowed to live (v. 13). However, some of the consequences remained; David and Bathsheba's first baby died (v. 14).

Remember these facts about sin and forgiveness from 2 Samuel 12:

- Doing evil despises the Word of God (v. 9).
- Sin has consequences (v. 10).
- Adultery is despising God (v. 10).
- Confession of sin results in God removing your sin (v. 13).
- Some consequences may remain even after confession (v. 14).
- God gives amazing grace and forgiveness when you return to Him (vs. 24-25).
- After God forgives and restores you, get back in the battle and obey Him (vs. 27-31).

Use the words from 2 Samuel 12:9-10 and 12-13 to pray over yourself and those for whom you stand guard as a faithful, prayerful watchman (Isaiah 62:6-7).

> *"LORD, do not let _____ and me despise*
> *Your Word by doing evil in Your sight.*
> *Keep the sword out of our house.*
> *Do not let us despise You by committing adultery or any other evil.*
> *Keep us from secret sins. LORD, take away our sins*
> *when we sin against You, and do not let us die.*
> *Because of You, Jesus~"*

Please read 2 Samuel 13.

Meditate on verse 21.

Now when King David heard of all these matters, he was very angry.

When David heard about Amnon raping Tamar he was angry, but he did nothing about the heinous violation. For two years, Tamar lived in disgrace; Amnon went unpunished; Absalom seethed at the injustice, and David still did nothing. Finally, Absalom took matters into his own hands and had Amnon killed.

After Amnon died, Absalom fled and stayed in Geshur for three years (v. 38). Five years passed after the rape of Tamar. Scripture records David as angry about the assault on his daughter, grieved by the report that his sons were dead, comforted concerning Amnon's punishment by death, and longing for Absalom. What Scripture did not record was David doing or saying anything that a father should have.

As Christmas get-togethers are happening, what can you learn from David's life to make you a better family member? Speak God's wisdom into your family. If your family is sinning, stop it. Seek God's blessings instead of incurring His wrath. If you are offended, give the offense to Jesus and seek reconciliation. With the power and wisdom of Christ, do what you can to stop Satan from getting a foothold in your family. And fathers, engage in your children's lives; speak up, and stop hoping the problems will disappear. God expects you to lead your family into Christlikeness.

Pray 2 Samuel 13:39 over yourself and those for whom you stand guard as a faithful, prayerful watchman (Isaiah 62:6-7).

"LORD, my heart longs to go out to _____.
Give me the courage to do it.
In Your name, Jesus~"

DECEMBER 14

Please read 2 Samuel 14.

Meditate on verse 14b.

> *Yet God does not take away life, but plans ways so that*
> *the banished one will not be cast out from Him.*

David's family problems continued. Absalom lived banished from his father for three years (2 Samuel 13:38). Joab, perceiving David wanted to be reconciled with his son, conceived a plan for reuniting them. David brought Absalom home, but refused to see him face-to-face. The estrangement continued for another two years. David longed for Absalom, but he did not take the courageous and humble steps necessary to bring reconciliation.

People are banished from God's presence because of sin, yet God longs for His people. In order to bring reconciliation, God acted with great courage and humility. He humbled Himself to earth as a human baby for the purpose of dying on a cross to remove people's estranging sins (Philippians 2:8). Jesus' sacrificial death ends the banishment, bringing face-to-face forever reconciliation with Him (2 Corinthians 5:18-21).

Have you accepted His incredible gift of reconciliation? Do you have family members who need you to act with courage and humility to bring reconciliation to relationships? Let this be the best Christmas ever as you walk face-to-face with Christ, extending His life to others.

Pray 2 Samuel 14:14 over yourself and those for whom you stand guard as a faithful, prayerful watchman (Isaiah 62:6-7).

> *"LORD, without You, _____ and I would surely die and be*
> *like water spilled on the ground which cannot be gathered up again.*
> *Yet You do not desire to take away life.*
> *Thank You for planning the Way that we,*
> *the banished ones, will not be cast out from You.*
> *Because of You, Jesus~"*

December 15

Please read 2 Samuel 15.

Meditate on verses 25b and 26.

> *If I find favor in the sight of the LORD, then He will bring me back again… But if He should say thus, "I have no delight in you," behold, here I am, let Him do to me as seems good to Him.*

The situation with Absalom grew worse. Plotting to take the throne from his father, he put doubt in the people's minds about David, claiming he would do a better job for them. Absalom stole their hearts. Panicking, David ran toward the wilderness, and as he ran, he came to the end of himself. He turned around and climbed up the Mount of Olives where he wept a prayer that would be echoed on that mountain 1,000 years later (vs. 25-30; Luke 22:39-42).

> *"LORD, do to me as seems good to You. My Father, if it is possible, let this cup pass from Me; yet not as I will, but as You will."*
> —2 Samuel 15:26; Matthew 26:39

Are you at the end of your rope? Are people lying about you? Turn to your Savior who knows and understands. In brokenness and humility, pray 2 Samuel 15:25-26 and 31 over yourself and those for whom you stand guard as a faithful, prayerful watchman (Isaiah 62:6-7).

> *"LORD, let _____ and me find favor in Your sight.*
> *Bring us back to You.*
> *Please delight in us, and do to us as seems good to You.*
> *O LORD, I pray, make the counsel of _____ foolishness.*
> *In Your name, Jesus~"*

DECEMBER 16

Please read 2 Samuel 16.

Meditate on verse 12.

> *Perhaps the LORD will look on my affliction and*
> *return good to me instead of his cursing this day.*

Things went from bad to worse for David. Not only had Absalom betrayed David, but he was told that Mephibosheth also hoped to usurp the throne. David was cursed and stoned by Saul's relative, Shimei, and his friend, Hushai, traitorously pledged his loyalty to Absalom. The chapter ends with Absalom having sex with his father's concubines on the roof of David's house "in the sight of all Israel" (v. 22).

Perhaps it was on this horrific day that David wrote:

> *O LORD, how my adversaries have increased! Many are rising up*
> *against me. Many are saying of my soul, "There is no deliverance*
> *for him in God." But You, O LORD, are a shield about me, my*
> *glory, and the One who lifts my head. I will not be afraid of ten*
> *thousands of people who have set themselves against me round about.*
> —Psalm 3:1-3, 6

Hopefully your day is not as bad as David's, but be encouraged even if it is, and pray Psalm 3:3 and 2 Samuel 16:12 over yourself and those for whom you stand guard as a faithful, prayerful watchman (Isaiah 62:6-7).

> *"You, O LORD, are a shield about _____ and me,*
> *our glory and the One who lifts our head.*
> *Please look on our affliction and return good*
> *to us instead of cursing this day.*
> *In Your name, Jesus~"*

Please read 2 Samuel 17.

Meditate on verse 14.

> *Then Absalom and all the men of Israel said, "The counsel of*
> *Hushai the Archite is better than the counsel of Ahithophel."*
> *For the LORD had ordained to thwart the good counsel of*
> *Ahithophel, so that the LORD might bring calamity on Absalom.*

Observe God's sovereignty in this chapter. Ahithophel gave Absalom a battle plan for overthrowing David. His advice would have secured the throne for Absalom, but Absalom's ego took over his better judgment, and he chose the advice of Hushai to personally fight his father. Absalom's choice was actually part of God's plan to ultimately secure and establish David's kingdom forever (2 Samuel 7:13).

God's sovereignty in preserving David's kingdom continued with the birth and death of Jesus. Through "the predetermined plan and foreknowledge of God," Jesus was "nailed to a cross by the hands of godless men and put to death" (Acts 2:23). When "God raised Him up again" (Acts 2:24), His promise to David was fulfilled; David's Descendant was indeed forever on the throne (Acts 2:30).

God's plans were "formed long ago, with perfect faithfulness" (Isaiah 25:1). Trust Him for the plans He has for your life.

Use 2 Samuel 17:14 to submit to God's ordained plans.

> *"LORD, I trust what You have ordained.*
> *Thwart what needs to be thwarted*
> *in order to be in Your will.*
> *In Your name, Jesus~"*

DECEMBER 18

Please read 2 Samuel 18.

Meditate on verse 33.

> *The king was deeply moved and went up to the chamber*
> *over the gate and wept. And thus he said as he walked, "O*
> *my son Absalom, my son, my son Absalom! Would I had*
> *died instead of you, O Absalom, my son, my son!"*

David wished he had died in the place of his son, Absalom. David's descendant, Jesus, fulfilled that desire.

> *Blessed be the LORD God of Israel, for He has visited us and*
> *accomplished redemption for His people, and has raised up a horn of*
> *salvation for us in the house of David His servant. For while we were*
> *still helpless, at the right time Christ died for the ungodly. For one*
> *will hardly die for a righteous man, but God demonstrates His own*
> *love toward us, in that while we were yet sinners, Christ died for us.*
> —Luke 1:68-69; Romans 5:6-7a, 8

Christmas is the celebration of God loving you so much He came to earth to die in your place so you can live forever with Him. Hear Him cry Your name:

> *"O My child, _____ ,*
> *My child, My child _____!*
> *I have died instead of you,*
> *O _____ , My child, My child!"*

Answer your Savior with thanksgiving. Then using the words from 2 Samuel 18:33, pray for those who need to hear the LORD say the same to them.

> *"LORD, thank You for dying instead of me!*
> *Let _____ hear You call them by name.*
> *Let them know You died instead of them.*
> *In Your name, Jesus~"*

DECEMBER 19

Please read 2 Samuel 19.

Meditate on verses 21b and 23.

> *"Should not Shimei be put to death for this, because he*
> *cursed the LORD's anointed?" The king said to Shimei,*
> *"You shall not die." Thus the king swore to him.*

Recall Shimei threw stones at King David and continually cursed him (2 Samuel 16:5-6). Of course he deserved to die for treating the LORD's anointed with such contempt, yet David in his mercy showed undeserved kindness to Shimei and allowed him to live.

> *But God being rich in mercy, because of His great love*
> *with which He loved us, even when we were dead in our*
> *transgressions, made us alive together with Christ (by grace*
> *you have been saved), and raised us up with Him, and seated*
> *us with Him in the heavenly places in Christ Jesus.*
> —Ephesians 2:4-6

Jesus was born to die for dead dogs, like Shimei and Mephibosheth, and for egotistical people, like Absalom, and for less-than-perfect fathers, like David, and for you. And like the thief on the cross, when you give your life to Jesus, He says to you, "You shall not die; today, you will be with Me in Paradise" (v. 23; Luke 23:43).

Pray 2 Samuel 19:16, 20-21, and 23 over yourself and those for whom you stand guard as a faithful prayerful watchman (Isaiah 62:6-7).

> *"King Jesus, _____ and I hurry and come to meet You.*
> *We are Your servants, and we know we have sinned;*
> *therefore, we come to meet You, our LORD, the King.*
> *We deserve death for cursing the LORD's Anointed.*
> *Thank You for saying, 'You shall not die.'*
> *Because of You, King Jesus~"*

Please read 2 Samuel 20.

Meditate on verses 15b-16.

> *All the people who were with Joab were wreaking destruction in order*
> *to topple the wall. Then a wise woman called from the city, "Hear,*
> *hear! Please tell Joab, 'Come here that I may speak with you.'"*

David reaped the consequences of his sin with Bathsheba (2 Samuel 12:10-12). His foolishness resulted in death and destruction and brought foolish fellows into his life, like Sheba (v. 1). Sheba wanted to divide David's kingdom. Joab, David's commander, nearly destroyed an entire city trying to stop him. God used a wise woman to stop Joab. Sheba lost his head, but everyone else kept theirs.

While the Christmas Holy days should be joyous, sometimes foolish family members come together, causing division. And perhaps a zealous relative will try to destroy the foolishness, resulting in more destruction. Ask God to make you a wise, peaceable, and faithful family member who speaks His counsel to others. Ask the LORD to give your family ears to hear His Word.

Pray 2 Samuel 20:15-17, 19, and 22 over yourself and those for whom you stand guard as a faithful, prayerful watchman (Isaiah 62:6-7).

> *"LORD, there are people wreaking destruction*
> *and trying to topple my family.*
> *Make me wise. Let _____ come and*
> *hear that I may speak with them.*
> *Let them listen to me. Make me a peaceable*
> *and faithful family member.*
> *Let _____ stop seeking to destroy us.*
> *Do not let them swallow up our inheritance from You, LORD.*
> *Make us wise and able to cut off the head of the*
> *problem without destroying our family.*
> *In Your name, Jesus~"*

Please read 2 Samuel 21.

Meditate on verse 1.

> *Now there was a famine in the days of David for three years, year after year; and David sought the presence of the LORD. And the LORD said, "It is for Saul and his bloody house, because he put the Gibeonites to death."*

This is a chapter about real life—dealing with mistakes from the past, dealing with the sins of others, and dealing with giants. David dealt with life by seeking the presence of the LORD. God explained to him the reason for the famine; it was punishment for Saul breaking a 400 year-old covenant with the Gibeonites (Joshua 9:1-10:21). Based on God's commands (Numbers 35:33-34), David avenged the blood of the Gibeonites and properly buried the dead. "After that God was moved by prayer for the land" (v. 14).

Christmas is the perfect time to seek the LORD's presence, asking Him to reveal to you and your family mistakes from the past and sins that need to be forgiven. Perhaps the best gift you could give is a written or spoken message to one who needs you to forgive them for sinning against you. The gracious gift of forgiveness topples giants just like Jesus' forgiveness toppled giants in your life.

Use the words from 2 Samuel 21:1, 14, 16, and 22 to pray over yourself and those for whom you stand guard as a faithful, prayerful watchman (Isaiah 62:6-7).

> *"LORD, I seek Your presence for my family.*
> *Please be moved by prayer for us.*
> *This giant intends to kill us.*
> *Let me kill the giant.*
> *By Your hand, Jesus~"*

Please read 2 Samuel 22.

Meditate on verse 47.

> *The LORD lives, and blessed by my rock; and*
> *exalted be God, the rock of my salvation.*

As Christmas approaches, think about Jesus and who He is (vs. 2-3):

- The LORD
- My Rock
- My Fortress
- My Deliverer
- My God
- My Shield
- My Stronghold
- My Refuge
- My Savior

What has Jesus done for you this past year?

- He drew you out of many waters (v. 17).
- He delivered you from your strong enemy (v. 18).
- He was your support (v. 19).
- He rescued you (v. 20).

"David spoke the words of this song to the LORD" (v. 1). Reread 2 Samuel 22 and say the words to Jesus as a gift of thanks to Him for coming to earth to rescue you.

> *"LORD, You are my rock and my fortress and my deliverer;*
> *my God, my rock, in whom I take refuge,*
> *my shield and the horn of my salvation,*
> *my stronghold and my refuge; my Savior…"*

Please read 2 Samuel 23.

Meditate on verses 2-3a.

> *The Spirit of the LORD spoke by me, and His word was on my tongue. The God of Israel said, the Rock of Israel spoke to me…*

The Rock of Israel is Jesus Christ (1 Corinthians 10:4). He spoke to David, and David called Him, "LORD" (Matthew 22:41-45). Jesus, the descendant of David, is also the LORD of David. "Jesus, the Messiah, the son of David" was born to "save His people from their sins" (Matthew 1:1, 21b). He made an everlasting covenant with David for salvation (v. 5), and that covenant is extended to you and those you love.

This is the Christmas story! Jesus is God; He was born in the flesh in order to be the perfect sacrifice for the sins of the world (1 John 2:2). The Sacrifice died and rose on the third day proving He is indeed God. When you, like David, call Him, "LORD" and enter into the everlasting covenant He made with you, your salvation is secured (v. 5).

Pray 2 Samuel 23:2-3 and 5 over yourself and those for whom you stand guard as a faithful, prayerful watchman (Isaiah 62:6-7).

> *"Spirit of the LORD, speak by me.*
> *Let Your Word be on my tongue.*
> *God of Israel, the Rock of Israel, speak to me.*
> *Truly, let my house be with You, God, for You have made*
> *an everlasting covenant with me, ordered in all things*
> *and secured; for all my salvation and all my desire.*
> *Make this covenant grow to include _____.*
> *In Your name, Jesus~"*

Please read 2 Samuel 24.

Meditate on verse 10b.

> *David said to the LORD, "I have sinned greatly in what*
> *I have done. But now, O LORD, please take away the*
> *iniquity of Your servant, for I have acted very foolishly."*

Sin is costly. Nine months and 20 days were wasted, and 70,000 men were dead because David disobeyed God (vs. 8, 15). God stopped the punishing plague when David built an altar on a threshing floor purchased from Araunah/Ornan (1 Chronicles 21:18-30). This place of sacrifice eventually became the location of God's temple.

> *Then Solomon began to build the house of the LORD*
> *in Jerusalem on Mount Moriah, where the LORD had*
> *appeared to his father David, at the place that David had*
> *prepared on the threshing floor of Ornan the Jebusite.*
> —2 Chronicles 3:1

David was not the first to offer a sacrifice on Mount Moriah. 1,000 years earlier, God called Abraham to take his only son Isaac "to the land of Moriah and offer him there as a burnt offering on one of the mountains" (Genesis 22:1-2). God provided a ram to replace Isaac that day, and He knew a day was coming, on that same mountain next to the temple built on a threshing floor, when He would die as the sacrificial Lamb for the sins of the world (John 1:29). The Baby you celebrate today is that Lamb who died to end the plague of sin and death for you.

Thank Jesus for the gift of Himself, and pray 2 Samuel 24:14 and 25 over yourself and those for whom you stand guard as a faithful, prayerful watchman (Isaiah 62:6-7).

> *"LORD, let _____ and me fall into Your hands,*
> *for Your mercies are great. Do not let us fall into the hands*
> *of men. LORD, be moved by prayer for our land.*
> *In Your name, Jesus~"*

Please read 1 John 1.

Meditate on verses 1, 2a, and 3b.

> *What was from the beginning, what we have heard, what we have*
> *seen with our eyes, what we have looked at and touched with our*
> *hands, concerning the Word of Life—and the life was manifested,*
> *and we have seen and testify and proclaim to you the eternal*
> *life, so that you too may have fellowship with us; and indeed our*
> *fellowship is with the Father and with His Son Jesus Christ.*

John was one of the three disciples closest to Jesus. He loved Jesus and knew his family well. In fact, on the cross, Jesus gave John the responsibility to look after Mary when He said to her, "Woman, behold your son!" and then to John, "Behold your mother" (John 19:26-27). John lived over 60 years beyond that time.

John spent years with Mary and her children. He knew the stories of the night of Jesus' birth, heralded by bright lights and hosts of joyful angels announcing The King of Kings, The Messiah, The Prince of Peace. John, the eyewitness of Jesus, joins in proclaiming this is the One who came so people can have fellowship with God and His Son Jesus Christ (v. 3).

Hear his Christmas message for you! John wrote to you, so you can know the fellowship with the Father and His Son Jesus Christ!

Pray 1 John 1:1-2 and 7 over yourself and those for whom you stand guard as a faithful, prayerful watchman (Isaiah 62:6-7).

> *"Word of Life, thank You for coming to be*
> *heard, seen, looked at, and touched!*
> *Help _____ and me to have eternal*
> *life and fellowship with You.*
> *Help us walk in the Light, as You, Yourself are the Light.*
> *I love you! Happy Birthday, Jesus~"*

DECEMBER 26

Please read 1 John 2.

Meditate on verses 28-29.

> *Now, little children abide in Him, so that when He appears, we*
> *may have confidence and not shrink away from Him in shame*
> *at His coming. If you know that He is righteous, you know that*
> *everyone also who practices righteousness is born of Him.*

Over the next few days as you prepare for the New Year, you will be challenged to prepare your life for living with the LORD. As you read during the next six days, you will see John refer to you as "children" 17 times and refer to the "children of the Devil" one time. It is a big deal to God who your father is.

In this passage of Scripture, John contrasts behaviors of the children of God and those who are not. Take a slow look at this chapter again. How do you see yourself in the comparisons? Even faithful believers will have areas of improvement, maybe areas of repentance and confession.

It is great to have a forgiving God. Look at 1 John 1:8-2:2. What a Christmas present! God gave you Jesus so you can be forgiven, become His child, and abide with Him.

Pray 1 John 1:9 and 2:28-29 over yourself and those for whom you stand guard as a faithful, prayerful watchman (Isaiah 62:6-7).

> *"LORD, _____ and I confess our sins to You.*
> *Thank You for faithfully and righteously forgiving us*
> *our sins and cleansing us from all unrighteousness.*
> *Help us abide in You, so that when You appear, we may have*
> *confidence and not shrink away from You in shame at Your coming.*
> *As Your children, help us practice righteousness.*
> *In Your name, Jesus~"*

December 27

Please read 1 John 3.

Meditate on verses 1-3.

> See how great a love the Father has bestowed on us, that we would
> be called children of God; and such we are. For this reason the
> world does not know us, because it did not know Him. Beloved,
> now we are children of God, and it has not appeared as yet
> what we will be. We know that when He appears we will be like
> Him, because we will see Him just as he is. And everyone who
> has this hope fixed on Him purifies himself, just as He is pure.

It matters a lot if your father is God. It is an enormous gift to become children of God. You become a child of God when you become a Christian. It is a rebirth. James 1:18 says that when you are reborn you are the first fruits of a new type or kind of creation. This is new DNA in the spiritual realm—unseen before Pentecost. 1 Peter 1:3-4 and 23-25 says you are born again into a living hope, to an inheritance which is imperishable, undefiled, not fading, and on reservation for you in heaven.

If you are a part of the family, you want to grow to become more like Jesus. Fix your eyes on Him. Grow each day to be more like Him.

Pray 1 John 3:1 and 3 over yourself and those for whom you stand guard as a faithful, prayerful watchman (Isaiah 62:6-7).

> "LORD, help _____ and me see
> Your great love for us,
> making us Your children.
> Help us and the world to know You.
> Help us fix our hope on You, Jesus;
> purify us, just as You are pure.
> In Your name, Jesus~"

DECEMBER 28

Please read 1 John 4.

Meditate on verse 8.

The one who does not love does not know God, for God is love.

Preparing for the New Year, you've had the opportunity to be in awe of God's gift of Jesus, His gift of forgiveness, and His gift of being His son or daughter. With these gifts, there is an expectation of living a changed life, not in order to earn salvation, that was God's free gift to you, but change comes because you have received salvation, and your heart is made new.

1 John 4 is a challenge to live your life abounding in love, God's love. He gave you Jesus, so you can love like the Father loves (vs. 9-10). He gave you the Holy Spirit to perfect His love in you and help you love right now (v. 12). The Holy Spirit inside of you is the proof God abides in you, and you abide in God (v. 13). What an amazing relationship you have with God and others!

The rest of the chapter builds on how important this loving relationship is to God. Make it important for every day of the rest of your life. Pray 1 John 4:8-13 over yourself and those for whom you stand guard as a faithful, prayerful watchman (Isaiah 62:6-7).

> *"LORD, thank You that _____ and I know You.*
> *Help us live through Jesus.*
> *Thank You for loving us and sending Your Son to be the*
> *propitiation, the sacrifice that satisfied Your wrath for our sins.*
> *Help us love one another. God abide in us.*
> *Perfect Your love in us.*
> *Thank You for the Holy Spirit,*
> *so we can know we abide in You.*
> *In Your name, Jesus~"*

DECEMBER 29

Please read 1 John 5.

Meditate on verses 14-15.

> *This is the confidence which we have before Him, that, if we*
> *ask anything according to His will, He hears us. And if we*
> *know that He hears us in whatever we ask, we know that*
> *we have the requests which we have asked from Him.*

As you abide in the LORD and prepare for the New Year, you want your prayer life to be dynamic. This year, come confidently to the LORD. Be the person who is the watchman on the wall for those you love.

Just as you expect a sentry on duty guarding a city to be faithful to their shift, hold yourself to the same standard of faithfulness. Make each day a day of faithful prayer for others. Make lists of individuals you can pray for each day.

A friend of ours who pastors in the Middle East showed us his prayer list on an oversized sheet of paper. There were hundreds of names in different categories. He had lists for salvation, lists for the sick, for ministers, family, friends ... He discerned which list needed prayer each morning and spent that day praying for those people.

Pray with purpose, 1 John 5:14-15 over yourself and those for whom you stand guard as a faithful, prayerful watchman (Isaiah 62:6-7).

> *"LORD, this is the confidence which _____ and I have before*
> *You, that, if we ask anything according to Your will, You hear us.*
> *And since we know that You hear us in whatever we ask,*
> *we know that we have the requests which we have asked from You.*
> *In Your name, Jesus~"*

DECEMBER 30

Please read 2 John.

Meditate on verses 5-6.

> *Now I ask you, lady, not as though I were writing to you a new
> commandment, but the one which we have had from the beginning,
> that we love one another. And this is love, that we walk according
> to His commandments. This is the commandment, just as you
> have heard from the beginning, that you should walk in it.*

John addressed the church (lady) with a command for all believers, to walk
in the commandment to love one another. Jesus said it this way in John
14:21:

> *"He who has My commandments and keeps them is the one who
> loves Me; and he who loves Me will be loved by My Father,
> and I will love him and will disclose Myself to him."*

There is a remarkable promise in that verse. If you obey the LORD, then
you love Him, and God loves you in a special way by revealing Himself to
you through Jesus. Walk with the LORD in step with the Spirit (Galatians
5:25), and you will be able to obediently walk in love everyday.

Pray, in the power of the Holy Spirit, 2 John 5-6 over yourself and those
for whom you stand guard as a faithful, prayerful watchman (Isaiah 62:6-
7).

> *"LORD, help _____ and me love one another.
> Help us lovingly walk according to Your commandments.
> In Your name, Jesus~"*

Please read 3 John.

Meditate on verses 1-3.

> *The elder to the beloved Gaius, whom I love in truth. Beloved, I pray that in all respects you may prosper and be in good health, just as your soul prospers. For I was very glad when brethren came and testified to your truth, that is how you are walking in the truth.*

John's letter to Gaius is positive and glad because he was walking in the truth. Poor Diotrephes gets his name in the Bible as someone who was seeking a place of prominence rather than for upholding the truth.

People like Diotrephes are still in the church today; they hurt the faith of others by sowing seeds of untruth. "The Bible is not really true." Or, "Jesus could not really be all God and all man at the same time, could He?"

As you enter the New Year this evening, enter with conviction to live by the truths of God. Let your abiding fellowship with God and your growing, prayerful, loving, obedient walk with the LORD work to make you a more truthful person. Be truthful with God, with the Word, with yourself, and with others. Next year, look back at this commitment and see what a difference walking with the LORD in truth has made in your life and the lives of those you love.

Pray 3 John 1-3 over yourself and those for whom you stand guard as a faithful, prayerful watchman (Isaiah 62:6-7).

> *"LORD, help _____ and me love in truth.*
> *In all respects, let _____ prosper and be in good health.*
> *Let our souls prosper as we walk in the truth.*
> *In Your name, Jesus~"*

$\mathcal{S}$CRIPTURE $\mathcal{I}$NDEX

TOPICAL INDEX

BLESSINGS FROM GOD

CHURCH/COMMUNITY

COURAGE

DEVOTED TO GOD

DISCIPLESHIP

FAITHFULNESS

March 10, March 18, March 22,
April 2, August 16, November 27

FAMILY/PARENTING

January 20, January 21, January 23, April 25,
April 27, August 2, August 17, August 24,
August 29, September 10, October 16, October 19, October 25,
November 13, November 21,
December 6, December 20, December 21, December 30

FAVOR

January 11, April 18, May 20, May 25,
May 29, June 5, July 30, August 19, August 25,
August 28, November 1, November 12,
November 26, December 15

FEAR/AFRAID

January 14, March 25, April 20, July 26, October 24

FEARING GOD

January 1, April 11, August 15, October 22, October 29, October 30

GOD'S PLANS/WILL

January 3, January 31, February 5, March 20,
April 10, May 2, May 10, August 20, September 9, September 14,
September 15, September 18,
October 7, November 22, November 24,
November 29, December 17, December 29

GOD'S WORD

May 3, May 22, September 12, September 16,
October 1, October 4, October 15, October 21,
December 12, December 23

HEALING

June 6, October 8, October 11,
Decmeber 4, December 16, December 31

HEART ISSUES

January 7, January 8, February 4, March 23, May 24,
September 3, September 17, September 19, October 2

HELP!

January 2, January 6, January 17, January 18,
March 21, March 29, March 30, April 12, April 29, April 30, May 27,
June 3, June 10, June 20, June 22, June 27, June 28, June 30, July 1,
July 2, July 5, July 8, July 10, July 12, July 13, July 14, July 16, July 24,
July 29, July 31, August 8, August 9, October 17

HOLINESS/INTEGRITY

January 22, January 27, January 30, February 9, February 11, February 17,
February 19, February 20,
February 21, February 27, February 28, February 29,
March 1, March 2, March 4, March 27, April 16,
June 15, June 26, July 4, September 1, November 23, December 27

HUMILITY

January 10, March 6, September 27, October 23,
October 26, October 27, November 5, December 7

INTERCESSION

January 28, March 31, May 7, May 14, May 21, May 30,
August 13, August 27, October 18, November 10

INTIMACY WITH CHRIST

January 25, January 26, February 2, February 26, March 11,
March 14, March 17, March 26, April 4, November 2,
November 20, December 25, December 28

LEADERSHIP

August 7, November 8, November 15, November 17,

LORDSHIP

April 22, April 26, May 1, May 5, May 23, May 31,
July 15, August 22, September 26, October 5,
November 4, November 7, December 2

MATURITY

March 13, March 24, March 28,
April 14, April 28, May 15, September 25

OBEDIENCE

January 4, January 5, January 9, January 24, February 7, February 8,
April 15, September 30, October 12, October 13, October 20,
November 11, November 14, November 30

PRAISE/WORSHIP

March 9, May 8, June 2, June 8, June 21, June 29, July 17,
August 4, August 23, September 4, November 3, December 22

PROTECTION

April 17, May 13, May 19, May 26, June 4, June 7,
June 9, June 12, June 16, June 17, June 18, June 23,
July 3, July 27, August 1, August 3, August 10,
August 30, September 28, November 16,
November 18, November 25, December 24

REPENTANCE

January 13, February 1, February 3, February 14, February 15,
February 22, February 24, March 15, April 13, April 24, May 18,
June 19, July 9, July 21, August 18, September 22,
September 23, October 3, October 9, October 14,
November 6, December 11, December 19, December 26

RIGHTEOUSNESS

January 15, January 16, June 1, June 11, June 14,
July 28, August 14, September 5, September 7,
October 28, November 28, December 1

SALVATION

January 12, January 19, February 10,
February 23, March 3, March 7, March 8, March 12,
July 19, July 23, August 26, September 6, December 3, December 18

STEADFASTNESS

April 3, April 6, April 19, July 25, September 2,
September 13, September 24, October 6, October 10, December 5

THANKSGIVING

February 12, February 13, February 16, February 25,
March 16, September 8, November 19, December 9, December 14

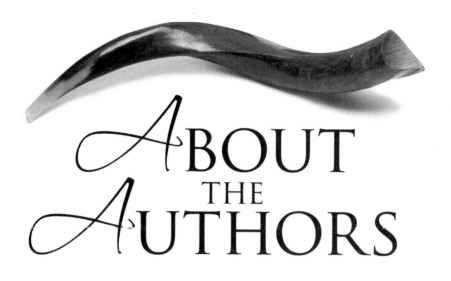

ABOUT THE AUTHORS

MARSHA HARVELL

Marsha Harvell has a passion for the LORD and treasures His Word. She has led more than 100 Bible studies. As an international trainer for Precept Ministries, she has taught hundreds of people in Germany, France, Qatar, Bahrain, India, Malaysia, and Japan how to study the Bible and lead Bible studies. Marsha is dedicated to helping others discover the promises found in Scripture.

She and her husband, Ron, recently returned to the States after serving for five years in Europe and the Middle East. Marsha is a missionary to the military as a chaplain's wife, appointed by the North American Mission Board (1991). Ron and Marsha

now minister to the military community from Barksdale Air Force Base in Louisiana.

With a Bachelors in Education from Hardin-Simmons University and a Masters in Gifted and Talented Education from Texas Women's University, Marsha Harvell is an accomplished woman who has taught in both public and private schools. She has helped plant churches and served as a worship leader and a women's ministry director. She is also a conference speaker; some of her favorite topics include: The Covenant Maker, Godly Relationships, Being a Godly Wife and Mother, Hearing and Heeding God, Being Complete in Christ, Knowing God, and How to Pray.

She is the author of *The Covenant Maker: Knowing God and His Promises for Salvation and Marriage* and co-author of *The Watchman on the Wall: Daily Devotions for Praying God's Word Over Those You Love* (Volumes 1 and 2).

Marsha and Ron have been married since 1984 and have two grown children, Stephanie (married to Jonathan) and Steven (married to Rachel). Both families serve the LORD overseas. They have five grandchildren: Nathan, Adilynn, Kik, Daniel, and Kyro.

RON HARVELL

Dr. Ron Harvell is a chaplain colonel in the United States Air Force where he is responsible for ministry to all Air Force personnel in Air Force Global Strike Command, Barksdale Air Force Base, Louisiana. From 2013-2015, he served as the Command Chaplain for all Air Force personnel serving in 22 countries of the Middle East.

Ron felt called to ministry when he was 17 years old. After being licensed to the Gospel Ministry by Circle Drive Baptist Church in Colorado Springs, he attended college where he met and married Marsha (1984). In June of 1985, he was ordained by Friendship Baptist Church in Weatherford, Texas. Following seminary, he pastored Northside Baptist Church in Kermit, Texas for four-and-a-half years. Since 1991, Ron and Marsha have lived in 13 locations around the world serving as commissioned missionaries by the North American Mission Board to the Air Force Active Duty Chaplain Corps.

Ron is an award-winning church growth pastor in both civilian and military organizations and a visionary leader serving God in His transformation of individuals, communities, and institutions. He is the co-author with Marsha of *The Watchman on the Wall: Daily Devotions for Praying God's Word Over Those You Love* (Volumes 1 and 2).

Ron has earned a Bachelors of Arts from Hardin-Simmons University in Bible and History, a Master of Divinity from Southwestern Baptist Theological Seminary, and a Doctor of Ministry from Asia Graduate School of Theology with a focus in Transformational Leadership for the Global City. He also has a Master of Science in National Security Strategy from National War College at the National Defense University and a Master of Arts in Organizational Management from The George Washington University. These academic experiences help to shape ministry opportunities and capacities for where his gifts and passions are: preaching, teaching, discipleship, church planting, and church growth.

Ron and Marsha have been married since 1984 and have two grown children, Stephanie (married to Jonathan) and Steven (married to Rachel). Both families serve the LORD overseas. They have five grandchildren: Nathan, Adilynn, Kik, Daniel, and Kyro.